*Edith Wharton and the Making of Fashion*

# Edith Wharton and the Making of Fashion

## Katherine Joslin

University of New Hampshire Press
Durham, New Hampshire

*Published by University Press of New England*
*Hanover and London*

UNIVERSITY OF NEW HAMPSHIRE PRESS

Published by University Press of New England,

One Court Street, Lebanon, NH 03766

www.upne.com

© 2009 by University of New Hampshire Press

Printed in the United States of America

5 4 3 2 1

The author and publisher gratefully acknowledge the support of the Coby Foundation, Ltd.

Frontispiece: Edith Wharton at Ste. Claire in 1933. Yale collection of American Literature, Beinecke Rare Book and Manuscript Library.

*Library of Congress Cataloging-in-Publication Data*
Joslin, Katherine, 1947–
    Edith Wharton and the making of fashion / Katherine Joslin.
        p. cm. — (Becoming modern: new nineteenth-century studies) (Reading dress series)
    Includes bibliographical references and index.
    ISBN 978-1-58465-779-8 (cloth : alk. paper)
    1. Wharton, Edith, 1862–1937—Criticism and interpretation. 2. Wharton, Edith, 1862–1937—Knowledge—Clothing. 3. Clothing and dress in literature. 4. Class consciousness in literature. 5. Fashion—United States—History—20th century. I. Title.
    PS3545.H16Z6855 2009
    813'.52—dc22        2009026509

*Becoming Modern: New Nineteenth-Century Studies*

SERIES EDITORS

Sarah Way Sherman
Department of English
University of New Hampshire

Rohan McWilliam
Anglia Ruskin University
Cambridge, England

Janet Aikins Yount
Department of English
University of New Hampshire

Janet Polasky
Department of History
University of New Hampshire

This book series maps the complexity of historical change and assesses the formation of ideas, movements, and institutions crucial to our own time by publishing books that examine the emergence of modernity in North America and Europe. Set primarily but not exclusively in the nineteenth century, the series shifts attention from modernity's twentieth-century forms to its earlier moments of uncertain and often disputed construction. Seeking books of interest to scholars on both sides of the Atlantic, it thereby encourages the expansion of nineteenth-century studies and the exploration of more global patterns of development.

For a complete list of books that are available in this series, see www.upne.com

## Reading Dress Series

SERIES EDITORS

Katherine Joslin
Department of English
Western Michigan University

Daneen Wardrop
Department of English
Western Michigan University

This series engages questions about clothing, textiles, design, and production in relation to history, culture, and literature in its many forms. Set primarily in the long nineteenth century, it examines the emergence of modernity by exploring the interweaving of material culture with social history and literary texts in ways that resonate with readers and scholars at the turn into the twenty-first century. The editors seek books that offer fresh ways of relating fashion to discourse and of understanding dress in the context of social, cultural, and political history. Such topics might include, for example, analyzing American, British, and/or European notions of style or tracing the influence of developing modes of production. As with the "Becoming Modern" series generally, the editors especially welcome books with a transatlantic focus or that appeal to a transatlantic audience.

Reading Dress is a subseries of Becoming Modern: New Nineteenth-Century Studies published by the University Press of New Hampshire

*To my daughters and granddaughters—*

Emily Katherine Joslin-Jeske,

Cullen Elizabeth Bailey Burns,

Caitlin MacDonald Bailey,

Bridget Cathleen Trost Bailey,

Emily Bailey Burns,

Margaret Elizabeth Burns,

& Clementine Constance MacDonald Trost Bailey

# Contents

# Reading Dress Editors' Preface

While innumerable literary studies have focused on class, economics, gender, and specific aspects of cultural history, the study of fashion in literary studies has remained in a nascent stage. The inaugural two volumes of the "Reading Dress" Series seek to reconfigure the study of Emily Dickinson and Edith Wharton by examining the stakes of fashion and the labor of producing clothing in the nineteenth and early twentieth centuries. Each volume follows a loose chronology of dress in the works of Emily Dickinson and Edith Wharton, whose lives spanned the years from 1830 to 1937, a century or so of considerable change in technology and fashion, moving from more to less restrictive garments for women in the middle and upper classes. Changes in production exacerbated the divide in labor between the working and the privileged classes, even as the lower cost of clothes made it more difficult at times to see differences in social class. We approach the project by attending to garments that encode cultural and historical issues; in the process, we renew our sense of each author's work.

The plainest of poets and the most luxurious of novelists, Dickinson and Wharton in many ways couldn't be more different. One bespeaks austerity and the other opulence, so that they seem almost to form polarities from which to see the pervasive and fluctuating nature of dress. In many ways, however, the differences between the two speak exactly to the point about the two literary redheads. Their works show a range of possibilities for reading literature more incisively through a study of costume. Many of the garments, typically, are no longer familiar to twenty-first-century readers, who have little sense of the texture of tulle or dimity and almost no experience with the lacing of corsets and bulk of bustles. By examining in depth one major nineteenth-century poet and one major twentieth-century fiction writer, we discern the many possibilities for fashion shifts as they occurred over a hundred years.

Dickinson and Wharton lived through times of prodigious change in gender politics as well as change in the technologies associated with textiles—both strikingly illuminated by the history of costume. This period marked radical changes in the production of fabrics and garments, moving from intense labor by human hands to labor with industrial machinery that required a different sort of human skill. Our study will look at the modes of production and the ways in which Dickinson and Wharton experienced dress as it intersected with the workplaces of home and industry. We have selected Dickinson and Wharton, too, because they are the most enduring female figures in the American literary canon, clearly iconic figures in the twentieth century, even before the retrieval work of feminist scholars at the end of the century. By combining the fashion resources depicted in their oeuvres, we hope to initiate a cross-disciplinary field of study that juxtaposes the history of dress and the analysis of literature. By setting ourselves in dialogue with each other, we invite others to join in the conversation.

# Acknowledgments

This book began on a walk in the woods with my colleague Daneen Wardrop who talked about Emily Dickinson and clothes as we wandered up a sunny hill along a leafy path. What better place could there be to muse on American literature? I begin by thanking Daneen for a lively collaboration—our many conversations over tea and wine—and for teaching me much about poetry and material culture. Many colleagues urged us on as we began a single volume on Dickinson, Wharton and the history of women's clothing from 1830 to 1930. I am grateful for the exuberant advice of Clare Goldfarb, who understood more clearly than we did the scope and promise of our research. I thank Shirley Clay Scott for her wise suggestion to separate our work into two volumes but to link them as a series called 'reading dress.' I would like to thank Irma Lopez and Barbara Liner for conversations about clothes, and Christine Gola for handing me a book by Edith Head and chatting with me about Patricia Marx. Wharton scholars have a tradition of collegiality and I would like to thank especially Janet Beer, Susan Goodman, and Donna Campbell for generous advice and encouragement. At the University Press of New England, I am thankful for the strong early support of Richard Pult and for his patience and enthusiasm for both books, and am grateful for the fine work of the staff, especially Ann Brash and Catherine Grabill. Linda Wagner-Martin and Patricia Cunningham read the manuscripts; I thank them for the care they took in suggesting ways to improve the books. Elizabeth Waterhouse gave countless hours to the task of copyediting, and I am truly grateful for her careful eye and thoughtful questions.

The material culture research for this book began at the Metropolitan Museum's Costume Institute. I am grateful to Elizabeth Bryan, senior research associate and collections manager, for her thorough knowledge of couture clothing and to Marci Morimoto, research assistant, for all she taught me about how to read garments. I thank Tatyana Pakhladzhyan, head of the Irene Lewisohn Costume Reference Library, for selecting articles and advertisements that precisely illustrated Wharton's clothes. At the Museum of the City of New York, I am grateful to the curator of costumes and textiles, Phyllis Magidson, who has designed exhibits of the fashions described in Wharton's novels. David Dashiell, director of publications at the Edith Wharton Restoration, gave me good advice about Wharton's own garments and I thank him for pointing the way. My research took me to the Mint Museum of Art in Charlotte, North Carolina, and I thank Charles Mo, director of fine arts, for talking with me about his detailed exhibit on dress in the nineteenth century. At the Beinecke Rare Book and Manuscript Library, I am grateful to Nancy Kuhl, associate curator of the Yale Collection of American Literature, for advice on Wharton's clothing. Collecting images to use in the book has been complicated. I thank Charles Mo; Anne-Marie Peylhard, conservateur du musée Agladon in Avignon, France; and Aimee L. Marshall, manager of rights licensing at the Art Institute of Chicago, for generously providing images without charge. Many people graciously helped me secure images and permissions, and I thank Andrea Collins, registration and photographic services assistant at the Mint Museum; Ben Fink and Dale Levinson of Ben Fink Photography; Faye Haun, head of rights and reproductions at MCNY; Joyce Fung, research associate, and Deanna Cross, assistant manager for images, at the Metropolitan; and Leah Jehan, public services assistant, at the Beinecke Library. In Kalamazoo, I would like to thank Western Michigan University, and specifically photographer Mary Whalen; David Dickason, director of the Upjohn Center for the Study of Geographic Change, and staff members Marilyn Johnson, Greg Anderson, and Angela Fortino; as well as Dave Marlatt and Anthony Minnema for their expertise in images.

I thank the Coby Foundation, Ltd. for their generous support.

My children, the daughters and granddaughters listed in the dedication together with Sam and Leo Bailey and Mike Burns, are indulgent of my eccentricities, and I thank them for the cushion of our blended family. I am most grateful for a happy marriage to my friend and colleague, Tom Bailey, who is always the best person to talk to about literature and, as it turns out, about clothes.

# Abbreviations

All abbreviations provided here refer to the works of Edith Wharton

| AI | The Age of Innocence |
|---|---|
| B | The Buccaneers |
| BG | A Backward Glance |
| BS | Bunner Sisters |
| CC | The Custom of the Country |
| CS | The Collected Stories |
| DH | The Decoration of Houses |
| FW | French Ways and Their Meaning |
| FT | The Fruit of the Tree |
| HM | The House of Mirth |
| "LaI" | "Life and I" |
| MT | Madame de Treymes |
| ONY | Old New York |
| SF | A Son at the Front |
| T | The Touchstone |
| WF | The Writing of Fiction |

*Edith Wharton and the Making of Fashion*

*Fig. I.1.* Sir Joshua Reynolds, "Mrs. Richard Bennett Lloyd," 1775–1776. *Private collection.*

# INTRODUCTION

## Remnant and Meaning

The remaining dresses, though they had lost their freshness, still
kept the long unerring lines, the sweep and amplitude of the great
artist's stroke, and as she spread them out on the bed the scenes
in which they had been worn rose vividly before her.
—*The House of Mirth*

Clothing is the closest sensation of the body. In perhaps the best
known scene of Edith Wharton's fiction, the doomed Lily Bart,
heroine of *The House of Mirth* (1905), spends her last evening unpack-
ing elegant Parisian gowns she considers survivals of splendor. Arranging the delicate remnants before her, she gazes on their unerring lines
that measure for her the "sweep and amplitude" of great art. In the sensual play of eye and skin against fabric, an "association lurked in every
fold: each fall of lace and gleam of embroidery was like a letter in the
record of her past."[1] At the bottom of the trunk lay the "heap of white
drapery" that had covered her body in the tableau vivant of Reynolds's
Mrs. Lloyd at the evening party given by the Willy Brys (figure I.1).[2]
The tactile sensation is heightened by smell and sound as the drapery
gives "forth an odour of violets" reminding her of "the flower-edged
fountain where she had stood." Her identity in New York is inextri-
cable from the gowns she holds. And, in repacking the garments, she
packs away her sense of self, "laying away with each some gleam of
light, some note of laughter, some stray waft from the rosy shores of
pleasure." Without her dresses, creations of the French couturiers
Jacques Doucet and Charles Frederick Worth, Lily sees herself as
"rootless and ephemeral, mere spin-drift of the whirling surface of existence" (*HM* 515). Her other garments, she explains, went to her maid
as "cast-off apparel."

  The ephemeral nature of garments, our tendency to cast them off or to pack them away to mold in trunks, has made the study of them difficult for readers and scholars who may not see, at first blush, the resilient and enduring nature of fashion. Specific articles of dress actually belonging to Edith Wharton are few and scattered, leaving us little to hold in the hand and inspect with the eye. We know that when she died on 11 August 1937, at the Pavillon Colombe, her country home outside Paris, she willed intimate items of jewelry and clothing to her closest female friends.[3] A favorite necklace she called a "dog collar," a star sapphire medallion encrusted with diamonds clasping strands of pearls, went to her close epistolary friend Daisy Chanler.[4] She left a chain with diamonds and pearls designed by Cartier, a piece she wore in nearly every photograph taken of her, to longtime friend Bessy Lodge. An array of antique lace caps and sheets, and organdy and silk bed linens in shades of pink, together with a Chinese scarf and tortoiseshell combs went to Beatrix Ferrand, her niece and last surviving relative. A sapphire and diamond brooch, chinchilla and sable wraps, other bejeweled dog-collars, and a crystal eighteenth-century watch went to friend Jane Clark. She gave a sapphire ring to Nicky Mariano, a moleskin coat and a coral necklace to Gabrielle Landormy, and a pearl Cartier watch to Jeanne Fridérich. We imagine the handing off of ceremonial goods—as Emily Dickinson put it: "I willed my keepsakes, signed away/ What portion of me I / Could make assignable"—and the bittersweet pleasure of the new owners in opening her gifts. The mortarboard from her regalia at the Yale University graduation when she received an honorary doctorate fell into the hands of Jacques Fosse, a historian from her village of St. Brice-sous-forêt who as a boy had known Wharton's gardeners. The garments of her later years, tailored suits, crocheted sweaters, and silken dressing gowns, some forty-five that survived, went by custom to her maid as what she and Lily Bart would call castoff apparel.

This is a book about castoff apparel, remnants of dress and ornament from the turn into the twentieth century and their meaning in American culture and literature, specifically in the writing of Edith Wharton. As Bill Brown in *A Sense of Things* (2003) contends, literary criticism "has hardly begun to bring material culture into view" and attention to the things we live among promises to refresh our reading of familiar texts.[5] What meaning can there be in clothing and how are we to discover it? The public has been reluctant to take seriously the notion of fashion design and the sewing of garments as forms of art. In contemporary culture, as has been true since the middle of the nineteenth century, the buying of clothes takes place as variations on couture designs make their way into department stores, a commercial ritual tainted by the power of money and the vagaries of the marketplace. How can easily pirated designs and mass produced goods constitute artistic endeavor? It is also true that scholars live in a world that valorizes the mind and looks askance at a well-clad body; perhaps that is why we have shied away from the glamour of fashion, preferring to consider the labor of clothing production. Social historians, in recent years, have looked closely at changes in the garment trade from the nineteenth to the twentieth centuries, especially changes in the United States, as industrial labor—much of it done by immigrant women and children—overlapped and competed with seamstress work within the home.

There are signs, however, that the scholarly reluctance to consider fashion is changing. Valerie Steele edits the journal *Fashion Theory*, a clear mark of academic interest. Fashion scholars, including Elizabeth Ann Coleman, have chronicled the history of haute couture garments even as museums have gathered notable collections.[6] The Costume Institute in New York City has become a prominent part of the Metropolitan Museum of Art and has in recent shows displayed the gowns of Charles Frederick Worth, Jacques Doucet, and more recently Paul Poiret that offer a visual and sensual proximity to the material culture that Wharton describes often lushly in her fiction.[7] In 1974, the Mint Museum in Charlotte, North Carolina, began a Historic Costume and Fashionable Dress Collection that now numbers 9,500 garments from three centuries, including haute couture designs by Worth, Doucet, Fortuny, Chanel, Dior, Ferrgamo, Givenchy, and Valentino.

The making of fashion, as museum collections attest, contributes to our understanding of social history as well as artistic design. Significantly for this study of fashion and literature, museum collections place actual garments within the reach of scholars who are able to view, if not always to touch, fabrics and designs. As a result of the increasing value of apparel from the turn of the last century, we have proximate objects and images at hand to study the relationship between garments themselves and their literary evocations. Another rich resource is the Internet, with its ready availability of images. It is exciting for a literary scholar to google "Jacques Doucet," for example, and to see in an instant a stunning black and white ball gown and to know from photographs that Edith Wharton owned a skirt very like it. The geometry of the bodice alone comprises forty-eight separate pattern pieces and dozens of separate strips form the skirt into what is called a chevron design (figure I.2).[8] Wharton posed in her chevron skirt for publicity photographs used in advertising *Italian Villas and Their Gardens* (1904). In various scenes, she places herself working in her garden and, as in this one, descending an ornate stairway (figure I.3). Material culture is vividly available online in digitized collections at museums, the Library of Congress, the New York Public Library, and at such places as Wikimedia Commons. The question at the center of this study is how to read such images and actual garments together with literary texts.

*Fig. I.2.* Jacques Doucet (1853–1929). Ball gown, circa 1890s; black silk velvet and white silk satin with black silk velvet ribbon. *The Mint Museum of Art, Charlotte, North Carolina, Historic Costume and Fashionable Dress Collection.* (Plate 1.)

*Fig. I.3.* Edith Jones before her marriage to Theodore Wharton in a black and white chevron skirt, 1884. *Yale Collection of American Literature, Beinecke Rare Book and Manuscript Library.*

Edith Wharton left readers remnants of social history and the culture of fashion in the body of her writing. Biographies, especially Cynthia Griffin Wolff's *A Feast of Words*, have stressed "the sureness of her eye for detail."[9] Wharton describes the palpable, even visceral effects that things have on the sense of self: "The truth is that I have always found it hard to explain that gradual absorption into my pores of a myriad details." In letters and memoirs, short stories and novels, and in books about design and decoration, Wharton offers sureness of eye and absorption of pore as she considers the making of fashion, the design and production of clothing, and the depiction of dress. Her sense of fashion is, at times, earnest as in her early work on household design, *The Decoration of Houses* (1897), and her scholarly studies, *Italian Villas and Their Gardens* (1904) and *Italian Backgrounds* (1905). In her fiction, she is more inclined to write about the making of clothing than she is about the digging of gardens or the crafting of home decor. The tone of her fiction is often satiric, even acerbic, as she dresses heroines and heroes and then measures each one by their selection of garments. In fiction and nonfiction she takes compatriots to task for aesthetic insensibility. As a writer during the Progressive Era, she measures the cost of luxury in human terms. John Amherst, the hero of *The Fruit of the Tree* (1907), gazes on the brilliance of Bessy Westmore's gown even as he is aware that young women in modest gingham dresses sacrifice youth and risk health working on looms and bobbins. During the years of the First World War, Edith Wharton opened *ouvroirs* or workrooms for Paris seamstresses who found themselves unemployed as some couture houses had to close for periods during the war years. Over the years following the war, she packed her fiction, more and more, with material culture, giving twentieth-century readers details of fashions no longer in style—and, she feared, no longer of interest to the women of the 1920s who shed corset and bustle in favor of loose, angular modes.

Remnants of her wardrobe come to us from publicity photographs that draw our attention away from the body and toward gowns, furs and jewels. If we were to read Wharton in our diverted gaze, focusing our eyes on a dress designed by Jacques Doucet or Charles Frederick Worth or Paul Poiret and on a hat by Madame Virot or a necklace by Cartier, seemingly superficial signs of fashion among Old New Yorkers, what might we learn about her as a writer? Looking closely at ornamental and decorative arts, we discover that Edith Wharton considered such seemingly peripheral elements to be central to her thinking and writing. As a measure of aesthetic value, fashion holds the key to authenticity of mind and strength of character. Pick up any of Edith Wharton's books, nonfiction as well as fiction, and you will find the same aesthetic ideas at work. That is why fashion inflects a text in ways that may enhance our reading.

This study focuses on both changes *of* dress and changes *in* dress at the turn into the twentieth century and offers through a study of apparel a fresh reading of Wharton's fiction. As an imaginative construct, dress creates the drama of the body. Wharton understood that an afternoon dress, in life and in fiction, invites the eye, and selecting one dress for the morning and another for the afternoon creates a sense of play in both the wearer and the viewer. Elisina Tyler, her legatee and close friend in later years, explained the relationship between Wharton and her clothes as a matter of personal taste as well as social and even political expression: "I see why Edith makes such a fetish of dressing. She considers it an absolute sign of civilization to dress in the evening."[10] Dress can be read as both fetish and sign. When the then young scholar Leon Edel interviewed Wharton in 1931, he found it quaintly ridiculous that she excused herself in the middle of his visit to change her dress.[11] Little did he understand the creative play that a change of clothes would signal to someone of her age and social class.

More significant than the imaginative, for a novelist of manners, may well be the symbolic realm of meaning. "Wharton knew what clothes have to tell us," notes Martha Banta, a savvy reader of American fashion and Wharton's fiction.[12] Sartorial codes carry nearly vestmentary meaning in a rigid society like Wharton's Old New York. Fashion theorists Dani Cavallaro and Alexandra Warwick argue that such codes are "designed to guarantee the socialization and institutionalization of personal identity and thus secure the cultural grooming of vision."[13] Wharton understood, perhaps more deeply than any American writer, the symbolic power of social grooming. "We lived in a hieroglyphic world where the real thing is never thought or said," Newland Archer famously declares in *The Age of Innocence* (1920).[14] In New York City an astute hero would never rely on what he thought he saw without thinking about the semiotic possibilities. Dress functions as hieroglyph: its material presence drapes the body, revealing and concealing intricate patterns easily read by members of the tribe and clearly setting limits on those included and excluded from its web of meaning. A canny eye, Wharton understands, sees the subtle shades of fabric and fabrication. What more sophisticated voice could American letters have to delineate fashion and the meanings of dress?

Wharton shopped along with other wealthy women in the couture houses of Paris in the rue de la Paix where ateliers employed hundreds of seamstresses in the making of rarified goods. The story of fashion over the years that separate us from her reveals the vulnerabilities of a consumer art that caters to the richest of patrons. In the twenty-first century, couture creations are copied from photographs and films and transferred into dresses that find their way into shops and online sales sometimes before a runway fashion show even takes place in Paris or New York, according to the filmmaker Margy Kinmonth. In her 2006 documentary *The Secret World of Haute Couture*, she notes that the number of couture houses in Paris had grown to more than one hundred at the peak of the industry in the years following the Second World War but has dwindled to merely a dozen today. As a result, the haute couture runway show in Paris in 2005 invited only two hundred shoppers, a select coterie of women who see garments as art objects to be worn rarely and then given to costume collections in art museums.[15] A handmade Paris creation can cost tens of thousands of dollars. Kinmonth interviews the collectors of haute couture "art," a group that includes Betsy Bloomingdale, whose fortune came from department store apparel; Bloomingdale values her own collection of garments at more than half a million dollars. In today's world, a couture garment purchased at a runway show arrives by private plane with a seamstress who fits it precisely to the buyer's body. The consumer art glitters with names like Karl Lagerfeld of Chanel, John Galliano of Dior, Valentino, Christian Lacroix, and the American Ralph Rucci.

In Wharton's day the House of Worth competed with the House

of Doucet for the business of wealthy Americans. The rise of couture in Paris followed the coup d'état on 2 December 1851, that restored the French Empire, called the Second Empire, and put Louis Napoléon Bonaparte (1808–73) in power with the Spanish countess Eugénie de Montijo de Guzmán (1826–1920), whom he married a year later, at his side. The emperor and his wife brought formal dress back to court life in a reprise of prerevolutionary France fashion and celebrated the panache of French style. The 1854 portrait of Empress Eugénie by Franz Xavier Winterhalter in the Metropolitan Museum of Art depicts her in a Second Empire gown reminiscent of styles worn by Marie Antoinette, a woman whose dresses she admired (figure I.4). Eugénie and her court patronized the emerging couture houses and thereby ensured the popularity of the designers the empress preferred. Ironically, it was an Englishman who first earned recognition as a Paris couturier. Charles Frederick Worth, then working for the clothier Gagelin-Opigez, designed for Eugénie a court train made of white watered silk and embroidered in gold; the train, valued at $3,000, won a medal at the 1855 Exposition Universelle in Paris. The empress placed orders with him for herself and others at court. As a result of her patronage, Worth collaborated in establishing the House of Worth and Bobergh at the famous address, 7 rue de la Paix. And with the opening of his house, the haute couture industry established fashion not only for Parisians but for all of Europe as well as North and South America. The Mint Museum holds a lush example of Worth's talent as a designer (figure I.5). The evening or reception gown of golden silk chiffon and net with Alençon lace appliqués flows in subtle lines that emphasize the small waistline with little, if any, hint of a bustle. The House of Worth served the empress and the queens of Europe, along with rich New Yorkers, including Lucretia Stevens Jones and, later, her daughter Edith Newbold Jones, who would always measure sartorial splendor by what she saw at the Houses of Worth and Doucet in the 1870s.

The Doucet family of French merchants established themselves in the early years of the nineteenth century as makers of fine fabrics, and by the 1840s Antoine Doucet (1795–1866) moved the shop to the rue de la Paix. Doucets gained considerable reputation as haberdashers, whose linens were purchased by the emperor. The women in the family established businesses throughout the century that featured ready-made accessories and individually made chemises, the sorts of items women would buy for themselves and their children. By the 1870s, the Doucet family provided ready-made lingerie to customers including Eugénie. Jacques Doucet entered the family business as a designer of women's couture fashions, creating gowns of silks and laces and delicate embroideries. Unlike the more conventional and respectable Worth styles, Doucet dresses gave subtle and supple play to a woman's

*Fig. I.4.* Franz Xaver Winterhalter (German, 1805–1873), the Empress Eugénie (Eugénie de Montijo, 1826–1920, condesa de Teba), 1854. *Metropolitan Museum of Art.* (Plate 2.)

body and attracted women of wealth who desired glamour and sensuality. Wharton's discerning heroine Lily Bart bought Doucet gowns when her budget would allow or when her Aunt Peniston would pay. A sign of her financial fall is when she can no longer afford the luxury of another Doucet gown. His are the gowns, the "fall of lace and gleam of embroidery," that Lily caresses at the novel's close with the odor of fabric evoking her fashionable past.

Edith and Teddy Wharton traveled to Paris to shop in the early years of their marriage after the Second Empire had fallen and as the financial depression of the 1880s dampened consumption. Wealthy patrons continued to want the cachet of Parisian designs and the luxury of handmade clothing. The richest of clients traveled to Paris for viewings of live models and individual fittings, under the eye of the de-

*Fig. I.5.* Charles Frederick Worth (1825–1895), evening/ reception gown, 1890; silk chiffon and silk net with Alençon lace appliqués over silk satin. *The Mint Museum of Art, Charlotte, North Carolina, Historic Costume and Fashionable Dress Collection.* (Plate 3.)

signer himself, and were courted at the Houses of Worth and Doucet with individualized attention that included the crafting of personalized wooden dress forms. Under the pressure of time and the prestige of wealth, ensembles could be made in a matter of hours and many were sewn within a day or two, boxed and mailed home. Wharton remembered that women of her social class had standing orders for French dresses, dozens at a time, that were discreetly left in their wrappings for two or three years until the styles were safely fashionable in New York City and Boston. Her clan wanted the status of Paris fashion without the taint of new money.

Other American women sampled Worth and Doucet designs without leaving the country. In the nineteenth century, New Yorkers could shop from models at the A. T. Stewart emporium, and Southern women, like the writer Kate Chopin, relied on the New Orleans establishment of Madame Olympé who made trips to Paris to shop for millinery and dress designs. Copies of dresses by Worth and other couturiers as well as combinations of styles became available to American shoppers at cheap prices as early as the 1870s. *Harper's Bazar* (later changed to *Harper's Bazaar*), a weekly fashion magazine that began publishing in 1867, catered to the taste and pocketbook of middle- and upper-class ladies. By the 1880s, the magazine featured Sandoz engravings of House of Worth garments with hats by Madame Virot. The American-made versions of couture gowns were often manufactured in cheap materials, sewn by fingers working machines, and sold everywhere at prices laborers might afford. Muslin and paper patterns in flat pieces or loosely sewn models were marketed, at first, in a single size, leaving household seamstresses to make them fit individual bodies. By the end of the century, Madame Demorest and Ebenezer Butterick drafted and mass-produced paper patterns in individual sizes that added to the uniformity of design. Much of the labor of sewing continued in the home as women shopped for patterns and fabrics and made family clothes themselves or, as the budget allowed, employed maids to make clothing and keep garments in repair. Tailors and dressmakers offered clients personalized service, copying Parisian styles and offering apparel in the latest fashions at considerable savings. Garment factories produced standardized goods for mass consumption that made fashion affordable for middle- and working-class shoppers. By 1905, the Philadelphia clothier John Wanamaker prepared a "Portfolio of Paris Costumes" in his New York City store, defining American fashion as French.

Chapters in this study focus on specific styles of clothing, imaginative and actual constructs, and place them in the context of Wharton's life and writing. The first chapter, "Dressing Up," considers how fashion lies at the core of Edith Wharton's aesthetics. Reading her nonfiction with fashion in mind reveals a remarkably coherent writing career in *The Decoration of Houses* (1897), *French Ways and Their Meaning* (1919), and *The Writing of Fiction* (1925), as well as in her autobiography, *A Backward Glance* (1934) and the unpublished memoir "Life and I." These studies remind us that fashion for Wharton moves well beyond clothing, the delicate drama between body and fabric, to include the placement of furnishings in a room, the draping of curtains at the window, the movement of the body, and the tone of the voice, as well as the conduct of a society and the endurance of art. She delighted in knowing the details of "every stick of furniture and every rag of clothing"; yet she observes what she calls a "tact of omission," giving readers only those details necessary to conjure objects in the mind's eye.

Chapters 2, "The Underside of Fashion," and 3, "Philanthropy and

Progress" examine Wharton's perception of ethics and her involvement in the means of production. The story of labor, its abuses, and the viability of Progressive reform emerge from a close reading of a single dress in the collection at the Costume Institute, a gown owned by Wharton's contemporary Caroline Astor Wilson. The delicate salmon-pink satin garment opens to reveal the elaborate stitching on its underside, the labor of its production. Looking closely at how textiles and garments are made, these chapters consider Wharton's depictions of women as owners and managers. She wrote the early tale *Bunner Sisters* (written 1892, published 1916) in the mode and mood of literary naturalism, as she did the millinery section of *The House of Mirth* (1905) and the Progressive Era industrial novel *The Fruit of the Tree* (1907). Wharton based stories about labor on visits to sewing and millinery shops around Stuyvesant Square in New York City, as well as on a tour of the Berkshire Cotton Manufacturing Company in Adams, Massachusetts, a motor ride from her summer home The Mount. What seems astonishing about the fashionable lady novelist is that in response to the chaos in Paris during the First World War, she constructed, managed, and supported a workroom for seamstresses as well as a lace-making school to train girls in the art of sewing and prepare them for a profession. Wharton's system of war charities looked much like Progressive settlement houses in Chicago and New York City.

Other chapters look at specific novels, especially ones written later in Wharton's career as she focuses on details of fashion. The third chapter, "Desire in the Marketplace," contrasts the shopping modes of Midwesterners with those of New Yorkers and sets American habits against the rituals of French patrons of fashion in *The Custom of the Country* (1913). Here more than in any other novel, Wharton depicts social class, even caste, as a matter of *things*, including the color of stationery, the texture of tapestries, and especially the cut of clothes. Items of dress, worn by men and women, are read in the context of shopping itself as characters become part of material culture, objects themselves of desire and fulfillment. Chapter 4, "Cut of a Gown," considers the case of a single garment, the Empire-style dress worn to the opera by Ellen Olenska in the opening scene of *The Age of Innocence* (1920). What catches the eye of every man is the large old-fashioned clasp that theatrically brings together yards of luxurious fabric to frame the slope of exposed breast. The plot of the novel moves on a single dress, a hybrid creation that links fashions of the 1870s and the postwar patriotic designs of Paul Poiret. The next chapter, "Dressing for Middle Age," contrasts the prewar tea gown and the postwar chemise, focusing on a perennial conflict of the twentieth century: how to dress mother and daughter. A study of fashion in *The Mother's Recompense* (1925) signals more than a clash over clothes: garments themselves reveal a primal struggle for youth and sexuality, culminating in the white dazzle of a wedding gown. Chapter 6, "Democracy and Dress" examines the last novel in Wharton's oeuvre, *The Buccaneers* (1938), an unfinished tale packed full of clothes. She sets the story, as she did *Bunner Sisters* and *The Age of Innocence*, in the 1870s of her youth. Wharton's tact of omission obtains in that she gives readers only details they need to reconstruct the world of her youth. To accomplish that imaginative task for readers in the twentieth century, she details "every stick of furniture and rag of clothing." Fabrication in a costume drama, such as this one, has the effect of preserving fabric, giving readers imaginative if not quite palpable garments to savor. The blurring of fashion in the novel makes clear, too, that the modern world of the 1930s is present in the portrait of the past.

Wharton's astringency of detail in early stories gives way in later writing to an abundance of things. As she put it in "A Little Girl's New York" (*Harper's* [March 1938]): "Everything that used to form the fabric of our daily life has been torn in shreds, trampled on, destroyed; and hundreds of little incidents, habits, traditions which, when I began to record my past, seemed too insignificant to set down, have acquired the historical importance of fragments of dress and furniture dug up in a Babylonian tomb."[16] Along with other recent scholars and theorists, I take the nature of things, here the designing and making of clothes, as serious study. *Edith Wharton and the Making of Fashion* centers attention on the veil of a hat, the button of a glove, the clasp of an opera gown, and the tulle of a tucker. I sift through remnants—"the fabric of our daily life" and especially "fragments of dress"—to find fresh meaning in literary texts.

## ❦ I

# DRESSING UP

[M]y newest Doucet dress . . . I can see the dress still—and it
was pretty; a tea-rose pink, embroidered with iridescent beads.
—*A Backward Glance*

Edith Wharton liked to dress up. We see her in our mind's eye
sculpted in very few lines, edges of lace and fur with jaw jutting
and hair knotted in a chignon pushed forward on her head like a
crown. The novelist eyed New York and Paris as keenly as any couturier and meant readers to see her as a woman of discerning taste and
personal style. She dressed smartly and yet faithfully in the fashions of
the moneyed class of Old New York, notably in the designs of Charles
Frederick Worth and Jacques Doucet. She comes to us handsomely
groomed in shimmering gowns with thick auburn hair (that resisted,
even as she aged, the turn into gray) and hawklike hazel eyes. Edith
Jones had the luck to have in her youth an hourglass figure—five-foot
three with a twentyish waist flanked by ample breasts and hips—the
defining female profile of the Gilded Age. By 1913, she would resist
tightening the stays of her corset, responding that the looser fit made
her "very comfortable."[1] As she grew thick with age, she ordered
clothes from dressmakers through her secretary, giving specific details
for suits and dresses that flattened her body into the conventional angles of the twentieth century. Always she dressed with a sense of moderation, fitness, and relevance, and we read her dress with these aesthetic principles in mind.

Edith Wharton wrote in her autobiography, *A Backward Glance*
(1934), that the "birth of her identity" had come as a child in the ritual of dressing up. Wearing a bright tartan velvet bonnet and clinging
to her father's hand, she entered the world as an ornamental being,
conscious of her beauty. Only after depicting her success as a fashionable female did she insist that "her first conscious moments" came as

imaginative play in the ritual she called "making up," or storytelling.[2] In her portrait, we see a preliterate child lugging a shaggy volume of Washington Irving's *Alhambra* across the floor of her father's library while her nanny Hannah Doyle and her mother Lucretia Jones listen in delight to the tales she made up: "At any moment the impulse might seize me and then, if the book was in reach, I had only to walk the floor, turning the pages as I walked, to be swept off full sail on the sea of dreams." Much of what readers and scholars have focused on over the years begins in this scene of fictive play. The imaginative child is the Edith Wharton we know well. This chapter considers the other image of the writer, the one who delights in dressing up, and places the ornamental woman in the context of the imaginative writer. How do the twin rituals, "dressing up" and "making up," create Wharton's sense of herself as a New Yorker, as an expatriate living in Paris, and especially as a writer?

Our image of her dressed as an adult comes, for the most part, from a handful of photographs taken as she made her way onto a public stage in 1905 with the publication of *The House of Mirth*, a novel of manners that would become a bestseller, and in 1907 as she tried to repeat her success with *The Fruit of the Tree*, a less successful industrial novel. In her forties she established herself as an American writer as well as a discriminating woman dressed in the French style. Through the icon she established in these photographs we think we know the writer. The image perhaps most familiar to us sets the scene, or the ostensible scene, of the artist at her task of writing. Wharton comes to us dressed, so it seems at first blush, somewhat preposterously for a woman at work: she wears an haute couture tea gown, sewn in a delicate geometric pattern of lace and silk, perhaps the creation of Jacques Doucet (figure 1.1).

I say perhaps because the identification of a specific designer from the remnant image of a photograph is akin to claiming that a photographic image of any work of art gives us enough evidence to determine its creator.[3] A scholar would need more than an image to make a judgment of, say, a painting by Monet; often having the object itself in hand is not enough to say for sure whose work it may be. Garments are especially difficult to identify given their reproducibility and the nature of their production that might well include the work of several seamstresses as well as the designer. Often the designer's identity comes down to the credibility of the label, as the Mint Museum identifies the Worth gown (see figure 1.5): "labeled 'Paris—C. Worth—Paris' and marked '56978' in ink on petersham." The trademark label is printed, that is to say, on Petersham ribbon, the finest of weaves that remains colorfast and resists shrinking. The label itself secures the value of the garment.

The tea gown that Wharton selects for the photo session brings together elements of what was variously called in the nineteenth century artistic, aesthetic, or reform dress. Over the course of the century, as the corset tightened the waist, and the cage crinoline (a framework worn under skirts) and bustle (a large cage or small pad worn over the derriere) exaggerated the hips, reformers advocated rational modes of dress that would allow women greater mobility, flexibility, and comfort. Patricia Cunningham in her study of fashion reform measures the distance between politics and the haute couture marketplace by the design of underwear. She notes that the cage crinoline and the bustle were actually reforms in allowing women to wear fewer petticoats and thus move about more freely in urban streets, a literal and symbolic movement that marked women's increasing activity and involvement in what was termed "the public sphere." Wharton's tea gown required an even lighter corset and no bustle at all. The design grew from the dressing gown, a garment meant to be worn in the privacy of the home. Tea gowns, according to Cunningham and Diana DeMarly, became the favored apparel for informal portraits because they suggested the comfort of the home and, too, because they suggested the pageantry of historic dress.[4]

Perhaps Wharton hoped for the relaxation of the garment to put her at ease in her new profession of authorship. She wears an elegant version of the dress, much like those designed by Jacques Doucet. He originally designed tea gowns for actresses—most famously Réjane—women of the demimonde who had the reputation of being "the tarts and hookers of their day, sometimes known as 'horizonals.'"[5] The silken texture and sinuous lines of Wharton's gown with elaborate lace inserts at the shoulders and across the bodice and skirt suggest intimacy. Still, she sits pensively on the edge of a caned chair at a desk that has neatly tapered legs, a leather pad, and an inkstand. Adorned with her Tiffany engagement ring (that according to biographer Shari Benstock included two bands of diamonds and one of rubies), her left hand gracefully cradles a book atop a manuscript situated between two brass and crystal candlestick lamps.[6] Completing the scene of literary intimacy, a discreet rack displays a single row of books. A marble bust, a mantle, and a sculpture stand sentry, and a Persian carpet creates the dais for the folds of her gown. Not one detail of the stage set escapes the writer's eye, intent on bending the reader's gaze to its will.

The stage that she and her publisher had in mind is one that Wharton would have known well from perusing fashion magazines. Ironically, the tea gown, which had begun as a garment meant for privacy and even seduction, had by the turn into the twentieth century come to be associated with serious female intellectual and artistic labor. Wharton's tea gown looks like an ensemble of skirt and blouse or shirtwaist with what was called a Dutch round neck and a long puffed sleeve, a style featured in Butterick's fashion magazine *The Delineator* in 1904 (figure 1.2). The language of the magazine might be used to describe Wharton's own garment in advertising her as a fashionable novelist: "An attractive waist, especially adapted to development in soft fabrics, is here shown in a make-up of white chiffon cloth and also in figured crêpe de Chine, lace lending a note of relief."[7]

In the privacy of one's home and office, the relaxed design of the tea gown signaled freedom of movement and mind. A writer supposedly had more pressing concerns than fashion. Wharton may well have had in her mind the attire of literary and artistic women featured in the popular French fashion magazine *Femina*. In April 1907, Mme. De Chabannes, Princess Armande de Polignac, appears seated in a caned back chair with her arms stretched across a manuscript on an uncluttered desk, gazing up at the camera in a thoughtful pose very like Wharton's own (figure 1.3).[8] *Femina* featured other bookish women in similarly styled shirtwaists: the novelist Mlle. Yvette Frost places her hand at the side of her head in a thoughtful pose, suggesting, no doubt,

Fig. 1.2. *The Delineator,* "Ladies' Costumes and Waists," December 1904.

Fig. 1.3. *Femina,* no. 149, (1 April 1907), Mme. De Chabannes, Princess Armande de Polignac.

the woman's intellectual strength, as does the same pose of the actress Mme. Simone de Bargy. The shirtwaist was popularized at the turn of the century by Dana Gibson who dressed his signature "girl" in what became an iconic image of the new woman (Figure 1.4).[9] Wharton's tea gown, viewed alongside the garments of other female artists, comes more clearly into its contemporary context. Her fashion and even her pose, as it turns out, are conventional, albeit an haute couture version of conventionality.

To the aspiring novelist, dressing up seems as important as making up. Another familiar vision of the writer shows her standing and gazing down into a book she holds in her hands (figure 1.5). The Christmas holiday pose situates the body, hangerlike, to display ceremonial goods, an ensemble brought together to make clear her social rank and distance from her readers. In sartorial elegance, she wears several objects that she will leave in her will to friends and family members. The dress appears to be beaded and adorned with Valenciennes lace at the bodice; the shoulders are draped in a cloak ruffled in yards of laces that flow from her lifted arm. Her shoulders support lush fur wraps, perhaps her sables, and her neck carries strands of pearls clasped in sapphires and diamonds, apparently the choker necklace or "dog collar"

*Fig. 1.4.* Charles Dana Gibson, woman sitting at a table.

she would leave to Daisy Chanler. The pearls repeat in earrings, a pendant, and a band woven through her hair. The last ornament is her gold chain of diamonds and pearls by Cartier, discreetly tethering a leather cigarette case. The layering of sumptuous vestments seems, at first glance, to fly in the face of moderation, and yet her dress leaves little

*Fig. 1.5.* Edith Wharton, Christmas 1905, dressed in holiday regalia, including beaded dress, antique laces, furs, and pearls. *Yale Collection of American Literature, Beinecke Rare Book and Manuscript Library.*

question about the fitness and relevance of her pedigree. In that way, her raiment is not merely decorative but structural, the sartorial marking of social place. There is no question about her knowledge of fashion among her moneyed class and no doubt that she writes with authority about Old New York.

Two other well-known images from the early years of her writing career appear to have been taken during a single photo session. The dates on the photographs are tentatively dated 1900 and 1907, but the column and the painting in the background are the same and the maturity of her face suggests the later date for both poses. The images show us a public woman no longer in need of a writer's props, no desk, inkstand, or book.[10] In the first shot, she poses as though arriving fresh from the outdoors to stand in front of the painting and column (figure 1.6). She wears a striped coat that has the lushly waled texture of a fabric from the House of Worth, and flat velvet hat with feathered brim that features the head of the bird itself peering down unto her face. The bird looks much like the detail on a hat by Madame Virot of Paris (figure 2.13). Lace scarves and ruffled silk cradle her neck and her hands remain tucked into a fur muff that matches the stole. If the photo is from 1907, it was the year that Mrs. Wharton arrived in Paris, settling into an apartment in the quietly posh rue de Varenne and taking on Morton Fullerton, a practiced and mercurial lover.

The second pose unveils the lady beneath the coat. She relaxes on a divan, hand behind her head, body reclining slightly against a lace pillow and what looks like the coat with its fur wrap and muff (figure 1.7). Wharton, even at rest, is a less than comfortable figure, restricted perhaps by a corset noticeably snug at a waist she had incentive to keep slim in 1907. The suggestion of repose comes, too, from exposed flesh of arm and throat. She dresses in a décolleté evening gown (her favorite style), but, for the sake of her reading audience, she wears a tucker of lace ruffles, covering the cleavage and capping the upper arm, leaving her shoulders provocatively bare. We see a beaded dog collar and pearl pendant. Her right hand grasps a fan at the end of what looks like the Cartier chain. The dress may well be a Doucet creation much like one he designed for Réjane at about the same time.[11] Both dresses have latticed straps across the shoulders and move snugly in at the waist; Réjane's tucker is dark like the dress and more revealing than Wharton's, but the styles are strikingly similar (figure 1.8). Wharton, we note, seems little concerned with the idea of being dressed in the gown of a worldly actress. Fashioning the self as seductress rather than novelist suggests the changes in her life from 1905 to 1907 in moving to Paris, abandoning her husband, and taking on a lover. As though waiting for Morton Fullerton, she appears sensually warm and socially cool.

Other photographs and paintings that have surfaced over the years

*Fig. 1.6.* Edith Wharton with fur collar and muff in a feathered hat, c. 1907. *Yale Collection of American Literature, Beinecke Rare Book and Manuscript Library.* Compare hat designed by Madame Virot, fig. 2.13.

*Fig. 1.7.* Edith Wharton in a black evening gown, perhaps designed by Jacques Doucet; compare Doucet gown, fig. 1.8. Photo dated c. 1900 but probably taken in 1907; compare background in fig. 1.6. *Yale Collection of American Literature, Beinecke Rare Book and Manuscript Library.*

place these familiar ones in context. Her hourglass profile comes into relief in a photograph from the 1880s of the young woman dressed in a Parisian gown trimmed in delicate lace at the bodice and sleeves with a skirt pulled across the front and bustled in the back, a design credited to Charles Frederick Worth (figure 1.9).[12] It is the pose that, as the man she would marry, Teddy Wharton, bragged, made it hard to believe that such a shapely female body could have written a line of poetry. Standing with an elbow on a podium and a graceful hand holding a fan, she seems concerned as much with fashion as poetry. An image of her in the 1890s reveals the depression she suffered in the early years of her marriage and before she emerged as a writer. Wharton wears a tailleur or walking suit with elaborate leg-of-mutton sleeves, the defining fashion detail of the decade, and a style that makes its way into *Bunner Sisters*, a story about seamstresses she was writing at the time. The wide shoulders are meant to slim the waist that for

Wharton seems not to require the illusion (figure 1.10). Her straw hat, perhaps the design of Madame Virot, also typifies the style of the decade, a flat brim sitting atop upswept hair and ornately trimmed in egret plume. Posing with her are a pair of lapdogs, their eyes as keenly as hers on the camera as it flashes. She and Teddy championed animal rights, belonged to the New York Society for the Prevention of Cruelty to Animals, and pampered their pedigree dogs. We note that even her choice of dogs signaled her wealth: over the years, she owned Pekingese, Skye terriers, Pomeranians, poodles, and papillons.[13]

The several candid photographs that have survived give another version of the fashionable writer, a woman intend on enjoying private pleasures. We have one surprisingly informal shot of her as an independent woman, much in the style of the Gibson Girl, standing under a tree, smoking a cigarette, dressed in a plaid skirt and shirtwaist with an elaborately feathered hat that blends into the tree in the back-

*Fig. 1.10.* Edith Wharton at age twenty-eight in a woman's suit or tailleur with leg-of-mutton sleeves and straw hat, 1890, together with two of her dogs. *Yale Collection of American Literature, Beinecke Rare Book and Manuscript Library.*

ground (figure 1.11). Hand on hip, taking a determined drag on the cigarette, she seems oblivious of her friends, the camera, and our gaze. She loved to smoke and gave cigarettes and cigars to her characters—often her favorite ones—as they indulged in conversation and intro-spection. Lily Bart, for example, opens her gold cigarette case at the end of its chain tether as she asks Lawrence Selden for a fresh supply during their first serious conversation, this one about the nature of fashion. Receiving an honorary degree from Yale in 1923, Wharton smiles broadly for the camera in photographs that show her draped in academic regalia. The day was an especially hot one, according to bi-

ographer Hermione Lee, and the open academic gown reveals a loose-fitting dress she had ordered through her secretary who had given precise instructions to Madame Denise, Wharton's dressmaker at the time.[14] Her Cartier chain no longer tethers a cigarette case but, more prosaically for the aging woman, a lorgnette.

In her sixties and seventies, Edith Wharton appeared in photographs wearing colorful sweaters, garments we might expect to find adorning the body of an aging woman. In a photographic session at the Pavillon Colombe in 1931, we return in delight to a reprise of the writer at her desk, perhaps the desk of the 1905 photograph, and sit-

*Fig. 1.11.* Edith Wharton smoking in Lenox, Massachusetts, in 1905, dressed in a plaid skirt and white waist or shirt with a feathered hat. *Yale Collection of American Literature, Beinecke Rare Book and Manuscript Library.*

ting in a caned chair, more angular than the early version (figure 1.12). She seems at ease, dressed in a crocheted sweater, as she works on a manuscript or on a letter to a friend; her lorgnette dangles from the Cartier chain. The profile is familiar to us but the smile is refreshingly new. Pictures of Wharton in her sixties and seventies show a relaxed woman, traveling and picnicking in intimate company with people she trusted and adored. She dresses in knit jackets and sweaters, wearing her crocheted favorite aboard the yacht *Osprey* during a Mediterranean cruise in 1926 with a group that included Daisy Chanler (figure 1.13). Wharton tends to be the central figure in photographs, drawing our gaze to her. On the deck, she is seated while the others stand around her: it was a trip, as the photo suggests, that she gave as a gift to her friends.

The last picture taken of her is, in many ways, the most honest image we have of the woman in the fashion of a novelist. She stands in the doorway of her country home Pavillon Colombe, no longer bothering to dress for the camera in an elegant tea gown. Rather, she wears an elegant dressing gown of silks and laces, hand on hip, beaming a full laugh at the camera (figure 1.14). She gives us no hint that she will die within the month. That image, more than any other, reveals the nature of the novelist. Edith Wharton wore a lace-trimmed dressing gown and cap every morning of her life as she wrote in bed, propped on feather pillows among linens in shades of pink with the

early morning sun lighting the pages, etched longhand in ink as they fluttered one by one to the floor to be scooped up later by her secretary and taken to the typewriter—*not* the machine but a woman she referred to as "the blond." The pages would be returned to her, typed and numbered, as she began the next day's writing by rereading and revising the pages as they piled up again on the floor.

Reading her books with fashion in mind, we find the same aesthetics of moderation, fitness, and relevance that we see in her photographs. She had a remarkably coherent writing career, one that we can trace in her nonfiction as well as in her novels and short stories. The first book she published was not a novel but a study of domestic fashion, *The Decoration of Houses* (1897), where she sketches the relationship between architecture and ornamentation. Form, she makes clear in example after example, underlies all valid decoration. Her insistence on structural integrity in that seminal book finds its way twenty years later into *French Ways and Their Meaning* (1919), a wartime study of French and American manners and morals. And in the next decade, she transfers ideas about decoration and culture to literary art in *The Writing of Fiction* (1925). A good writer understands the relationship between decoration and structure.

Decoration must "rhyme to the eye," she schooled her compatriots, much as poetry satisfies the ear. *The Decoration of Houses*, written with the fashionable Newport architect Ogden Codman, Jr., begins

*Fig. 1.13.* Edith Wharton, wearing a crocheted sweater and cloche hat, aboard the yacht *Osprey* with friends, including Daisy Chanler, on 11 April 1926. *Yale Collection of American Literature, Beinecke Rare Book and Manuscript Library.*

*Fig. 1.14.* Edith Wharton, Pavillon Colombe, St. Brice-sous-forêt, July 1937, just days before her death, wearing a silk and lace dressing gown and sleeping cap. *Yale Collection of American Literature, Beinecke Rare Book and Manuscript Library.*

with the very principle of design that they believed functions in all of art. Although Wharton developed ideas along with Codman, the voice in the prose is recognizably hers as she passes judgment on cornices, windows, and doors that serve, as well, as judgment on people and culture. We imagine the writer leaning forward in the caned chair and talking intimately with her readers. "Rooms may be decorated in two ways," she declares without a hint of hesitancy, "by a superficial application of ornament totally independent of structure, or by means of those architectural features which are part of the organism of every house, inside as well as out."[15] A structure comes to life if it grows from the inside out. She castigates decorators for "the piling up of heterogeneous ornament" and the abandoning of the architectural organism (*DH* xx).

Lest the well-to-do reader, sinking into an elaborately stuffed chair in a Newport summer house, have in mind the crassness of the middling throng, Wharton insists that we do not require money to be fashionable. Simplicity of line and honesty in form are available to owners of even a modest cottage. Fashion does not require wealth but taste: "[I]t is easy to make a room with tinted walls, deal furniture and dimity curtains more beautiful, because more logical and harmonious, than a ball-room lined with gold and marble, in which the laws of rhythm and logic have been ignored" (*DH* 16). Those in the leisure class, in truth, are more culpable than those in the working class. The rich, she charges, have grown callous to the beauty of architectural form and have, consequently, furnished their costly homes with vulgar decoration, the symbolic drapery of wealth and status. And perhaps more to the point, the rich bear the burden of setting the example. She sternly adds, "Every good molding, every carefully studied detail, exacted by those who can afford to indulge their taste, will in time find its way to the carpenter-built cottage" (*DH* xxii). Imaginary and symbolic meanings come to us down the generations and across social classes, passed from hand to hand. The Rhinelanders and Joneses who formed her family had come from England and Holland and had been in the United States long enough to have little memory of European ways. They made money as merchants and bankers in New York, a city whose immigrant population produced the very goods that marked social rank. Even as the economic system churned out a vast array of goods, New Yorkers understood little about the subtle acquisition of taste, or so she feared.

Wharton believed that women by virtue of their gender (and we have to assume that many if not most of her readers were women) are not any surer of taste than the rich are by virtue of their wealth. She is especially rough on women because they seem to her too easily led by popular taste. "Men, in these matters, are less exacting than women," she needles, "because their demands, besides being simpler, are uncomplicated by the feminine tendency to want things because other people have them, rather than to have things because they are wanted" (*DH* 17). Wharton's men care about comfort—light, heat, and access—and convenience as the central features of household decoration. Her women too quickly abandon comfort for frill. "Lingerie effects do not combine well with architecture," Wharton chides female readers, "and the more architecturally a window is treated, the less it need be dressed up in ruffles" (*DH* 72). The frilling of a window in order to create a frame on the inside of a house is wrong because it lacks a structural purpose; outside the house, the lace obstructs the view and constitutes an unseemly display of luxury. Women make a mistake—and an equal one—in falsely ruffling a window as in ruffling their bodies in garments that may be fashionable without being tasteful.

Wharton arrives at the idea that will govern all her writing in the future, fiction as well as nonfiction, when she declares that the heart of household decoration, indeed the heart of all art, is simplicity: "Moderation, fitness, relevance—these are the qualities that give permanence to the work of the great architects. *Tout ce qui n'est pas nécessaire est nuisible*" (*DH* 198). What is not in a room or on a page determines the value of what remains, the mark of a master's hand, the "tact of omission." Tact, the skill of avoiding offense and winning trust, measures maturity, delicacy, discernment, and acumen. An imaginative creation—fiction, architecture, decoration, fashion, and any other art—is spoiled by excess detail and useless ornament. A painting becomes art in what is *not* on the canvas, just as a narrative becomes a novel by the force of the words that are not on the page. A master knows the art of conjuring.

The aesthetic principle of tact makes its way into her analysis of culture in *French Ways and Their Meaning*, a book she wrote during the war years to introduce Americans to France. For her, what appears at first sight to be mere decoration signals cultural and artistic sensibility. A stroll around Paris in the evening, she declares, will give a tourist a view of buildings that "bear the stamp of the most refined taste the world has known since the decline of the arts in Italy."[16] To acquire and, more specifically for Americans, to reacquire taste, one must turn to the European city street. Fashion and architecture measure refinement. Taste, for her, finally comes down to the "way the women put on their hats, and the upholsterers drape their curtains" (*FW* 39). Gesture and movement evince cultural integrity. At the heart of French taste is the knowledge that the curve in the brim of a woman's hat is the same as the curve Auguste Rodin sculpted in marble, and the drapes hang so agreeably at the window because they mimic the lines of a tree branch. In many ways, Wharton's ideas were belated: since the middle of the nineteenth century, when the Houses of Worth and Doucet had opened in the rue de la Paix, stylish people worldwide agreed that the French defined fashion. Wealthy women in Europe and the Americas traveled to Paris to buy their clothes, and the French sense of style worked its way into a marketplace that was becoming, then as now, defined by an increasingly global culture. Magazines in the United States, especially *Vogue*, glorified Parisian designers, whose labels transformed any dress into a desired style.

Wharton admired a country that designed and constructed beautiful clothes. Taste in clothing, to her mind, expresses a culture's long embrace of balance, suitability, harmony, and grace, features that can be seen in the portal of a cathedral, or along the banks of an urban river, and in the traditions of political institutions. "For it must never be forgotten that if the fashion of our note-paper and the cut of our dresses come from France," she insists, "so do the conceptions of liberty and justice on which our republican institutions are based" (*FW* 113). Surprisingly, she links notepaper and dresses, seemingly superficial expressions of value, to fundamental political ideas of liberty and justice. Reading fashion, the seemingly superficial wrapper, is the way to read the underlying structure, the interweaving of manners, values, politics, and morals. We cannot drape ourselves in fabric and, thereby, conceal our nature. The choosing of fabric, the draping of a dress, and veiling of a hat reveal more than they conceal.

Dressing up, decorating a room, and designing a political system are kin to making up fictional stories. A writer relies on a sense of moderation, fitness, and relevance, the same principles that guide an architect: "*Tout ce qui n'est pas nécessaire est nuisible.*" In *The Writing of Fiction*, she bemoans the creation of writing courses at universities that promise the maturing of literary skill over a semester, as though the art of writing could be had for the price of tuition and in the company of academics. And yet, we note, she confidently offers her own primer. Here too she argues that the French have led the way by creating the genre of literary realism: "Balzac was the first not only to see his people, physically and morally, in their habit as they lived, with all their personal hobbies and infirmities, and make the reader see them, but to draw his dramatic action as much from the relation of his characters to their homes, streets, towns, professions, inherited habits and opinions, as from their fortuitous contacts with each other."[17] She praises Balzac and Stendhal for their understanding "that the bounds of a personality are not reproducible by a sharp black line, but that each of us flows imperceptibly into adjacent people and things" (*WF* 7). The realist novel juxtaposes people and things; yet such details, she warns, must not intrude on the narrative.

Just as window treatments rely on architectural form and ball gowns on the body's bones, so too "adjacent people and things" in a novel must be supported by the frame of the story. In making her argument, Wharton strings together a dazzling set of analogies: between writing and acting ("the cleverest actresses put on the least paint"); writing and sketching ("a great draughtsman gives the essentials of a face or landscape in a half-a-dozen strokes"); writing and cooking ("the seemingly simple sauces are those that have been most cunningly combined and then most completely blent") and, finally, writing and fashion ("the simplest-looking dresses [are] those that require most study to design") (WF 54). Acting, drawing, cooking, and fashion—all require an eye for moderation, fitness, and relevance, the sort of tact she advocates. She cautions writers, just as she had cautioned decorators, to consider a story's architectonic structure before indulging in the "indolent habit of decorating its surface." The established writer in her sixties gives the same advice she had given as a novice decorator in her thirties that the "secret of success" lies in the "instinct of selection" (*WF* 142). A good writer "uses every scrap of colour, every picturesque by-product of his subject which that subject yields; but he avoids adding to it a single touch, however decoratively tempting, which is not part of the design" (*WF* 138). An astute realist knows how to evoke the drape of a gown without explicitly drawing one.

Early in Wharton's writing career, heroines and heroes parade on stage with a tint of color, a sweep of fabric, and a wisp of scent. In *The Touchstone* (1900), the would-be hero Stephen Glennard affords a wife by selling the letters of his dead lover Margaret Aubyn and seems as blind to fashion as he is to ethics, preferring a "civilized uniformity of dress clothes."[18] Clothes, it is fair to say, function as metaphors more than actual garments; as his wife uncovers the truth, he sees himself doing "penance naked in the market-place" (*T* 153). Hint of color and whiff of scent link generations in *Sanctuary* (1903), where Kate Orme sees her stepmother as "a scented silvery person" and later views the "silvery flexible furs" of her son's fiancée.[19] And as Fanny de Malrive arrives on stage in *Madame de Treymes* (1906), John Durham sees "a mere stick to hang clothes on (but they *did* hang!)." She has forgotten to pull on her gloves in spite of the fact that she was "the kind of woman who always presents herself to the mind's eye as completely equipped, as made up of exquisitely cared for and finely-related details."[20] Sartorial details elude us, however, leaving only "the very fall of a flounce and tilt of a feather" (*MT* 18) to evoke images of actual dresses and hats.

Reading the depiction of dress in Wharton's writing, we find that the later a novel was written and the earlier the setting of the story, the more precise and even lavish the detail about garments and accessories. In the opening of *The House of Mirth*, a early novel set in the contemporary era, we stand with Lawrence Selden and gaze on Lily Bart's desultory body with little sense of what she has on: "Her vivid head, relieved against the dull tints of the crowd, made her more conspicuous than in a ball-room, and under her dark hat and veil she regained the girlish smoothness, the purity of tint, that she was beginning to lose after eleven years of late hours and indefatigable dancing" (*HM* 4). It is Selden who is reading dress for us, and the male eye notes color and texture; Lily is vivid in a dull crowd and her skin seems smooth under a dark veil. Throughout the novel, Lily Bart's gowns exist in suggestion rather than precise design and fabric. At the novel's end, the heroine, rather than the less observant hero, gazes on the couture collection that has defined her as a social being, draping each delicate fashion across the bed. Yet here, too, Wharton gives us a delicate sketch rather than a heavy drawing. Lily senses "the long unerring lines, the sweep and amplitude of the great artist's stroke." The delicate textures and subtle smells, like Proust's *petite madeleine*, elicit memories. Even the gown she wore for the Reynolds tableau vivant exists in muted suggestion of smell rather than clear line; its "long flexible folds, as she shook them out gave forth an odour of violets." The truth is that readers in 1905 would need little else in bringing vividly to mind Lily's clothes.

We know that Wharton struggled against the popular images of femininity idealized by Gibson's drawings, even as she wore the fashions herself. What irritated her as novelist and a woman was the fraudulence of the Gibson drawings themselves, presenting a lavishly dressed female body, tightly corseted and yet supposedly agile. The heroines of her fiction suffer the misconception that a culture that would tightly lace the body would offer free social and political movement. Wharton struggled to keep such images out of her novels as she worked to establish her reputation as a writer. Readers, then perhaps as now, bought magazines and books that were rich in illustration. The turn into the twentieth century, after all, was recorded in photographs and increasingly defined by motion pictures. *The House of Mirth* came out, as was the custom, first in serialized form in *Scribner's* magazine and included illustrations by A. B. Wenzell. He drew Lily Bart in the conventions of a commercial marketplace that was saturated with the "Gibson Girl" (figure 1.15). As the scholar Edith Thornton explains, Wharton lamented her decision to allow the illustrations into the printed book and confided to her editor William Brownell, "I sank to the depth of letting the illustrations be in the book—& oh, I wish I hadn't now."[21] To salve her conscience, she insisted that several copies of the book be printed without the offending images for distribution to her friends. What she hoped for was the strength of language over illustration as she dressed her heroine in the sinuous folds of Parisian gowns.

Edith Wharton, as an artist, balances eidetic memory and aesthetic tact. The question in her mind was, How much detail does a story need? After the First World War, many of her heroines come gowned in rich fabrics and specific styles from the late nineteenth century. She wrote to her sister-in-law Mary Cadwalader "Minny" Jones (who helped over the years with research for Wharton's fictional accounts of the past) about the 1921 dramatic production of *The Age of Innocence*, a novel set in the 1870s: "I am very anxious about the staging & dressing. I could do every stick of furniture & every rag of cloth myself, for every detail of that far-off scene was indelibly stamped on my infant

brain."[22] The novel's heroine Ellen Olenska makes her reentry into Old New York in sharp focus as a slim young woman with curly brown hair held by a diamond tiara: "The suggestion of this headdress, which gave her what was then called a 'Josephine look,' was carried out in the cut of the dark blue velvet gown rather theatrically caught up under her bosom by a girdle with a large old-fashioned clasp" (*AI* 19). Not much is left to the imagination.

Wharton's writing changes over time as she stages dramas that rely on a knowledge of things, the detail of dresses and carriages and houses. Even so, I argue, she never changes her sense of moderation, fitness, and relevance. Between the writing of her two most famous novels, *The House of Mirth* (1905) and *The Age of Innocence* (1920), the world changed in cataclysmic ways. The First World War threatened every writer's sense of order. Edith Wharton, who was living in Paris and organizing war relief, felt the battle acutely, describing the scene as a house on fire. In response to the destruction she witnessed, her fiction in the 1920s and 1930s is full of the things she felt needed saving. She salvages precise details of opera houses and ballrooms, broughams and landaus, waistcoats and gowns, tulle tuckers and handmade laces, the artifacts of Old New York she had allowed readers of her earlier novels to imagine for themselves. In her sixties and seventies, Edith Wharton wove into her fiction and nonfiction astonishing fashion detail.

In the quartet of stories that make up *Old New York* (1924), for example, Wharton draws her tales in thick lines. Mrs. Raycie, wife of a "full-rigged" commodore, in "False Dawn" arrays her "pale amplitude" in "her best watered silk (the kind that stood alone), and framed her countenance in the innumerable blonde lace ruffles and clustered purple grapes of her newest Paris cap."[23] Likewise in "The Old Maid," Delia Lovell Ralston, at twenty-five, comes draped in a grey silk stretched across her bosom, causing "her heavy gold watch-chain— after it left the anchorage of the brooch of St. Peter's in mosaic that fastened her low-cut Cluny collar—to dangle perilously in the void above a tiny waist buckled into a velvet waist-band" (*ONY* 81). The sweep and amplitude of her breasts rest under a scarf of cashmere. Still, Wharton displays tact in giving her readers only what she thinks they need to know in order to dress her characters.

Her last novel, posthumously published, *The Buccaneers* (1938), leaves little to the imagination. The aging Mrs. St. George, sitting on the verandah of the Grand Union Hotel in Saratoga, New York, thinks back to a time when crinolines were worn to bell the shape of long skirts. Her delight comes to us filtered through Wharton's sarcasm. "What," Mrs. St. George muses, "could be prettier, or more suitable for a lady, than a black alpaca skirt looped up like a window-drapery above a scarlet serge underskirt, the whole surmounted by a wide-sleeved black poplin jacket with ruffled muslin undersleeves, and a flat 'pork-pie' hat like the one the Empress Eugenie was represented as wearing on the beach at Biarritz?"[24] What indeed? Wharton's irritation with skirts rigged up like window-drapery, we note, lasted a lifetime. The heavy layering of fabrics may well have seemed necessary as she schooled readers much younger than she about the American sense of fashion—or lack thereof—in the Gilded Age.

As a septuagenarian, Wharton wrote two memoirs, a manuscript fragment "Life and I," and the autobiography *A Backward Glance*, that tell the story of how she came to be conscious of her twin desires to look beautiful and to write well. In her portraits of life at the turn into the twentieth century, she worked to rebuild a culture that had become lost in the collective consciousness of her compatriots. She abandoned "Life & I," probably because it drew too personal a portrait of the artist as a young woman. Instead, she published *A Backward Glance* because in that version she managed to move away from the private "I" and into the literary "Life" she had come to inhabit. Just as her publicity photographs divert our gaze, so her autobiography diverts our attention. She looked upon the Depression years following the cataclysm of war as a time of considerable material and cultural loss. The hieroglyphic world of Old New York had little resonance for Americans of any social class as they struggled with the prosaic problems of bare survival. Too, the very fabrics, textures, colors and designs of garments in the late nineteenth century of her youth and even the fashions at the turn into the twentieth century had fallen out of style, out of favor, and indeed out of memory. Parisian haute couture houses, even before the war, had begun to loosen the lines of women's clothing and abandon the tight corset that had defined the outline of the female body for a century. During the war, many houses in Paris closed briefly; when they reopened, designers continued to create shorter, looser, more angular female styles that would by the 1920s have the effect of freeing the body and blurring gender. Even as she settled her own thickening waistline into the modish straight lines, Edith Wharton sought to replenish the collective memory of apparel in the Gilded Age. That impulse seems to have led the writer, who had earlier warned against the piling up of ornament, to bring items into the light, displaying each one before readers.

"Life and I" rustles with fashion. She describes herself as a child who had perfect pitch, not in her ear but in her eye, beauty and ugliness standing as absolute poles in her mind. The young Edith Jones, called by her baby name Pussy, wears the "very handsome bonnet made of bright Tartan velvet with a white satin ground, with a full ruffling of blonde lace under the brim" (compare the hat and coat in figure 1.16). [25] At the tender age of four, Pussy wants more than anything "to look pretty" and measures victory in the prize of a kiss from her cousin. She celebrates the power of her vivid memory: "I always saw the visible world as a series of pictures, more or less harmoniously composed, & the wish *to make the picture prettier* was, as nearly as I can define it, the form my feminine instinct of pleasing took" ("LaI" 1071). The goal of her writing is to detail the precise elements of the bonnet, its velvet texture, the tartan colors, even the blond ruffling, in a seemingly superficial discussion of fashion that suggests a depth of cultural understanding. The little girl, young as she was, had been schooled in Europe on the nature of beauty; on returning to New York, she had proclaimed, "*How ugly it is!*" (see figure 1.17). The juxtaposition of cultures heightened her sense of living two lives, one of normal childhood play and the other "parallel with it, but known to

*Fig. 1.16.* Edith Jones at five years old, 1867, dressed in a stylish hat, coat, and boots. *Yale Collection of American Literature, Beinecke Rare Book and Manuscript Library.*

*Fig. 1.17.* Edward Harrison May, painting of the red-headed Edith Wharton at age eight, 1870, in a blue satin dress with sash and fur trim at the neck and cuff. *Yale Collection of American Literature, Beinecke Rare Book and Manuscript Library.* (Plate 4.)

none but myself—a life of dreams & visions, set to the rhythm of the poets, & peopled with thronging images of beauty."

The autobiography, *A Backward Glance*, depicts the same scene in which the young New Yorker dons the bonnet for a walk with her father that culminates in the kiss from her cousin. Remembering the

Fig. 1.18. Edith Wharton's great-grandmother, Mrs. Rhinelander, in *A Backward Glance*.

Fig. 1.19. Edith Wharton's great-grandmother, Mrs. Stevens and her son, painter unknown, in *A Backward Glance*.

reflection in the hall mirror as she walks out of the door, Wharton describes her finery as much from imagination as memory in that the bonnet itself changes from its earlier iteration. The scene explodes with colors and textures: "The bonnet (I can see it today) was of white satin, patterned with a pink and green plaid in raised velvet. It was all drawn into close gathers, with a *bavolet* in the neck to keep out the cold, and thick ruffles of silky *blonde* lace under the brim in front. As the air was very cold a gossamer veil of the finest white Shetland wool was drawn about the bonnet and hung down over the wearer's round red cheek like the white paper filigree over a Valentine" (*BG* 777). As she revises the earlier description, the bonnet comes into sharper view—white satin background with pink and green plaid embossing veiled in white filigree—as a valentine. Dressing up awakens her to the importance of adornment: "so that I may date from that hour the birth of the conscious and feminine *me* in the little girl's vague soul" (*BG* 777–778). The pudgy little cousin lifts the woolen veil to kiss young Edith Jones, defining her for herself, as the story goes. The heart-shaped bonnet signifies beauty—and surprisingly, given the fact that she was only four years old, hints at sexuality, the essential elements of female knowledge for a young girl in Old New York.

All her female ancestors are likewise defined by dress, the details of their garments coming from paintings of individuals and family groups (figures 1.18 and 1.19). Reading dress in the portraits, Wharton tells us that the women in her mother's family, the Rhinelanders, wore beaver hats and woolen dresses that marked their middle-class status at the turn into the nineteenth century: "In winter their 'best dresses' were low-necked and short-sleeved frocks, of pea-green merino, with gray beaver hats trimmed with Tartan ribbons, white cotton stockings and heelless prunella slippers" (BG 792). The seemingly superficial details of dress—pea-green merino frocks, gray beaver hats with tartan ribbons, heelless prunella slippers—constitute the only knowledge a woman may have of the females who preceded her, a knowledge based solely on fashion and what it might symbolize for the viewer who gazes upon the portraits decades later. The only other hints come from her mother's stories that define such garments as old-fashioned and, more so, signs of relative poverty. After Lucretia Rhinelander married the wealthier George Frederic Jones, she came to distinguish herself as the best-dressed woman in New York society—or so her daughter believed. On her tour of Parisian couture houses, as the family story goes, she was intent on rectifying the indignities of the humble apparel she had been forced to borrow from her mother.

Lucretia Jones shopped at the House of Worth, where ladies of assorted lineages gained passage by virtue of their pocketbooks. Wealthy American women liked doing business with Charles Frederick Worth because he spoke to them in English, putting them at ease as he subdued and seduced them into luxury. The shopping ritual began by marching sometimes bewildered women through a maze of spaces, colors, and textures configured to urge them toward a considerable purchase. They ascended a red-carpet stairway and waited in a black and white vestibule, to cleanse the visual palate, before being paraded through Worth's private collections of snuffboxes and fans.[26] The women were then allowed into the recesses of his lair, rooms full of watery silks, rich brocades, dense velvets, and finely woven woolens, where wooden models dressed in the year's fashions stood surrounded by mirrors tempered in soft light. The men accompanying the ladies had the luxury of distance. Many male observers noted the absurdities of Worth's stagecraft and his personal style; he dressed in beret and smock to pass himself off as a sort of Rembrandt (figure 1.20). Hippolyte Taine wrote a skit in 1867 that caricatured the designer as a man who "receives in a velvet jacket, lounging on a divan, cigar in mouth." Charles Dickens mocked supposedly modest ladies who allowed male couturiers to "robe them, unrobe them, and make them turn backwards and forward before them." In an 1871 interview, Charles Frederick Worth observed smugly that "the women who come to me want to ask for my ideas, not to follow their own." He manipulated the ironies of the exchange as women spent the riches of the Gilded Age on French garments, designed by an Englishman, in order to mark

*Fig. 1.20.* Charles Frederick Worth by Félix Nadar, 1895, in Rembrandt's style of dress. *Commons.wikimedia.org.*

their social status and cultural refinement in America. The couture industry, then as now, offered elaborate drama for observers and writers of all sorts.

Edith Wharton's mother Lucretia Stevens Rhinelander struggled, as her daughter noted, to become New York's best-dressed woman. Even before her marriage, family photographs reveal a handsome young woman dressed in the fashion of pre–Civil War America: she appears in an elaborate day ensemble with a crinoline bell-shaped skirt, outlined in a cascade of contrasting fabrics that emphasize the wide hem and sleeve and, as a consequence, slenderize the waist. We note that the bonnet, pulled back slightly and tied in a bow under her chin, mimics the valentine shape of the girlhood bonnet Edith remembers herself wearing (figure 1.21). Her desire to dress as well as her mother dressed—that is, literally for the Jones daughter to keep up with the Joneses—is clear in the family album as well as in Wharton's autobiography.

In *A Backward Glance*, she details her mother's triumphant Paris shopping tour after her marriage that included a "white satin bonnet

trimmed with white marabout and crystal drops in which the bride made her wedding visits, and a 'capeline' of *gorge de pigeon* taffetas with a wreath of flowers in shiny brown kid" (*BG* 796). Such shopping was not cheap and, for women of Wharton's class, several changes of outfit would be worn each day, making it necessary to buy dozens of gowns and coats and suits and hats at a time. Valerie Steele in *Paris Fashion* records a typical order of seven day ensembles, including a dark blue poplin outfit, a black velvet suit with sable hat, a brown coat trimmed in sealskin, a purple velvet dress with pheasant feathers and coat to match, a grey velvet gown with chinchilla coat and hat, a green hunting costume, and a dark blue traveling suit. For the evening, the same order included a dress of light green tulle embroidered with silver, one in light-grey satin trimmed with Brussels lace flounces, another in black lace over white tulle, and yet another in light blue tulle with Valenciennes lace. And for the afternoon, the same woman purchased gowns in lilac faille, light café au lait, green faille with a Charlotte Corday sash, red faille, and a final one in grey.[27] As Wharton notes, with only a trace of characteristic irony, it is such booty that marks social rank.

Wharton claims three hundred years of colonial history on her father's side of the family, and here, too, the Jones women are knowable only through fashion. Looking at family paintings, Wharton notes a wedding dress of "a gauzy Directoire web of embroidered 'India mull'" (*BG* 783) and precious little else. She concludes that "so it happens that I know less than nothing of the particular virtues, gifts and modest accomplishments of the young women with pearls in their looped hair or cambric ruffs around their slim necks, who prepared the way for my generation" (*BG* 788). A woman is known and remembered for her fashion; her virtues, gifts, and accomplishments count as "less than nothing." We note, however, that Indian embroidery, looped pearls, and cambric ruffs mark the status of the Jones clan (Edith herself would weave pearls through her hair). The Directoire gown (the cut of Ellen Olenska's opera dress in *The Age of Innocence*) was the style favored by Josephine, the wife of Napoléon Bonaparte; thus, the fashion carries the name of the Directoire or Empire period in France. The chemise style with its high waist replicated the draping of fabric on Greek statues and came into and out of style over the nineteenth century, having the clear advantage of providing women relief from the bite of a corset. We note, too, from Wharton's descriptions of female dress that although the Joneses were wealthier than the Rhinelanders, nothing in the paintings suggests that any female forebears ventured beyond conventional fashion.

The paintings provide Wharton a frame for telling the story of her own life, the dual strivings for beauty and accomplishment, as a portrait of the female artist in America. The elegant woman in the 1905 pose, sitting on the edge of the caned chair with her tea gown forming a dais at her feet, is the symbolic heir of generations of the materially successful in the New World. The decorative, moneyed world of Old New York with an elite society that summered in Newport, Rhode Island, gave birth to a woman who understood the intricacies of adornment. Yet Edith Wharton claims that only through the art of fiction did she achieve a true sense of self. "I had yet no real personality of my own," she insists, "and was not to acquire one till my first volume of short stories was published—and that was not until 1899" (BG 868). That's a strong claim: no real personality until editors, publishers, and readers discovered her literary talent. Her aesthetic principles—she is adamant about this point—developed quite apart from her social and cultural birthplace. Old New York provided nothing to nourish and nurture the soul of a young female artist. "I have often wondered," she muses, "in looking back at the slow stammering beginnings of my literary life, whether or not it is a good thing for the creative artist to grow up in an atmosphere where the arts are simply nonexistent" (BG 874). She suffered through years of neurasthenic illness and depressive doubt, years she numbered as twelve, and battled "through a thick fog of indifference" to emerge as the successful lady novelist (BG 875).

In the photograph of 1905, what the writer allows her reader to see is the lady in her library, sitting stiffly in what may well be a Doucet tea gown. Wharton claimed that she had worn one of his dresses to woo Henry James when she attended a party in the 1890s given in Paris by Edward Boit, "the brilliant water-colour painter whose talent Sargent so much admired" (BG 913). The dress was chosen by her discriminating eye to capture the gaze of the distinguished literary figure who strove to be one on whom nothing is lost. Following the ritual of her class, the shy ingénue selected the Doucet gown. "I can see the dress still—and it *was* pretty; a tea-rose pink, embroidered with iridescent beads," she remembers in noteworthy detail in *A Backward Glance*. She may have had in memory the delicate gown she had worn in a photograph from the period (figure 1.22). She appears here mature, fashionable, handsome, and confident; yet, as her story goes, James missed the cue, ignoring both gown and woman. On a second occasion, she donned a *"beautiful new hat!"* designed perhaps by the French milliner Madame Virot: "I was almost sure it was becoming, and I felt that if he would only tell me so I might at last pluck up courage to blurt out my admiration for 'Daisy Miller' and 'The Portrait of a Lady'" (BG 913).

The great man's acknowledgment of her fashionable hat, she suggests, would have echoed her cousin's attraction to her valentine bon-

net. Henry James, however, remained oblivious to both gown and hat—but not because he never thought about fashion. He was himself meticulously bearded at those Parisian parties: Wharton described him as "the bearded Penseroso of Sargent's delicate drawing, soberly fastidious in dress and manner, cut on the approved pattern of the *homme du monde*" (BG 914). Even years later after he had gained too much weight to carry off a youthful style of dress and had drifted into more comfortable clothes and shaved his beard, Wharton tells the story of his lingering fastidiousness in choosing a hat, a selection that signaled as much for a man as it did for a woman. Henry kept everyone waiting as he puzzled over styles, arguing that he wanted one like everybody else's, until Edith eased him into a decision by joking that what he sought was a hat "'*pour l'homme moyen sensuel*'" (*BG* 915). An Old New York sense of fashion held them both in its grip.

We do know that every word that Edith Wharton had to say about fashion needs to be read with the sort of care she took in selecting it. Take the dropping of the name Jacques Doucet; an urbane figure shown here in a caricature by Leonetto Cappiello (1875–1942), an Italian illustrator and advertiser who lived in Paris (figure 1.23). For any sophisticated reader in the early twentieth century, the name Doucet suggests much more than a dress designer. By the 1890s, when Mrs. Wharton selected a gown to meet Henry James, the hallmark of Doucet gowns was a contrast of textures—*gros point de Venise* lace, feathers, beadwork, embroidery, flowers and ribbons—in distinctive geometric patterns. What Wharton does not tell us is that Jacques Doucet was a connoisseur of other arts and an avid collector of eighteenth-century French furniture. Charles Frederick's son Jean-Philippe Worth saw Doucet as a rival, cattily charging that the money he made came from his art collection and not from his couture designs. Biographer Fran-

*Fig. 1.23.* Leonetto Cappiello (1875–1942), "Caricature de Jacques Doucet (Paris 1853–1929), couturier, collectionneur et mécène." *Avignon Musée Angladon, ADAGP 2008.*

çois Chapon claims Doucet liked to think of himself as an art collector and connoisseur and not a designer of women's clothes: "No one was ever absent as Doucet was from all the professional situations where one would have expected to find him."[28] He bought rare manuscripts by Apollinaire, Baudelaire, Cocteau, Gide, Mallarmé, Verlaine, and Stendahl and commissioned Pierre Legrain and Rose Adler to design stunning Art Deco bindings for his collection, a project that changed the face of bookbinding design, first in France and then in Europe and America.[29] According to most accounts, it was Legrain who induced Doucet in 1912 to sell his collection of eighteenth-century furniture and spend the money collecting contemporary art. Doucet's apartment became known as a temple of modern art for his collection and its interior decoration. He bought works by Impressionists and Post-Impressionists, including Braque, Derain, Laurencin, and Matisse. His most remarkable acquisition was Pablo Picasso's *Les Demoiselles d'Avignon*, which he placed in his staircase. Fascination with cubism influenced his dress designs, too, as he began, along with other couturiers, most notably Paul Poiret, Jeanne Paquin, and Madeleine Vionnet, to drape a straightened female torso in loosely layered angles.

For all the scholarly work that sees Edith Wharton as a writer of the nineteenth century, we see in her wardrobe a move toward the modernity of the twentieth century in which she lived half her life and wrote her novels. Although images from the 1890s and 1990s show her dressed in couture French designs that require a firm corset and ample bustle, photographs from the twentieth century reveal a woman increasingly content to loosen the stays of her corset and shed the bustle altogether. In these clothes, too, she follows the fashion conventions of her day, allowing dresses to drape from the shoulder and follow the body's more natural lines as she thickened into middle age. She was never a flapper, of course, but her dresses retain the flair of fashion in the rue de la Paix. A photograph from the 1920s shows a matronly Mrs. Wharton in a cubist-inspired dress, a fluttering of loose-fitting angles that may have been the creation of Doucet or another modern designer (figure 1.24). The corset no longer grips her waist and the shortened asymmetrical hemline reveals stylishly heeled shoes with pointed toes.

A casual remark, seemingly peripheral to Wharton's story about how Henry James did not notice her at parties, is a clear signal of how she wanted readers to see her as an artist. In her autobiography, the Doucet dress, iridescent with beads, gains significance precisely because it fails to catch the eye of the master, Henry James. The scene between the two writers is marvelously incongruous: a shy American woman, dressed by a Parisian couturier, desires the attention of a literary compatriot more interested in men than women and in the fashion of London more than Paris. He noticed her finally not for her

*Fig. 1.24.* Edith Wharton in the 1920s wearing a cubist-style dress with asymmetrical hem and holding two of her dogs. *Yale Collection of American Literature, Beinecke Rare Book and Manuscript Library.*

dress but for her short fiction, strongly admiring "The Pelican" and the writer who could tell such a story. He encouraged her to write, as she was already doing, about life in the United States: "And I applaud, I mean I value, I egg you on in your study of the American life that surrounds you."[30] Even as he had expatriated literally and literarily, he admonished her: "Let yourself go in it and *at* it—it's an untouched field, really: the folk who try, over there, don't come within miles of any civilized, however superficially, any 'evolved' life."

Does it matter that Edith Wharton had herself photographed in Doucet dresses to lure readers or that she used them to ensnare Henry James? Her dressing up for us in publicity photographs and her dressing up for James at a literary party have the same effect. A stylish lady in a Parisian gown might be just the writer to "*Do New York!*" We side, as she wants us to, with Henry James, who knows that as an artist, expert in the art of making up, she has no need of finery, even as we admire the lady's clothes.

❧ 2

# THE UNDERSIDE
# OF FASHION

There were twenty of them in the work-room, their fagged
profiles, under exaggerated hair, bowed in the harsh north light
above the utensils of their art; for it was something more than
an industry, surely, this creation of ever-varied settings for the
face of fortunate womanhood.
—*The House of Mirth*

Garments have many stories to tell. The Costume Institute at the
Metropolitan Museum of Art houses collections of gowns, capes,
suits and hats from Wharton's era; although the garments never belonged to her, they offer proximate knowledge to us as we read dress.
The delicate fabrics are frail and brittle with age and come carefully
wrapped in sheets of muslin, stacked like shrouds on shelves where
from a distance they appear as shrunken bodies in an ancient tomb.
Unfolding the muslin wrappers and looking at gowns and hats from
the 1880s and 1890s with their iconic shapes, one reads the textures
and stitches as sartorial signs of class distinction. The delicately lovely
dresses and hats adorned the bodies of wealthy women and, at the
same time, embodied the expertise of seamstresses and milliners. In *The
House of Mirth*, Wharton describes labor in a millinery shop: "fagged
profiles" work long hours, often in harsh light and unwholesome air,
to create "ever-varied" garments to ornament the bodies of women
fortunate enough to afford such luxury. Finding herself working
among such workers, Lily Bart considers prescient questions. As the
young women bow over "the utensils of their art," are they engaged
in the production of art? And, if so, is their work "more than an industry"? What power do women of any social class have in the exchange? Ceremonial goods tell the story of ownership *and* of produc-

tion. Both tales come to mind as one examines the fragile garments that have survived over time.

Edith Wharton's early fiction, much of it in the mode of literary naturalism, includes tales about the production of garments in the Gilded Age. Old New York, after all, was a world full of finery, much of it purchased with money that had been amassed from the manufacture and sale of apparel. Wharton often uses fashion detail to satirize class mobility. In the short story, "His Father's Son," for example, she depicts the life of a father who worked his way up in a button factory and his son who luxuriated in what became the dynasty from his father's signal invention, the Grew Suspender Buckle: "The Buckle had been Ronald's fairy godmother," the narrator sardonically puts it.[1] And in another tale, "The Daunt Diana," the hero's capriciously acquisitive instinct is financed by two or three million dollars he inherited from an uncle who had patented the Mystic Superstraight corset (CS 2:54). Her most American novel, *The Custom of the Country*, features an acquisitive heroine, Undine Spragg, whose family money has come from an invention. Even her name comes from "*un*doolay, the French for crimping" and its association with her grandfather's patented "hair-waver" (CC 80). She is, in the eyes of her family, already a product.

Two early works focus seriously on female experience in the textile and garment trade, depicting the struggles of women to own and manage the means of production. She wrote the novella *Bunner Sisters* in the early 1890s about a pair of semiskilled seamstresses who struggle to stay in business. Her first bestseller, *The House of Mirth* (1905), is about Lily Bart's search for a profession, first as wife, then as social secretary and cultural adviser, and finally as a milliner, a craft requiring sewing skills that she fails to master. This chapter looks at the underside of the fashionable clothes that Wharton and others of her social class wore; it considers how, as a writer, she sought to tell the story of labor.

Biographers agree that we don't have a collection of clothes that Edith Wharton actually owned; we do have, however, apparel belonging to her contemporaries in Old New York.[2] The Costume Institute houses garments that were once the property of Caroline Schermerhorn Astor Wilson, the daughter of Mrs. William Astor (née Caroline Schermerhorn), perhaps the defining female figure of the Gilded Age. As Ward McAllister coined the term, the "Hour Hundred" formed the inner circle of a nascent American aristocracy eager to restrict membership and secure elite status based on family name.[3] In her autobiography, Wharton carefully situates herself among the wealthy families: "The Schermerhorns, Joneses, Pendletons, on my father's side, the Stevenses, Ledyards, Rhinelanders on the mother's, the Gallatins on both, seem all to have belonged to the same prosperous class of merchants, bankers and lawyers" (*BG* 784). Caroline, called "Carrie" by her family, dressed, as Pussy Jones was taught to do, in French couture fashions. She and her mother shopped at the Houses of Worth and Doucet, ordering dozens of dresses a year from Paris as well as from American seamstresses who copied French designs.

Apparently, Carrie looked pretty in pink and had, at least in her youth, an enviable waistline of twenty-two inches (I measured her gowns). She married Marshall Orme Wilson, the son of a banker and railroad magnate, in 1894. The *New York Times* detailed what such a society wedding meant in terms of fashion. Eight bridesmaids and eight groomsmen were on display before thousands of guests (listed by the newspaper to include Theodore Roosevelt). The bridal gown was made of silver brocade and white satin, trimmed in orange blossoms, with a veil of antique point lace, secured with diamonds and matching blossoms. The most visible sign of wealth and fashion, however, was Carrie's diamond necklace with a pendant that consisted of a ruby, a pearl, and a sapphire in a cluster of large diamonds; the ensemble gift of the groom to his bride was "said to have cost $75,000."[4] Mrs. Astor, Carrie's mother, also wore a white satin gown, hers with an overskirt of point lace and a waist "literally covered with diamonds." Carrie's wedding was the sort of opulent New York occasion that Wharton would detail in *The House of Mirth* and *The Age of Innocence*. The mansion that Carrie Astor Wilson and her husband would later build for themselves on 64th Street, discreetly placed just east of Central Park (because to live directly on the park was considered vulgar), contains forty rooms, including a ballroom in the style of Louis Seize.[5] In 1904, three hundred New Yorkers attended the housewarming party where Enrico Caruso sang arias. Perhaps with the color of her dresses in mind, Mrs. Astor Wilson selected a dull rose velvet fabric to upholster the gilt settles, or low benches, in the white marble entrance hall.

It is a strange experience for a literary scholar, schooled in the subtleties of language, to research actual garments and literally to read dress. Gazing on Carrie Astor Wilson's dresses in the Metropolitan Museum more than a hundred years later, the eye first sees color, finely differentiated shades of pink and coral and salmon, and then the hourglass shape of the gowns, ample in the bodice and slender at the waist. The beige brocade of a Doucet opera cloak, hanging next to the examination table, is strikingly embroidered in coral, gold, and orange rose motifs and lushly cushioned by a yoke of wild mink. The gowns are placed, one by one, on the table and unwrapped from their muslin wrappers for inspection. One two-piece ball gown (figure 2.1) vividly exemplifies the opulence of Worth designs. The tightly fitted, boned basque of the bodice dips to a point below the waist in the front and is finished by a double box-pleated peplum at the back. The gored shirt

*Fig. 2.1.* Charles Frederick Worth (born in England, 1826–1895), *left*, ball gown of pale green and ivory silk satin and yellow, pink, and ivory silk chiffon with embroidered sunburst pattern in silk, glass, and metallic thread; label "Worth, Paris," c. 1887; *right*, ball gown of pink damask with crystal embroidery, designed by Jean-Phillip Worth, 1892. *The Metropolitan Museum of Art, gift of Orme Wilson and R. Thornton Wilson, in memory of their mother, Mrs. Caroline Schermerhorn Astor Wilson, 1949 (49.3.25a,b; 49.3.28a,b). Image © The Metropolitan Museum of Art.* (Plate 5.)

is floor-length in the front with deep folds on either side. The drama of the gown, however, comes in the net insets of the skirt's front, embroidered with tiny gold sequins, white and gold glass beads, and silver threads in a pattern meant to simulate a cloud and sunburst. In several dresses, owned by Carrie Astor, we see the colors and textures that had delighted her eye. As we move closer, focusing on the detail of the fabrics, we pick out woven textures as well as appliqués, sequins, and embroidery. Closer still, patterns emerge, ribbons and bows and floral motifs, woven into fabrics or sewn onto them in layers. Bending over the table top, looking yet more closely, we note delicate variations of silk, chiffon, and lace, the most mysterious of the fabrics, here in bits of handmade designs dating to the eighteenth century, when both men

*Fig. 2.2.* Jacques Doucet (1853–1929), two-piece ball gown of salmon-pink self-patterned satin in large bow motif, trimmed with ecru-colored lace and black velvet ribbon decorated with paste buttons; label "Doucet, Paris," 1897. *The Metropolitan Museum of Art, gift of Orme Wilson and R. Thornton Wilson, in memory of their mother, Mrs. Caroline Schermerhorn Astor Wilson, 1949 (49.3.26a,b). Image © The Metropolitan Museum of Art.*

and women wore lace, and in yards of machine-made laces stitched at angles into skirts to soften the outline of the body. Machines made lace affordable in the nineteenth century even for seamstresses laboring to make gowns such as these.

Another of Carrie's gowns typifies the sinuous designs of Jacques Doucet. Carrie's ball gown from 1897, inspired by eighteenth-century designs, brings together a bodice and skirt of silk and velvet and lace, adorned with paste buttons and artificial roses (figure 2.2). The salmon-pink satin brocade features a motif of bows, signifying that the woman's body is, after all, a gift. The hourglass shape of the gown is framed by ecru-colored lace in the sleeves and black velvet ribbons in the skirt. The gown is boned to hold its shape even without the support of a body and includes a long pointed stomacher of black velvet that traces the vital middle of a woman's body. The décolleté neckline is wide and rounded, covered for modesty's sake with a large satin and lace bow that echoes the motif in the fabric and a corsage of artificial roses. Matching satin ruching borders the sides of the stomacher and the neckline. The satin sleeves are short and puffed with ruffles of lace. The skirt opens like curtains on a stage, exposing the underskirt, and drapes into a dramatic train in the back. Black velvet ribbons stitched in patterns of three horizontal stripes emphasize the underskirt and provocatively highlight the hips and ankles. One imagines the body's twirling on the dance floor as the black velvet ribbons direct the gaze to the most private spaces of a woman's body.

The glittering garment lying on the examination table tells the story of seamstress and mistress. On the underside of the fashion, we find signs of the labor it took to craft the gown as well as the labor it must have taken Carrie Astor to wear it. The weighted skirt hem flips up to expose a pink taffeta ruffle that still bears traces of dirt from the dance floor. The hidden dust ruffle carries the burden of sweeping up debris, an unintended consequence of wearing floor-length apparel. Upon arrival at a door, a lady would by custom lift her skirt, an act that would allow a servant to remove anything she may have inadvertently collected from the street. Her seamstress would have spent hours pinking the edges of the taffeta ruffle, dyeing it to match the gown, and basting it into place to be worn, discarded, and replaced relatively cheaply.

The underside of the gown, too, reveals contraptions, including a drawstring at the neckline and a row of hooks and eyes along the bodice, that create the fiction of the gown's seemingly natural flow across the body. The bodice opens along the edge of the stomacher to reveal the work of many hands brought together in a concerted effort to clothe the female body, pressing it into the shape of fashionable beauty. Opening the bodice of the dress allows the eye to move over private layers of labor meant for the eyes of women only, those stitching it together and those lifting the garment across the body of the woman ornamented by the whole production. It is a surprise to learn that the inner garment remains relatively roughly hewn. We can see, for example, stitches on the rows of hooks and eyes, reversed every other one, a design that makes the opening of the garment difficult for Carrie Astor and requiring the deft hand of a maid. The underside of fashion need not be neatly finished because a lady supposedly would never expose body and gown to the gaze of anyone other than her maid.

The underside of fashion is like the back of a tapestry where, as Lily Bart remarks, "the threads were knotted and the loose ends hung" (*HM* 445). The value of the dress is secured by the hours of labor performed on the inside. One imagines the hours of attention by eyes and muscles of a seamstress as she selects colors and threads needles and then pulls them through the fabric over and over, tying knots, rethreading, and patiently repeating the process. Hands and eyes baste yards of ribbon and secure unwieldy sequins, and gather laces in tuckers and sleeves and skirt. A quick hand tediously hems satin ruffles or pleats a skirt to a waistband with precision; no doubt, the hand is calloused and perhaps aching at the end of the long labor. One sees in the stitches the melding of hand and machine in a regular, efficient punch of needle into fabric, guided by precise movements. The lining of the garment lies against the outer fabric, the two sewn together in the seams, cut and moved through a sewing machine and then pressed open and overcast in handstitches to keep the rough edges from fraying. The finished gown keeps its shape without a body's being in it, even a hundred years after its creation, because it was crafted to stand alone with stays slipped into its seams and weights sewn into its hemline. The surprise is that so little time elapsed between the order of a gown and its delivery, perhaps as the buyer completed days touring Paris museums and evenings strolling along the Seine.

In the rue de la Paix, the average Parisian dressmaker, and there were many, employed forty seamstresses who usually lived on the premises. Some women slept beneath stairways and under counters so that they would be on call, ready to complete orders on any customer's whim at odd hours and under pressure of time. The House of Worth established itself as the center of couture fashion in the 1850s with twenty seamstresses; by the 1870s the staff had grown to twelve hundred, a number that would remain constant until the beginning of the First World War.[6] At the large houses women workers lived in dormitories or in workhouses scattered through nearby neighborhoods. Apparently Charles Frederick Worth and his family had little interest in industrial conditions and were "never in the forefront of reform for staff." Seamstresses began apprenticeships at the age of thirteen or fourteen, working twelve-hour days; if luck and skill and health allowed, they made their way into positions as second "hands." They assisted first-hand seamstresses and, in time, might rise to the premier level of skill. Even then, women workers in the late nineteenth century were paid an average of two francs, twenty-five centimes, per day, even as men in the tailor trade earned twice the money for similar labor.

One would think that this speed of production would concern couturiers, who depended on giving wealthy patrons the impression that gowns were tailored to their individual bodies and suited to their unique desires. To the contrary, standardization of fashion became essential to the growth of the industry. Worth built his reputation by mass-producing dresses for Empress Eugénie's court. To streamline the production, he utilized basic designs for bodices, sleeves, and skirts, and then reshuffled components made in various fabrics with differing ornaments, a practice that gave the impression, each time, of freshness and originality. An important job in his establishment was the strict keeping track of customers and designs, a system that sustained the illusion that a lady's gown was a pure expression of her beauty and taste. Worth was savvy, too, about advertising haute couture fashions, dressing his wife, Marie Worth, in sumptuous clothing and designing gowns for actresses whose celebrity added cachet to his business.

The House of Worth, along with neighboring houses in the rue de la Paix gained international fame and prestige by displaying designs at the World's Expositions in 1878, 1889, and 1900, held in Paris and featuring French haute couture garments with the goal of establishing and maintaining fashion hegemony (figure 2.3). The Paris Exposition of 1900, especially, ushered in the modern era in its exhibits of the combustion engine. Intellectual men of the era, most notably Henry Adams in his influential essay "The Virgin and the Dynamo," contemplated the mechanical and symbolic changes at the turn into the twentieth century wrought by the creation of the combustion engine; Adams feared that science was displacing Christianity and specifically the Virgin Mary as the generator of human culture. At the Palace of Costume in 1900, however, modernity was defined by the shape of couture fashions. The movement of a woman's body into more lissome designs signaled the progress of the new century.

The display of fashion in the Palace of Costume posed essential questions about the relationship between the aesthetics of dress and

*Fig. 2.3.* Paris Exposition, Palace of Costume, Paris, France, 1900, side view of the façade of the Palais des Fils, Tissus et Vêtements, Champ de Mars. *Brooklyn Museum Archives. Flickr.com.*

ethics of production. Is fashion an art form? Do garments belong at an international exposition or in collections at the Metropolitan Museum and the Mint Museum? If so, what are we to think of Worth or Doucet or Poiret or Virot as artists? What is the nature of sewing as a craft, and how do we value the handwork that produces the garment itself? To what extend is clothing a mere commodity, copied and manufactured as a commercial enterprise? The garment industry, as historian Nancy L. Green puts it, "offers a perfect vantage point" in the study of art in an era of mass production.[7] The tension between "uniqueness," the quality associated with art, and "reproducibility," the value associated with business, is especially keen in the dresses of Wharton's era. Are we to assume that haute couture fashion is art and prêt-à-porter or ready-to-wear fashion is not? In either case, what credit goes to garment workers and how are conditions of labor to be considered? And how, we might ask, does the history of fashion production shed light on such questions?

The term *couturière*, coming from *couture* or needlework, is feminine in the French because the making of clothing had been traditionally the work of women. Before the middle of the nineteenth century, women designed and sewed clothing for women, based on the desires and needs of the female customer. Households managed their own sewing, and middle-class daughters were expected to sew, crochet, and embroider. To accomplish such skills was a female achievement; households with servants hired women to stitch family clothes. As was true for other domestic laborers, seamstresses were paid little for their craft. The term *couturier* became masculinized in the 1850s to acknowledge and accommodate the rise of couture designers, first Charles Frederick Worth, and then his colleagues, including Jacques Doucet. Even as men came to define female fashion, much of the labor of sewing remained in female hands. Victorian ideology constructed separate gendered spaces: a private and domestic sphere for women, a public and political sphere for men. Supposedly, the design of fashionable clothing and the industrial production of garments were men's jobs. The idea of female ownership of the means of production seems at odds even with language itself; the term business*man* denotes male activity in English, much as *couturier* marks masculine endeavor in French.

Recent historians have found evidence that such strict division of labor may have been more ideological than real. In a comparative study, *Ready-to-Wear and Ready-to-Work* (1997), Nancy Green looks at working conditions for garment workers in Paris and New York from the nineteenth through the twentieth century.[8] She concludes that in the labor market, "gender roles have never been fixed." Making garments in the home was a female preoccupation that over the course of the nineteenth century moved toward a male occupation that employed female seamstresses. By the turn into the twentieth century, however, industrial labor was performed primarily by women and then, in turn, by male and female immigrant workers in both New York and Paris. Work, that is to say, became more a matter of economics than gender. Ownership, apparently, was not defined exclusively by gender either; a businessman may well have been a woman. Wendy Gamber, whose research focuses on dressmakers and milliners, enumerates a wide variety of nineteenth-century female entrepreneurs, including "sellers of female finery, purveyors of food and lodging, keepers of houses of ill repute, proprietors of grocery and variety stores, dealers of books and newspapers, apothecaries, tobacconists, and jewelers, midwives, healers, and fortune tellers, even silversmiths and embalmers."[9] Nancy Dye, looking across lines of social class and gender, reports that at the turn into the twentieth century, some 350,000 women worked in New York City, many of them doing domestic sorts of labor—cleaning, clerking, waitressing, laundering—in the public sphere. A substantial number of women (she counts the exact number as 132,535 in 1900) worked in manufacturing, and most of those females labored in the garment trade.[10] As these studies show, the making of clothing involved both male and female labor and, at times, ownership of production.

*Fig. 2.4.* B. Kuppenheiner & Co. Spring Book, 1900, man's ensemble, period about 1815. *New York Public Library Digital Gallery.*

The making of fashion has likewise crossed the gender divide. Growth of the ready-to-wear clothing industry in the nineteenth century evolved from the production of men's clothing. The basic cut of a man's suit, as it was designed at the beginning of the nineteenth century after the French and American Revolutions, changed very little over the century. The flannel outing suit popular in Wharton's era consists of lines very like those in vogue during the age of Jane Austen in spite of the protest of tailors in advertisements for "new" men's fashions (figures 2.4 and 2.5). We see from the flannel suit that men's fashion has changed very little even into the twenty-first century. In the public world, male tailors have traditionally made clothing for men; perhaps as a consequence, male styles of attire have been more uniform than the clothing worn by women. The height of the hat may be raised or lowered, the jacket sometimes styled with a longer tail or tucked in slightly at the waist, and the trousers may cling tightly to the leg or flair away from the ankle, but the man's suit has always been designed with freedom of movement in mind, reflecting the active and public life that men have traditionally enjoyed. And, of course, masculine apparel has been influenced by military fashion. The American clothing industry grew under the pressure of producing uniforms for use during the wars of the nineteenth century. Manufacturing clothing for soldiers during the Civil War made New York City the dominant garment center in the country and a major producer, along with London and Paris, in an increasingly global market.

Tailors, who had established themselves as makers of male attire, turned toward the female market during the nineteenth century, as was evident in the overlapping businesses of the Doucet family as they expanded a couture line of women's clothing. We can see the results of the blending of genders in a Jones family photograph of Edith and her brother Harry, standing behind their mother Lucretia (figure 2.6). All three faces, rigidly angled, bear close resemblance in feature and facial gesture. All of the Joneses, we note, are dressed for the street in neatly buttoned jackets and formal hats. There is very little difference in the cut and fabric of the suits won by the siblings; Lucretia sits draped in furs, the sign of the Jones family wealth and her status as mother (Edith will inherit fur stoles and muffs and will leave them, as we have seen, to close friends in her will). As historians have noted, the idiom "keeping up with the Joneses" may have applied to the visages and vestments portrayed grandly in Jones family photos like this one.

We imagine Edith and Harry moving about the streets of New York City in day ensembles like these that would have given her nearly as much flexibility and visibility as they offered her brother. The movement of middle- and upper-class women into the open air of city streets had the unintended effect of necessitating such male-styled apparel. The full bonnets popular in the middle of the nineteenth century restricted peripheral vision in congested urban spaces; as a consequence, women's hats of later in the century flattened and moved upward on the head with veils across the face for a privacy that still allowed the eyes relatively clear views. Also, heavy petticoats and long skirts had had the effect, intentional or not, of hampering the movement of the female body and restricting activities in the public square, a complaint lodged by dress reformers throughout the century in attempts to move women into trousers and out of corsets.

In the reform of women's fashion, perhaps more persuasive than political and practical rhetoric about mobility in urban spaces was the increasing popularity of sports, especially among those in the moneyed class where "free" time allowed and even encouraged leisure activities, among them horseback riding, bicycling, skating, archery, and tennis. Sports became de rigueur for women at resorts in places like Lenox, Massachusetts, and Saratoga, New York, and Wharton recorded such activities in her novels. For example, she compares May Welland's lithe body and physical agility to the goddess Diana in *The Age of Innocence*; the young New York debutante distinguishes herself as an archer even before she takes the literal name in marriage to Newland Archer. Teddy Wharton loved horses and dogs, and Edith also rode (although

*Fig. 2.5.* B. Kuppenheiner & Co. Spring Book, 1900, flannel outing suit, no. 9, the "new" breakwater summer suit. *New York Public Library Digital Gallery.*

we see her in photographs as an awkward equestrian). In her novel *The Fruit of the Tree*, she gives Bessy Westmore a passion for riding that will result in a catastrophic accident. Athletic movement required in archery and horseback riding called for flexibility in women's clothing, including shorter skirt lengths and split legs, the very styles that fashion reformers advocated. The active life thus influenced the fashion of an elite class that had previously desired sedentary styles. Thorstein Veblen in his landmark study, *The Theory of the Leisure Class* (1899), reported that the mark of a family's status could be measured by a woman's use of leisure as well as her consumption of material goods: "Its ascendancy is furthered by the fact that leisure is still fully as effective an evidence of wealth as consumption."[11]

As affluence came to be marked by sport activity, American as well as French designers responded to the practical styles of dress reform. We see in an example from the Mint Museum, a fashionable sporting ensemble that features bloomers (figure 2.7). The red wool twill and flannel jacket with silver buttons, from perhaps 1895, comes from Brooks Brothers, an American company that had been founded in 1818. And the black woolen sports bloomers from 1895 complete the athletic outfit. Amelia Jenks Bloomer (1818–1894), a resident of Seneca Falls, New York, had championed various reforms throughout the nineteenth century, including temperance, education and suffrage, but her signal achievement was in fashion. As the story goes, one day she saw two feminists, Elizabeth Smith Miller and Elizabeth Cady Stanton, dressed "somewhat in the Turkish style—short skirt, full trousers of fine black broadcloth; a Spanish cloak, of the same material, reaching to the knee; beaver hat and feathers and dark furs."[12] Bloomer, a founder and editor of the reform and fashion magazine *The Lily*, was working on an editorial featuring fashion reform. She decided to join her colleagues by donning the Turkish ensemble and the name of the "bloomer" trouser stuck. Throughout the 1850s, she advocated the wearing of the

*Fig. 2.7.* Sports jacket in wool twill and wool flannel with silver commemorative, c. 1895–1905, by Brooks Brothers Company; and American-made wool bloomers, c. 1895. *The Mint Museum of Art, Charlotte, North Carolina, Historic Costume and Fashionable Dress Collection.* (Plate 6.)

male-styled garment that became an easy target of humorists. She and other reformers had hoped to challenge traditional dress and, thereby, hasten political ends, but bloomers became an icon of caricature and ridicule. Responding to critics and humorists, leaders in the suffrage movement shied away from bloomers and, indeed, trousers of various styles for everyday attire. Feminists hoped that conservative dress would give their political aspirations more gravity.

Uniformity of clothing, the blending and blurring of differences across gender and class lines, resulted in large part, too, from technological changes. Speed of production and mass distribution of garments were enhanced by the invention of the sewing machine, produced in France by Barthélémy Thimonnier in 1830, though his model was never widely used. In the 1850s an American machinist, Isaac Merritt Singer (1811–1875), was working in a shop on an awkwardly designed and therefore unmarketable version of a sewing machine. It is Singer who figured out how to change the design—moving the shuttle in a straight line with a straightened needle—that made the machine commercially viable.[13] By the end of the 1850s, after several patent disputes, I. M. Singer & Co produced thousand of machines a year, and in the 1860s the Singer Manufacturing Company developed into an international corporation (figure 2.8). As a result, Isaac Singer became an astonishingly wealthy man in the New York of Wharton's youth; he was also an unconventional fellow, notorious for having several wives and sets of children.

Sewing machines transformed the making of garments in the home as they became affordable for middle-income households. The Singer, too, changed garment-making in tailor and dress shops, where the dexterity of the hand was quickened by use of the machine. Even so, individually owned shops retained a close business relationship between customers and tailors or seamstresses. Each person in the exchange had a hand in the designing and making of specific garments. Nonetheless, increasingly mechanized modes of production had the effect of severing the link between the maker and the wearer, as well as between the maker and the garment itself. The most dramatic shift in the late nineteenth century was in the establishment of sweatshops and factories. The new speed of sewing and the relatively unskilled nature of industrial labor furthered a rift between those who saw fashion as a handcraft or even an art and others who saw it merely as a trade. Ready-made garments came in standard sizes and uniform designs. As a result, a garment could be put together from presewn parts, produced as "piecework," a process whereby jobs were assigned according to the complexity of the labor. Sleeves were constructed in one workroom and bodices in another. Not only did those wearing the garments have little to do with their production; the piecework sys-

*Fig. 2.8.* Advertisement for Singer sewing machines, "The Cycle of a Century," 1800–1900. *Prints and Photographs Division, Library of Congress, Washington, D.C.* (Plate 7.)

tem often prevented seamstresses from seeing the garment assembled. The mass production of clothing, as labor reformers lamented, alienated workers; yet, at the same time, it democratized fashion by placing material goods within the economic reach of working and middle class shoppers. By the end of the nineteenth century, New York had established itself as the center of clothing production and, as Wharton's novels record, had also become the defining city in American fashion.

Edith Wharton is a pivotal figure in understanding fashion as well as fiction in the United States at the turn into the twentieth century. She preferred the work of French designers, even during much of her early life in New York City, where fashion design lagged behind production. She ordered gowns from Worth and Doucet and also patronized seamstresses and milliners in New York City, gathering material not only for dresses but—significantly—for fiction. The questions we are asking about the nature of fashion as a form of art permeate the fiction of Edith Wharton. Heroines and heroes, too, can be judged by their choice of apparel. A subtle mind and substantial character comes clothed, according to her aesthetics, in relatively unadorned gowns featuring, as we have seen, form over flounce.

Her first long piece of serious fiction, the novella *Bunner Sisters*, opens, as *The Age of Innocence* will open three decades later, on the streets of 1870s New York. The city grew rapidly in the decade following the Civil War and Wharton's novels record her memory of the changes in society, art, and culture taking place in her youth. A horse's pace determines the flow of traffic, Christine Nilsson's voice sets the standard for opera, and the artist's eye from the Hudson River School marks sophistication in painting. The two opening scenes differ as a brougham delivers the reader at a doorstep, one an inconspicuous seamstress shop in the basement of a deteriorating building on the border of Stuyvesant Square, and the other a conspicuous portico of the Academy of Music (1854–1886) in Union Square at 14th Street and Irving Place. Much of Wharton's early fiction is about the juxtaposition of these two worlds, one established for the making of garments and the other for the ceremonial display of goods.

Wharton knew both addresses well. In the novella, we catch a glimpse of a character walking into the seamstress shop run by Ann Eliza and Evelina Bunner. The sisters sell a bonnet to the character they refer to as a "lady with puffed sleeves," a distinguished and interesting woman who lives on the square, a lush garden then as it remains today with a statue of Peter Stuyvesant, the portly, one-legged patriarch of New York, as the garden's defining feature. The lady with the puffed sleeves seems, as critics have noted, a sly self-portrait of the artist as a young woman in the 1890s. The narrator tells us "she was elegant (as the title they had given her implied), and she had a sweet sad smile about which they had woven many histories."[14] The comment, of course, is playfully ironic in that it is the lady with the puffed sleeves, Wharton herself, who is weaving the history of the luckless Bunners.

Elizabeth Coleman says of fashion designs that revivals "always carry a bit of their own time" (*Opulent Era* 157). That seems to be the case here as Wharton anachronistically dresses her character. The puffed sleeve, a Romantic design that appeared in 1824, is cut on the bias of fabric, full at the top and gathered into the arm opening, producing the swell of fabric. Over time, such puffing grew preposterously in size and shape, supported by horsehair stiffening on the underside, until the contraption collapsed of its own weight and went out of favor in 1833 as sleeves narrowed. For decades, puffed sleeves were out of style, although ensembles designed by Worth in the 1870s sometimes included bodices with horizontally banded sleeves that echoed seventeenth-century designs. The filmy fabric of an "undersleeve" would be pulled out or puffed to complete the look, and such a sleeve may have been in Wharton's mind as she placed the enigmatic lady into the frame of the story. As styles always do, the puffed sleeve came back into fashion in 1889 and grew again to enormous size as the gigot or what become known as the "leg-of-mutton" sleeve became a fashion icon early in 1890s before shrinking again at the turn into the twentieth century.

Wharton's sweet sad lady may well be clothed in a tailleur or suit much like one that she herself owned (figure 2.9 and compare figure 1.10) The tailleur design is credited to John Redfern, a British tailor, who in the 1870s began designing jackets for women that included lapels and buttons on the sleeves, elements used in making men's jackets.[15] He made one in 1880 for Princess Alexandra, who was the queen consort of England from 1901 to 1910, and another for a granddaughter of Queen Victoria to include in her trousseau.[16] Fashion historians note that the tailored suit was England's signal achievement in fashion at the turn into the twentieth century (of course, we note that Worth was British although he is thought of as a French designer). The tailored suit offered women more freedom of movement and became a significant part of an urban woman's wardrobe. In the Parisian couture business, the tailleur became a signature design of Jacques Doucet, and Wharton may have shopped with him for the one she owned in the period, a slim-waisted version with gigantic leg-of-mutton sleeves.

*Fig. 2.9.* Henri Boutet, *Les modes féminines du XIXe siècle, interprétées en cent pointes sèches aquarellées au pinceau, 1801–1900* (published in 1902), fashion plate 99; compare Wharton's tailleur or suit in fig. 1.10. *New York Public Library Digital Gallery.* (Plate 8.)

Wharton's use of the puffed sleeve would have signaled to contemporary readers an overlapping of time, bringing together the social history of the 1870s and the economic realities of the 1890s, an era of depression and hardship for laborers and owners who struggled to stay in business. What exactly did the lady with the puffed sleeves see? There was before her a gathering of businesses in a brick-fronted, three-story building and other struggling establishments crowded into a row of deteriorating brownstones that had once housed well-to-do families. The Bunners are seamstresses who manage to make ends meet by renting the basement of the brownstone, downstairs from the first-floor dressmaking establishment of Miss Mellins. The women in the story are single and satisfy their sexual desires vicariously through reading and gossip. Miss Mellins reads the *National Police Gazette*, an activity that takes up much of her time. Women in the *Gazette* are well dressed and strong-willed but also the center of highly colored tales, like those that Miss Mellins repeats and embellishes throughout the novella.

Edith Wharton's tale of female vulnerability challenges such popular narratives by offering an unsentimental realism, even a lurid naturalism. The women live in an immigrant neighborhood where the Mendozas, a Spanish Sephardic family, run a hotel in an adjacent brownstone that is "cracked and blistered" with "cast-iron balconies and cat-haunted grass-patches behind twisted railing" (*BS* 280). Immigrants and working-class people living in the Mendoza Hotel are, the narrator explains, as fastidious as their meager incomes allow, and the lady in the puffed sleeves would have noted the general character of a street that "rapidly fell from shabbiness to squalor" (*BS* 280). The butcher is described as a "gory-aproned" fellow whose clients include an old woman "in an antiquated bonnet and mantle" and "a blowsy Irish girl." The litter of an American city remains at the day's end, in "a mosaic of coloured handbills, lids of tomato-cans, old shoes, cigarstumps and banana skins, cemented together by a layer of mud" (*BS* 280). Wharton's portrait of urban, immigrant life reveals the usual prejudices of her day, much as Jacob Riis's *How the Other Half Lives* depicts ethnic type as a matter of order and cleanliness. The Bunners, apparently British in ancestry, scrupulously wash their windows and organize their merchandise, providing customers refuge from the chaos and filth of the street.

Wharton is drawing a portrait of New York City at a time of intense population growth. According to the Bureau of Immigration, the peak year for the decade was 1873, a year that brought 459,803 immigrants into the country, especially from Ireland and Germany, as Wharton's story depicts. The heaviest years of immigration, however, came in the 1880s with 788,992 in 1882 alone, and the numbers climbed in spite of laws to curb or (in the case of the Chinese) to bar entry. As Wharton was writing *Bunner Sisters*, 560,319 immigrants arrived in 1891 and another 579,663 in 1892; many of whom were Jewish Poles, Russians, Austrians, and Germans, fleeing anti-Semitism in Europe. The Bunner sisters live in a once-prosperous neighborhood near Stuyvesant Square, the original property of Peter Stuyvesant given to the city by his heirs. The area's proximity to the tenement neighborhoods of the Lower East Side made it attractive to immigrant laborers seeking more spacious housing. Wharton depicts the blight of poverty and the stresses of industrial labor.

The culprit in the case of the Bunner sisters is the mechanization of the sewing industry that called for the parceling out of piecework. The Bunners live meagerly because they have few sewing skills and those they have are not worth much money. Their living space, a relatively commodious version of a tenement sweatshop, is a single room that serves as bedroom, kitchen, and parlor. The sisters operate two machines, one for sewing and the other for pinking. They depend on income from mending clothes, such as "a brown merino wool seam," making baby-waists, fashioning bonnets with artificial flowers, and cutting heaps of flounces, pinked rather than hemmed and no doubt used to make dust ruffles under skirts. The pinking machine was a hand-operated device that attached like a meat grinder to a worktable. Moving its wheel and directing the fabric required little skill; consequently, the job of pinking yards of material earned little cash. It is the sort of work that the older sister, Ann Eliza, can manage. The more expert of the two sisters is the younger, Evelina, who does millinery work with implements "suggestive of dental art" (*BS* 299–302). She fashions a "bright array of muslin petals, yellow stamens and green corollas" and twists "a rose-petal into shape" as fresh garnishments for ladies' hats. But she, too, lacks the nimbleness and imagination of a true milliner. Their business, these details reveal, is marginal and represents a "shrunken image of earlier ambition" (*BS* 281). The sewing industry, in truth, is changing during the 1870s and, in the process of industrialization, squeezing out small businesses. Female workers with the skills of the Bunners are expendable. They make ends meet by keeping garments made by others in repair, as they do for the lady with the puffed sleeves.

Mass-produced garments supposedly democratized fashion because goods could be sold in the marketplace at prices workers might be able to afford. One of the ironies of the story is that the sisters are so poor that they are not able to buy even machine-made dresses for themselves. Wharton dresses the sisters in working-class garments that are, as Diana Crane details in her study of clothes and class, among their most valuable possessions.[17] On special occasions they wear black silk dresses with mantles of cashmere. Ann Eliza's "pre-Raphaelite" body is arrayed in a double-dyed and triple turned black silk dress with "a *patine* worthy of a Renaissance bronze," a hint of its "sacerdotal" significance (*BS* 282). The silk dress, symbolism aside, has been dyed and the fabric turned several times in order to extend the garment's life. Ann Eliza believes that her younger and more ornamental sister Evelina was meant by providence to marry, have babies, and wear "silk on Sundays" (*BS* 293). Carefully crimping her hair, we note, has not attracted a man. When the German immigrant Herman Ramy arrives in the story, Ann Eliza feels a "sudden heart-throb [stretch] the seams of her flat alpaca bosom" and Evelina pins "a crimson bow under her collar" (*BS* 295). What if, as both sisters seem to envisage, he is their one chance at a fully sexual life?

The central piece of art in the apartment is a "chromo of a young lady in a nightgown" clinging to the "Rock of Ages" (*BS* 281). The "devout young lady in dishabille" is a fashion cue to the sort of story Wharton intends to tell about female sexual vulnerability in the city. This is a novella about fashion and desire much in the mode of a "white slave" narrative, a sensational tale that features the luring of an innocent and always white "girl" into the world of sex and violence. Often the young woman in such tales is abducted and drugged or courted and conned into a sham marriage. Once in the clutches of the panderer or procurer, the woman loses her maidenhead or her good reputation, leaving her vulnerable to further sexual bartering. She becomes in the process a slave in the sex trade. Lurid images of seduced and abandoned women triggered a national crisis at the turn into the twentieth century that spurred purity campaigns. Writers who experimented in literary naturalism, the radical style of the 1890s, wrote stories about sexual slavery.[18] Stephen Crane's *Maggie, A Girl of the Streets* is an Irish version of the tale and Wharton's *Bunner Sisters* provides an English/German variation on the literary pattern. In the years before the First World War, white slavery would become as big a cause as the ills of liquor, the two vices featured together in fiction and social tracts, such as *Fighting the Traffic in Young Girls; or, War on the White Slave Trade* (1910; edited by Ernest Bell) and *A New Conscience and an Ancient Evil* (1913) by Jane Addams. Ironically, the white slave narrative led purity leagues to keep their eye on fiction that attempted to tell the story of white slavery. Crane self-published *Maggie* because of controversy and Wharton would not publish *Bunner Sisters* until 1916 when the world was more receptive to literature that was considered radical in the 1890s. Normally considered a conservative writer, Wharton, as Hermione Lee points out, may be seen rather as an experimental one—especially when one considers *Bunner Sisters* as a first text.

We read the story according to the bits of fashion that Wharton reveals. The villain Herman Ramy, a German with a pale beard, had immigrated to the United States in the 1850s when he was nineteen and also worked in the fashion industry, as a watchmaker at Tiffany's. He wears a "thread-bare overcoat and shabby hat" and keeps his shop "tumbled and tattered and grimy." His clothes and shop signal character; the Bunners are as poor as he, but the fact that he is shabby and grimy suggests a decadence that the sisters have not been trained to read. Once the German intrudes, the spinster life grows "intolerably monotonous" to the seamstresses who only feel "the treadmill routine of the shop" and the colorless and aimless existence as they labor at their sewing and pinking machines (*BS* 303). The dress shop is "doomed to decline" (*BS* 279). Wharton focuses on the nature of Ann Eliza's sexual awakening and then the sacrifice of her own desire in order to give Evelina the supposed comfort and fashion of married life.

Evelina and Ramy's wedding features white chrysanthemums, dishes of oranges and bananas, and an iced wedding cake. Miss Mellins comes "profusely spangled and bangled" and has designed the bridal gown in grey cashmere. The white wedding bonnet is, no doubt, the creation of Evelina herself and a mark of her craft (*BS* 343). Clair Hughes argues that well-detailed wedding finery is a sign in a novel that the marriage is not much good, and that is certainly the case here.[19] And, too, expenditure of money on lavish events in a naturalist novel always portends a financial fall. The bride looks like "a faintly washed sketch beside a brilliant chromo"—reminding readers of the "Rock of Ages" chromo—and "like a drowned face on a sunset-dabbled sea" (*BS* 343). The couple disappears from sight, and Ann Eliza learns from the manager at Tiffany's that Ramy had been fired for drug addiction. The lady with the puffed sleeves may have been of help but shows up in mourning, even sadder and more remote. A year later, as the yellow jonquils bloom and the shop continues to decline, the lady reappears "in sleeves of a new cut" as she, apparently, lightens her mourning garb. Ann Eliza's eye catches the change in the sleeve design but her hands lack her sister's skill to turn the sight into a pattern. Fashion designs move in the story as they do today: by a quick eye and a knack for pirating.

The naturalistically drawn tale comes to its inevitable close as Ann Eliza catches "a slim dark figure" approaching that she, at first, believes is the lady with the puffed sleeves and then discovers is the prodigal sister dressed in clothes that tell "a tale of poverty" (*BS* 369). "I've been to hell and back," Evelina reports, as she details her work as a milliner, the death of her baby, the physical abuse of her husband, his desertion, and her work as a waitress, a housekeeper, and finally a beggar. Wharton hints at prostitution: "It was a tale of misery and humiliation so remote from the elder sister's innocent experiences that much of it was hardly intelligible to her" (*BS* 370). And Wharton, true to the naturalist mode of presentation, brings Evelina home to die and leaves Ann Eliza unable to earn enough money to remain in business. As brutally as Emile Zola might have done, Wharton pushes Ann Eliza into the street, homeless and in search of a job. On Broadway, she sees a help-wanted sign and she enters a shop, "festooned with muslin, a varied assortment of sofa-cushions, tea-cloths, pen-wipers, painted calendars and other specimens of feminine industry" (BS 387). It is the very image of the shop that she and her sister had hoped to establish.

And much in the mood of literary naturalism, Wharton gives health and exuberance to the plump proprietor who looks up from her task of fastening bows on a basket and beams, "We want a bright girl; stylish, and pleasant manners. You know what I mean. Not over thirty, anyhow; and nice-looking" (388). The social Darwinism of American business at the turn into the twentieth century brings the tale to its logically grim ending. What sort of future does a woman over thirty have? We note that Wharton creates *Bunner Sisters* as she herself moves into her thirties. Her marriage to Teddy was never a happy one, and they will separate and divorce as Edith's writing career succeeds. She finds, in her own experience, that a woman over thirty may be able to keep herself, even to take on a lover and shed her husband. But the fiction she is writing mulls over questions of female vitality and posits grim consequences for women who find themselves outside the economic protections of marriage.

Wharton's first novel about New York, *The House of Mirth* (1905), is likewise a story about a woman's quest for a livelihood. Lily Bart is bright and stylish with fine manners, discriminating taste, and a handsome face and figure, but she is also twenty-nine and thus on the very cusp of her usefulness, as the plump proprietor put it to Ann Eliza Bunner, "'Not over thirty, anyhow.'" Here, too, the heroine is "doomed to decline" and lives on the very edge of elegance. Lily tries her hand at millinery work and longs to own a shop, much like the one the Bunners envisioned, a green-shuttered establishment that would be "fresh and gay and thriving" (BS 388). She imagines presiding "over the charming little front shop—a shop all white panels, mirrors, and moss-green hangings—where her finished creations, hats, wreaths, aigrettes and the rest, perched on their stands like birds just poising for flight" (HM 477). James Tissot's *The Shop Girl* from the 1880s depicts the very sort of female establishment that Ann Eliza and Lily have in their minds but not within the reach of their expertise or financial power (figure 2.10).

Perhaps no piece of apparel has signaled fashion and social class more than a hat. The felt hat, made from animal pelts, was the main product of the fur trade during the eighteenth and nineteenth centuries. The beaver, especially, provided a pelt that could be made to hold its shape and shed water. But the hunting of the animal caused its

*Fig. 2.10.* James Tissot, *The Shop Girl*, 1883–1885. *The Art Gallery of Ontario. Commons.wikimedia.org.* (Plate 9.)

extinction in Europe and stimulated the fur trade in North America. A finely crafted beaver hat, however, put millinery workers in peril from a step in the process that called for "nitrate of mercury" to be brushed into the fur to strengthen the fibers and prepare them for shaping. That process, known as "carroting," exposed workers to mercury vapors; hence the phrase "mad as a hatter."[20] The process had changed by the middle of the nineteenth century when Wharton's family shopped for hats with care, in the knowledge that fur and feather carry substantial sartorial meaning.

The premier designer of women's hats at the turn into the twentieth century was the Parisian milliner Madame Virot, whose shop stood at 12 rue de la Paix. Her hats were popular with contemporary artists who used them on models, most famously Henri de Toulouse-Lautrec's various depictions of the actress Jane Avril, shown here (figure 2.11). Survivals of Madame Virot's work at the Museum of the City of New York remain more than a hundred years later remarkably fresh. A black velvet bonnet from 1885 is small and close-fitting, adorned with black beads and jet trimming with a white satin ribbon that ties under the chin. The style of the bonnet of the 1880s, like Wharton's bright tar-

*Fig. 2.11.* Henri de Toulouse-Lautrec, *Divan Japonais*, 1892–1893, color lithograph, featuring feathered hat designed by Mme. Virot, Paris. *Commons .wikimedia.org.* (Plate 10.)

tan velvet bonnet with the lace ruffle, gave way to more flattering designs in the 1890s that highlighted upswept chignons, giving a clearer view of a woman's face. A hat owned by Mrs. Louis Comfort Tiffany, née Louise Knox, is flat and brimmed, made of natural straw trimmed with pale artificial pink roses. To highlight the face, the hat brim is faced with black chiffon and a narrow band of black straw.

Later Virot hats feature elaborate ornaments made of artificial flowers and feathers of real birds, like the two examples shown here from the Museum of the City of New York. The silver-crowned style brings orchid plumes together with an aigrette or tuft of a vividly white egret tail feather (figure 2.12). The other hat comes wrapped in green iridescent feathers dramatically highlighted by the very head of the bird with its beady eye gazing on the viewer (figure 2.13). The positioning of the bird is much like the one on the hat that Wharton wore in the publicity photograph nearly a decade later (see figure 1.6). The Metropolitan collection holds a somewhat later hat, a small tricorn design of black velvet. The flat-topped crown is higher in front and pulled down in back and built over a wire frame, trimmed inside and out with baby ostrich feathers set off by an egret brush. Looking closely, one notes the painstakingly regular handstitches that hold each feather in place.

It is clear that the millinery craft relies on precise eyes and deft hands that have mastered a long period of apprenticeship.

Looking at the astonishing plumage on the hats—wings spread and eye open—we can see, as well, the cost of the hat to the natural world. On a day in 1886, the founder of the first *Audubon Magazine*, Frank Chapman, decided to study the ornithological ornaments on women's hats in fashionable New York; he recorded parts of "3 bluebirds, 2 red-headed woodpeckers, 9 Baltimore orioles, 5 blue jays, 21 common terns, a saw-whet owl, and a prairie hen."[21] The woman's hat seemed to him the culprit in the decline of bird populations, especially the egret population in Florida. The magazine credits Mrs. Augustus Hemenway of Boston as the most insistent voice in the founding of the Audubon Society: she decried the hunting of the egret, and she and other members of women's clubs linked the conservation of birdlife to the conservation of femininity. Club member Orinda Hornbrooke posed the question, "Do women who wear birds ever stop to think what an injury to the . . . moral influence of our sex they are inflicting?" Female activists joined politicians—most notably Theodore Roosevelt, who had been an ornithologist even as a child—in supporting the Lacey Act in 1904. The law made it a federal offense to kill wild species illegally in one state and then ship them across state lines for sale in another. The Lacey Act made it difficult for milliners in New York and other cities to buy bird carcasses for their trade. The federal movement was echoed in various state and city laws. In New York, the Audubon Plumage Bill of 1911 banned the sale of native birds, and the 1913 Tariff Bill made it illegal to import the plumes of wild birds. And in the Migratory Bird Act of 1913, migratory birds

*Fig. 2.12.* Madame Virot, Paris, hat comprising aigrette (the tufted crest of an egret), ostrich plumes, silver embroidery, and pearls, 1896. *Museum of the City of New York, gift of Mrs. S. Breck Parkman Trowbridge (49.125.2). Ben Fink Photography Inc., New York City.* (Plate 11.)

*Fig. 2.13.* Madame Virot, Paris, hat fabricated of an entire Quetzal (a vividly colored, long-tailed Central American bird) and silk velvet, c. 1898; compare Wharton's hat in fig. 1.6. *Museum of the City of New York, gift of Susan Dwight Bliss, 1937 (37.252.4). Ben Fink Photography Inc., New York City.* (Plate 12.)

were placed under federal jurisdiction. We note in photographs that Wharton's hats over the years of the twentieth century feature fewer and fewer birds (although we see feather trim even into the 1920s).

Wharton's stories about millinery concern themselves with the cost of hats in human terms. Evelina Bunner knows how to trim hats but lacks the skill of a professional milliner. Little wonder that Lily Bart at twenty-nine cannot train eye and hand to do such meticulous work. The garment industry requires youth and energy. The Progressive social settlement founder Jane Addams describes such young women who labor in the city and desire to wear the fashions they produce: "As these overworked girls stream along the street, the rest of us see only the self-conscious walk, the giggling speech, the preposterous clothing. And yet through the huge hat, with its wilderness of bedraggled feathers, the girl announces to the world that she is here. She demands attention to the fact of her existence, she states that she is ready to live, to take her place in the world."[22] A woman might prefer to work in a factory or in a shop, Addams explains, because a job in the public sphere allows freedom from household labor performed in relatively private spaces where men may press young women to provide sexual favors along with domestic tasks. Lily Bart discovers that Gus Trenor is such a man. What Lily hopes to establish is a business of her own, a millinery shop where her sense of style will attract customers.

*The House of Mirth* is, in many ways, a novel about the wearing and making of hats. From the opening scene on the train platform, Lily is shown in contrast to "sallow-faced girls in preposterous hats, and flat-chested women" of the working class that Addams describes, a group that our hero Lawrence Selden sees as dingy and crude (*HM* 6). In musing about the differences between wearer and maker, he sounds much like John Amherst in having "a confused sense" that Lily Bart "must have cost a great deal to make" and that the cost could be measured, as he puts it, in the labor of "a great many dull and ugly people" who had been "sacrificed to produce her" (*HM* 7). Lily is the product of American industry and commerce, the ultimate piece of material culture, a finely crafted woman formed into a seemly futile shape. She appears first wearing a dark hat and veil, and Selden observes other accoutrements, including a jeweled watch, antique laces, and a sapphire bracelet that has the look to him of a manacle "chaining her to her fate" (*HM* 10). Who is most at risk in the making and wearing of goods: the laborer who produces the bracelet, in this case, or the woman who places the bracelet on her wrist? The working title of the novel, "A Moment's Ornament," reinforces Wharton's intention to create a heroine who is herself an object, much like the hat she buys. Percy Gryce desires to make her part of his American collection and Simon Rosedale would collect her, too, were she not tainted by scandal.

The first conversation Lily and Selden have is about fashion. A man can be shabby but the tatters of his coat or the clutter of his study cannot diminish his commercial value; they may even enhance his social status as a man so well-off that he need not pay attention to the details of dress. Lily lectures Selden on the social and commercial value of a lady's clothes, the very goods that Selden has been eyeing. She schools him in a woman's perception of clothes as "the background, the frame" of her worldly success. "Who wants a dingy woman?" she asks, turning to study her image in a mirror. The truth is, as she bluntly puts it: "If I were shabby no one would have me; a woman is asked out as much for her clothes as for herself" (*HM* 17–18). The charwoman appears in the next scene as a grim illustration; she has a sallow face pitted with smallpox scars and clothing so dirty and crude that Lily pulls her skirt up to avoid contact.

Lily jokes in a later flirtation with Selden that should they marry and be poor, she would at least be able to trim her own hats. That is a joke that will turn sour over the course of the novel. Imagining one can trim a hat is very different from acquiring the actual skill to trim a hat. The first job that Lily thinks herself qualified to hold in Madame Regina's hat shop is as a live model in the showroom, "a displayer of hats." The truth is that she has performed as a displayer of goods throughout the novel and has changed garments to fit into various scenes, dressed in a red crêpe de chine for card playing, a gray "devotional-cut" gown to lure Percy Gryce on his way to church, and a woodland ensemble for her walk in the woods with Lawrence Selden. Although malleable, Lily is not so pliable as Bertha Dorset as a "live model." Bertha dresses "as if she could have been crumpled up and run through a ring"—that is, crumpled as a delicate gown and run through a wedding ring—and glitters in "serpentine spangles" (*HM* 36).

The social worker Gerty Ferrish, herself an independent woman, inspires Lily to think of herself as a milliner rather than a live model. The business that Gerty and Lily have in mind is one owned by Madame Regina, a New York version of Madame Virot. Regina employs twenty workers in her New York millinery shop. Lily believes, at first, in the ability of "her charming hands" to knot a ribbon or select an artificial flower as the finishing artistic touch on a lady's hat. Subordinate workers would, she imagines, shape hat forms and stitch linings, the drudge work that requires "blunt, grey, needle-pricked fingers" (*HM* 456–457). Her apprenticeship in the craft that will require knowledge and skill in such needlework begins ominously in January and drags out over the winter season. After two months of training, Lily's hands fail to find the rhythm of sewing spangles on hat frames (figure 2.14). It puzzles her that her "untutored fingers were still blundering over the rudiments of the trade." What she does learn

*Fig. 2.14.* A. B. Wenzell, illustration for Wharton's *The House of Mirth*. Madame Regina instructs the novice Lily Bart with the caption: "Look at those spangles, Miss Bart, —every one of 'em sewed on crooked."

is that the delicate art of shaping and trimming the hat comes from long years of labor. In a millinery shop only talent and expertise can lift Lily from the inexorable routine of preparation.

Wharton takes up many questions about fashion in the episode at Madame Regina's hat shop, a typical establishment. Is millinery an art? As the narrator puts it, "[I]t was something more than industry, surely, this creation of ever-varied settings for the face of fortunate womanhood" (*HM* 455). Can art come from the labor of less fortunate womanhood, "fagged profiles" with exaggerated hairdos, sallow faces, and dull, colorless personalities—the very workers that Jane Addams describes on the street of Chicago? Although they are fairly well paid and dressed, the environment, especially the quality of air, is unwholesome, and the young women labor at sedentary tasks. The "underworld of toilers" in the novel follows the social season of the Trenors and Dorsets with genuine excitement. Each worker "knew to whom the headgear in her hands was destined, and had her opinion of its future wearer, and a definite knowledge of the latter's place in the social system." Judy Trenor's hat is festooned with a green bird of paradise plume. Bertha Dorset's blue tulle hat is French from the millinery House of Madame Virot, and the shop has taken it in simply to refresh its ornament of artificial flowers. Women in the working class, as Wharton depicts them, buy the "gross tangible image of material achievement" every bit as much as the Trenors and the Dorsets do. "Miss Bart, if you can't sew those spangles on more regular I guess you'd better give the hat to Miss Kilroy," the forewoman commands and Lily has to agree. She was hired as a "fashionable apprentice" at "the temple of art" where raw beginners were more malleable than an experienced soul. Lily goes back to binding edges, the most menial and least demanding of tasks. As the day ends, she finds herself aloof from the values and ethics of the throng, "shrinking from all that was unpolished and promiscuous," as she experiences life on the underside of fashion. And it is on the "dirty and unpropitious corner" among the "tumult of trams and wagons contending hideously" that she runs into Simon Rosedale for a moment of tea and conversation.

In the background of the novel, Wharton is working with Progressive ideas that will come into clearer relief in her next novel, *The Fruit of the Tree*, an industrial novel that depicts and considers solutions to harsh working conditions for laborers (whom she refers to as "hands"). Unlike many of her contemporary novelists, Wharton is never quite comfortable with the idea that the human condition is remediable. For example, she satirizes Lady Cressida Raith, who dresses in Liberty silks and ethnological trinkets as she does missionary work in London's East End (*FT* 83). By the 1880s Liberty & Company on Regent Street in London designed flowing silk tea gowns, the style associated with reform or aesthetic dress; Wharton adds the ethnological trinkets to emphasize her point that Lady Cressida follows radicalism through fashion more than substance. And yet it was East End London poverty that had spurred Jane Addams to establish the Hull House social settlement on Chicago's Halstead Street in 1889 and to become a major Progressive figure at the turn into the twentieth century.

Photographs taken of Wharton in tea gowns and shirtwaists reveal, as we have seen, her own comfort in wearing reform apparel: Reading dress, we note that Lily Bart's costume in the tableau vivant scene (figure 1.1) is an example of reform or aesthetic dress very like fashions being designed about the same time by Mariano Fortuny, an artist born in Spain and raised in Paris who worked in Venice as a painter, costume designer, photographer, and architect.[23] His dress designs, particularly the "Delphos Robe" which he patented, followed the contours of artistic dress by releasing the female body from the corset and draping the gown from the shoulders (figure 2.15). Fortuny's goal, as biographer Guillermo De Osma puts it, was to "liberate the body, allow for complete freedom of movement, provide comfort and warmth, and above all, be beautiful."[24] Lily Bart seals her letters with the word "Beyond!" set below the image of a ship, and Wharton makes it clear that the heroine seeks a world beyond convention. In

*Fig. 2.15.* Mariano Fortuny (Mrs. Condé Nast) in Delphos robe, c. 1907; compare background, gown, and pose of Reynolds's Mrs. Lloyd in fig. I.1. *Prints and Photographs Division, Library of Congress, Washington, D.C.*

the Reynolds gown she stands in a natural landscape next to a force-fully phallic tree and for a moment defines herself as a truly modern woman. Her friends agree that the gown portrays the "real" Lily Bart.

Wharton's ambivalence toward social reform is signaled, too, in her dressing of the charity worker Gerty Farish in subdued, sensible garments. Her gowns are, as the narrator frankly puts it, ugly to look at even as her charity work is laudable. Mlle. Lily's Hat Shop is Gerty's idea, and she acts as social worker to Lily just as she has worked to save the typist, Nettie Struther, from financial ruin when she became pregnant and could not work. Ironically it is Nettie who explains to Lily, "Working girls are n't looked after in the way you are, and they don't always know how to look after themselves" (*HM* 509). She articulates precisely Lily's dilemma, and the Darwinism of the novel brings about the dour ending.

In her early fiction, Wharton depicts the struggle of working-class women to make their own way in the world. The truth is that the Bunner sisters can run a marginally viable sewing establishment as long as the two of them remain together, unmarried, and healthy. Any break from the pattern of dull duty results in economic disaster, as Wharton's story depicts and as reports on working conditions in late nineteenth-century America record. Even into the twentieth century, the situation for wage-earning women isn't much better. Madame Regina has the expertise to run a millinery shop, Gerty Ferrish makes a lusterless living as a social worker, and Nettie Struther secures a job and a marriage in order to create financial security. Wharton's ornamental heroine, Lily Bart, lacks the training and skill to become self-supporting even as she has the audacity to resist marriage. Her fate, as Elaine Showalter and other critics have noted, begs the question. Does Wharton really want a well-clad lady to be a worker in the garment trade, much less a businesswoman? Over the next ten years, in her fiction and in her own life, she will find the answer.

❦ 3

# PHILANTHROPY
# AND PROGRESS

Her dress could not have hung in such subtle folds, her white chin
have nestled in such rich depths of fur, the pearls in her ears have
given back the light from such pure curves," he concedes, "if thin
shoulders in shapeless gingham had not bent, day in, day out,
above the bobbins and carders, and weary ears throbbed even
at night with the tumult of the looms.
—*The Fruit of the Tree*

During the years leading into the First World War, Wharton
weighed ethical issues surrounding the making of the very fashions she wore. The manufacture of cloth and the production of garments became increasingly mechanized in the late nineteenth century,
a sign of industrial progress that lowered the costs of goods even as it
diminished the value of skills like carding, spinning, weaving, cutting,
and sewing. A manufacturer's goal of increasing profit often came at
the price of safety for garment workers who were, in turn, paid meager salaries for their labor. It is the very set of pressures that created the
union movement at the turn of the last century and led to legislation
to curb abuses, especially for the protection of children and women
who performed much of the work. Progressive changes in the design
of mills and the conditions of sweatshops seemed to Edith Wharton,
as they did to any prescient observer, laudable and perhaps viable. Yet
she was not wholeheartedly a Progressive reformer; in the end, she
doubted that legislative or paternal mandates could solve complex
human problems. This chapter considers two of Wharton's experiments, one fictional and other real, with ownership and management
of the means of production. Her industrial novel, *The Fruit of the Tree*
(1907), places a fashionable widow, Bessy Westmore, in ownership of
a textile mill and, after her death, leaves a professional nurse, Justine

Brent (married to Bessy's second husband) in an awkward partnership of the mill. In that tangle of love relationships, Wharton sorts through conflicting desires: on the one hand, to make money and to dress well; on the other, to ameliorate the conditions of workers whose labor provides such comfort and luxury. A striking feature of Wharton's life is that during the war in Europe, she herself turned to the practical business of running sewing rooms and a lace-making school as part of her network of charities, an expansive philanthropic enterprise that resembled an urban settlement house.

The Fruit of the Tree is Wharton's most revealing study of industrial conditions and factory reform in the garment trade. To do research for her novel, she traveled the five miles or so from her house, The Mount, in Lenox, to Adams, Massachusetts, to tour the Berkshire Cotton Mill. The mill was situated along the Hoosac River in the small New England industrial town that had grown first from a gristmill in 1772 and later from cotton mills that developed there largely as a response to the War of 1812 and the resulting restriction on the importation of cotton from England.[1] As businesses prospered, the Adams South Village Cotton Manufacture Company opened in 1814 with three floors, 708 spindles, and 26 looms. The Berkshire Mountains became a center for industrial towns that produced textiles along with other manufactured goods, especially shoes. Looking at the map of manufacturing in the Berkshires at the turn into the twentieth century, we see that Wharton lived close to industries in Pittsfield, including the J. L. Peck Cotton and Woolen Mills and the Pontoosuch Woolen Mills, as well as the Johnson Manufacturing Company Mills in North Adams. A railway system and a tunnel through Hoosac Mountain provided a gateway to New York, and by 1878 the town of Adams had grown significantly and split into the twin towns of Adams and North Adams. An Adams entrepreneur, W. B. Plunkett, began to manufacture textiles in the 1830s and was followed in business by his sons who opened the Berkshire Cotton Manufacturing Company in 1889.

The Plunketts built what had the reputation of being the largest fine goods business in New England, with four mills running by 1900 that were considered state-of-the-art. According to an article in the New York Times, President McKinley laid the cornerstone of the fourth mill in the summer of 1899. At a ball in December to mark the opening of the mill, the Boston Festival Orchestra played in "the new weaving room, which is 530 by 225 feet, the largest in America."[2] Ten thousand celebrants, including the governor-elect, attended, and two thousand of them had room to dance in the vast weaving room that elegantly doubled as a ballroom, illuminated with a thousand lights. Marking the clear distinction between owners and workers, the Times reported, "The whole affair was in charge of the operatives of the mill," a group numbering 2,500 whose wages had been raised twenty percent that month. The millworkers, rewarded with a raise in pay, had the honor of working the event—without, we assume, the benefit of dancing on the floor of their weaving room.

The enormity and sophistication of the mill attracted visitors, Edith Wharton among them. The operation she would have seen looked much like the photographs taken by Lewis Hine (1874–1940). Known for iconic images of New York City taken atop the Empire State Building as it was being built, Hine also photographed immigrants at Ellis Island and child laborers in the Berkshire Mills, among other factories. He had studied sociology at the University of Chicago and Columbia University and had taken pictures for the National Child Labor Committee and for the reform magazine *The Survey*. His camera recorded the Berkshire Mill in much the way Edith Wharton would have seen it; figure 3.1 shows a fifteen-year-old boy sweeping the floor of the spinning room.

Wharton's eye noted problems in the mill's configuration of carding machines, a compression of space, no doubt, caused by the eagerness of owners to increase output and thereby make more money. The carding machines looked to her as though they were jammed together too tightly in patterns that put workers in danger. In the process of carding, workers brush, wash, and mesh together fibers of cotton or wool or animal hair so that they can be spun into yarns or threads and then woven into fabrics. Carding by hand requires two brushes and a skilled movement of fibers between the bristles to tease out workable strands. A carding machine, like the one Wharton observed, could take up a full room in a series of drums or rollers that move fibers through many cycles, refining them into bats or flats stretched to usable thinness. Lewis Hine photographed young women working at a carding machine in 1908 (figure 3.2). This image shows a scene much like the one Wharton would have seen in the Berkshire mill at about the same time. The danger to a worker, of course, would be the handling of the fiber as it makes its way through the series of drums. Without precaution, and in the early days of manufacturing without safety devices, a worker could be at considerable risk of injury, especially to a hand caught up in a mechanized roller. The novel Edith Wharton wrote after touring the mills begins with just such an industrial accident. The hand of a worker, someone she refers to as a "hand," is caught in a carding machine, an injury that causes him to lose not only a hand but an arm. Her telling of the story raises the Progressive Era issues of safety in the workplace and workman's compensation. The maimed worker is of little value without the ability to earn a living for himself and his family.

As in other naturalist novels, the relentless and even monstrous jaws

*Fig. 3.1.* Lewis Wickes Hine (1874–1940), photograph of a fifteen-year-old sweeper in the spinning and spooling room, Berkshire Cotton Mills, Adams, Massachusetts, 10 July 1916. *Prints and Photographs Division, Library of Congress, Washington, D.C.*

of the machine set the plot into motion. Wharton depicts the sounds and smells and sights of the grand monster unleashed by the power of the dynamo (the engine that had awed Henry Adams at the Paris Exposition of 1900). Many novelists of her day used the machine as a metaphor of modern life in its power to both dazzle and cripple an individual. The novel's hero, John Amherst, sees the mill in such terms as both a beautiful and a terrifying force: "It was not only the sense of power that thrilled him—he felt a beauty in the ordered activity of the whole intricate organism, in the rhythm of dancing bobbins and revolving cards, the swift continuous outpour of doublers and ribbon-

*Fig. 3.2.* Lewis Wickes Hine (1874–1940), photograph of Bertha Bonneau, fifteen years old, working in the card room, King Philip Mill, Fall River, Massachusetts. *Prints and Photographs Division, Library of Congress, Washington, D.C.*

laps, the steady ripple of the long ply-frames, the terrible gnashing play of the looms—all these varying subordinate motions, gathered up into the throb of the great machines which fed the giant's arteries."[3] Under the power of its engine, the machine comes to life, dancing and gnashing and throbbing. What if, Wharton's novel posits, a Progressive reformer had the power to subdue the dynamo? The novel is about that epic battle, a modern version of dragon slaying.

At the heart of the battle is a clash of clothes. Amherst has committed himself to a career in mill management, a decidedly unglamorous profession with little need for sartorial fussiness, and the plot moves as he stumbles against the sumptuous attire of the mill's owner, a young woman newly widowed. A man supposedly not interested in fashion, we note, reads dress closely as he measures the value of female garments in terms of the cost to the laborers who produce them. "Her dress could not have hung in such subtle folds, her white chin have nestled in such rich depths of fur, the pearls in her ears have given back the light from such pure curves," he concedes, "if thin shoulders in shapeless gingham had not bent, day in, day out, above the bobbins and carders, and weary ears throbbed even at night with tumult of the looms" (*FT* 49). And here is the ethical dilemma of the story: what is to be done about his sexual desire for Bessy Westmore in the face of his professional obligations to run the mill that produces the income to buy her gowns and indeed manufactures the very fabrics to make them?

John Amherst thinks he has the answer in two overlapping ideas. One idea is based on economics: the problem of the textile business is "the ultimate substitution of the stock-company for the individual employer" (*FT* 48). A clear-eyed entrepreneur would have the power and, presumably, the inclination to run his business in ways that would ensure continuing prosperity for himself and protection for his workers. The other idea is based on ethics: "Till he entered personally into [the workers'] hardships and aspirations—till he learned what they wanted and why they wanted it—Amherst believed that no mere lawmaking, however enlightened, could create a wholesome relation between the two." The new ethics he seeks is based on the old relationship between "master and man," modernized in an enlightened collaboration between them that will have the effect of ameliorating harsh conditions and establishing Progressive reform in the workplace. He sees beauty in the subtle folds of a lady's gown and also in the ordered activity of the textile mill. The clash between individualism and mutualism is heightened as he marries Bessy Westmore and becomes not only the manager but the putative owner of the textile mills and of property in the factory town.

Consider how Amherst describes the economic issues to Bessy: "Financially, I don't suppose your mills could be better run; but there are over seven hundred women working in them, and there's so much to be done, just for them and their children" (*FT* 51). What he hopes to instill in his wife is a sense of maternalism patterned after the paternal system of mill ownership. She might, he believes, be taught to act beyond her individual profit through a blossoming of her motherly instincts. "'Do you leave it to your little girl's nurses to do everything for her?'" he asks early in the novel. Good question for a woman who has married into luxury and is quite comfortable leaving her daughter in the care of a nurse; indeed, she herself is comforted by being in the care of a nurse. Bessy has been infantilized by the cushion of wealth that surrounds her. Amherst guides Bessy through the mills, much as Wharton herself toured them, amid the monstrous energy and throb of the looms. He exposes her to what he sees as "the dark side of monotonous human toil . . . the banquet of flesh and blood and brain" (*FT* 56–59). His job and that of the novel's heroine, the nurse Justine Brent, is to reveal the meaning of the industrial accident to Bessy and thereby awaken her sense of responsibility and obligation, as a mother and an owner, to the worker and his family. Not surprising in a Wharton novel, the enlightened progressivism of Amherst and Brent never works on Bessy Westmore.

Wharton uses clothes to tell the story of textile manufacturing but, governed by her own sense of tact, omits unnecessary fashion details. This is a contemporary novel and, therefore, her readers would have the clothes already in mind. The novel focuses, instead, on sartorial details that signify social class and individual character. Justine Brent measures John Amherst by the cut and care of "his shabby clothes—carefully brushed, but ill-cut and worn along the seams" (*FT* 5–6). He appeals to her because although he is shabby, he is carefully brushed. For him, as for many of Wharton's men who do the looking for us, Justine is defined in simple lines, first by her dark blue linen nurse's uniform. When he sees her again in street clothes, his imagination fails "to identify the uniformed nurse with the girl in her trim dark dress, soberly complete in all its accessories" (*FT* 8). He is attracted to the darkly sober dress; no doubt, he feels affinity with its trim style and her attention to accessories. Justine's clothes are complicated to read as she moves from uniform to street dress, the transition that baffles John Amherst: she is "as cool as a drum-major till she took off her uniform—and then!" (*FT* 27). Over the long course of the novel he comes to discover the feminine being ("—and then!") beneath the professional attire. The fact that Justine Brent will move from nurse's uniform to couture fashion perhaps signals Wharton's own proclivities more than those of the novel's hero.

The moral fiber of her characters is reflected in their garments. John Amherst's mother, for example, knits throughout the novel, "shaping garments" and "darning rents" (*FT* 24–25). Likewise, she is a nurturing, maternal presence. Her son's clothes may be shabby but she makes sure they are clean, mended, and well brushed, the very qualities that attract Justine Brent. The mill manager's wife, Mrs. Truscomb, is "a large flushed woman in a soiled wrapper and diamond earrings" (*FT* 30). One needs little more than the sartorial juxtaposition of soiled bedclothes and glittering diamonds to read her character and social standing (her husband is, after all, merely an overseer). Mr. Tredegar, Bessy Westmore's lawyer, luxuriates in the "careless finish of his evening dress and pearl-studded shirt-front" (*FT* 73). His status comes, as his manner of dress suggests, from the wealth of his client. Bessy Westmore's father, Mr. Langhope, is another man who lives off the Westmore pocketbook. We see him sitting with "one faultlessly-clad leg crossed on the other" (*FT* 33) and revealing the "glossy tip of a patent-leather pump" (*FT* 75). In the details of grooming—"careless finish," "pearl-studded," "faultlessly-clad," and "glossy tip"—Wharton signals that the men are in league to draw as much money as possible from the Westmore mills. Halford Gaines, the central figure in the consortium of business owners in the town of Hanaford, comes dressed suspiciously in "jeweled-shirt-front and padded shoulders" (*FT* 110) and everyone notes "the official majesty of Mr. Gaines's frock-coat" (*FT* 154). As the bejeweled shirt and padded shoulder suggest, however, society in the New England town lacks authenticity. We note that his son and heir, Westy, longs to live in New York City, and the Gaines daughters arrive absurdly dressed in "the latest philanthropic fashions" (*FT* 122). Wharton cannot resist satire in dressing the townsfolk. The family friend Mrs. Ansell, more a mirror than an actual presence, is gently gowned under a lace sunshade (*FT* 172).

The very garments that arouse the hero's passion come at a high human price, and he is perplexed by his responses. In truth, Bessy may never have taken notice of John Amherst had he not "taken unusual pains with his appearance" by allowing his mother to dress him up in "carefully brushed Sunday clothes" (*FT* 39). He frets over when and where his well-brushed dress clothes ought to be worn. What if Bessy should shun him because of his clothes and place him outside "the little circle of people who gave life its crowning grace and facility" (*FT* 68)? Our hero wants to reform the garment industry even as he yearns to live in the graceful style of the moneyed class. We know few details of Bessy's dress, only that she wears black in the beginning because she is in mourning for her husband and that the fashionable shape of her widow's veil turns everyone's eye in Westmore. For Amherst, "her beauty was like a blinding light" and her hair "bubbled up," causing an "electric flash" from his eye to his brain (*FT* 42–43). He is as dazzled by the electricity of sexual desire as he is by the power of the dynamo. Amherst notes the subtlety of her gown and the purity of its form and muses over the gingham frocks of the young women who slave above the bobbins in the mill to produce the fabrics of the garment. Luxurious clothing is the product of the "monstrous energies of the mills" and "the dark side of monotonous human toil" and "the banquet of flesh and blood and brain" at the "meaningless machines" with humans performing like "automatic appendages" (*FT* 56–59). Amherst has done his reading of naturalist texts and sees the evils of mechanized production, even he desires the beauty that labor creates.

Bessy Westmore is described more by accoutrements than specifics of dress. She lies in bed on embroidered pillows and linens edged in delicate laces, and she dresses in lace wrappers and rose-lined slippers, details very close to those we would find in Wharton's own boudoir. We note, too, that the Westmore family home is decorated in ways that Wharton admired: warm light and old pictures and bronzes with "soft mingling of tints in faded rugs and panellings of time-warmed oak" (*FT* 221). Bessy enjoys riding and golfing and playing tennis—all activities that moved women's fashion, as we have seen, toward the reform of petticoats, corsets, and bustles. Bored after her marriage to John Amherst, Bessy makes plans to use mill money to build a pleasure house that includes a gymnasium and spa for herself and her friends. She delights in riding her horse, aptly named Impulse. It is her passion for hard riding that brings about the accident that leaves her paralyzed. In Amherst's absence, Nurse Brent makes the ethical decision to euthanize Bessy who is in much pain without hope of recovery.

Looking at wealth and dress in the novel, we find Justine Brent also appreciates the beauty and luxury of the moneyed life. In response to John Amherst's reformist zeal, she confesses, "I'm not philanthropic" (*FT* 231). She had been a girlhood friend of Bessy's and, as she comes to live in Hanaford, she comes to see her utilitarian self as ornamental. Early in the novel, Justine dresses up for a ball, Cinderella-like, in the wealthy Mrs. Dressel's gown of Irish lace and ponders the advantages of dress as she views herself in her first good frock. In the "festal raiment, which her dark tints subdued to a quiet elegance, she was like the golden core of a pale rose illuminating and scenting its petals" (*FT* 145). And she imagines herself back in her own clothes as "no more than a little brown bird without a song" (*FT* 146). Just as John Amherst has puzzled over the meaning of fashion, Justine wonders whether such finery will restrict her encounter with a kindred soul: "don't you remember the fable of the wings under the skin, that sprout when one meets a pair of kindred shoulders?" (*FT* 148). Justine "disguised as a lady" and Amherst dressed in Sunday clothes may seem to be kindred souls, but the artifice of their costumes belies the legitimacy of their union. It is true that both yearn for the beauty and luxury that Bessy's money provides. Both understand, too, that the mills were for Bessy, in essence, "a vast purse in which to plunge for her pin-money" (*FT* 181). That pin money has made the Westmore family comfortable and promises the same tainted luxury to Amherst and Brent.

How are the two would-be reformers to balance aesthetics and ethics? That is certainly in Wharton's mind as she crafts the novel that she always thought of as ill-conceived, what she called episodic and not architectonic in design.[4] The ethical questions at the core of the novel concern the workers who are sacrificed to the making of goods and the earning of fortunes. To ameliorate working conditions in the mills and living conditions for workers in the town, Amherst plans to establish a Mothers' Club, a recreation-ground, an emergency hospital, a night school, a library and, finally, the spa and gymnasium that he mistakenly believes Bessy planned as the crown on his reforms. He wants healthy conditions in the mills themselves, more space for equipment, and worker ownership of the tenement houses that surround the mills.

Amherst believes, along with Progressive reformers in the early years of the twentieth century, that the "roots of the baneful paternalism" had choked out "every germ of initiative in the workmen" (*FT* 194). The Hull House social settlement founder Jane Addams, in her first book, *Democracy and Social Ethics* (1902), assessed George Pullman's culpability in the 1894 violent strike against his company in much the same way: "He built, and in great measure regulated, an entire town, without calling upon the workmen either for self-expression or self-government."[5] Pullman had built a "Utopian" mill town near Chicago to house his Palace Car Company, that manufactured railway cars, and also house his four thousand workers. Progressive reformers, like Addams and Wharton's Amherst, understood the irony behind the construction of mill towns without consulting those who were to live in the towns and the arrogance of men like Pullman who "honestly believed" that they knew better than the workers themselves what was "for their own good." The Hanaford consortium of owners, managers, and lawyers fear the power of a "low mongrelly socialist" and keep a distance from the "mongrel populations of lay labourers" (*FT* 216 and 308). The truth is that Amherst, too, spends very little time listening to the workers and considering their ideas.

In the background of the novel stand garment workers, especially in New York and Chicago, who were forming unions that threatened to bring socialism to capitalist America. Several unions comprising Jewish, Italian, and Irish immigrants as well as garment workers born in the United States formed a coalition in 1900 that established the International Ladies' Garment Workers' Union.[6] Wharton's novel is distinctly modern in its depiction of textile mills and hints of worker unrest, although she moves the plot away from unionizing and toward the act of euthanasia, another controversial topic of her day. What Wharton could see around her in New York, however, were the festering relations between workers and owners, the hints of socialism that reverberated across New England, even into her fictional town of Hanaford. In 1909, workers in the Triangle Shirtwaist Factory walked off the job in a conflict that would build over several weeks into an "Uprising" of 20,000 laborers; that strike was followed the next year in a "Great Revolt" of 60,000 cloakmakers. Strikers demanded higher wages, health benefits, and union recognition by owners, the reforms that workers needed in the fictional Westmore mills. A devastating fire at the Triangle Shirtwaist Factory in March 1911 resulted in the deaths of 146 garment workers, most of them women and children, trapped on the eighth floor because doors had been locked to keep them at their tasks. Many of the young women leapt from windows rather than perish in the fire. In a memorial held in the Metropolitan Opera House, Rose Schneiderman rebuked owners and consumers: "This is not the first time girls have been burned alive in the city. Every week I must learn of the untimely death of one of my sister workers. Every year thousands of us are maimed. The life of men and women is so cheap and property is so sacred." Wharton's novel depicts harsh conditions in the mills and, in that way, anticipates the unionizing of textile and garment workers in a movement that would demand reform. Yet the novelist was not philosophically a progressive, much less politically a socialist.

The heroine Justine Brent, after her marriage to Amherst, becomes something of an owner herself and, in the luxury of her new wealth, as Kimberly Chrisman and other scholars have noted, comes to dress as Wharton herself dressed. Justine was "always finished and graceful in appearance with the pretty woman's art of wearing her few plain dresses as if they were many and varied" and shunning what Wharton condemned as "the upholstery of life" (*FT* 450).[7] She admires Amherst's desire to remake the mill town in the image of Progressive reform: "his whole scheme hung together, harmonizing the work and leisure of the operatives, instead of treating them as half machines, half man, and neglecting the man for the machine" (*FT* 458). And yet she understands more clearly than Amherst does the contradictions in any system of reform. In what is perhaps the core line in all of Wharton's fiction, Justine concludes "life is a series of pitiful compromises with fate" (*FT* 624). Reading dress, we see Justine Brent as the embodiment of both her author's sense of fashion and her philosophical realism.

Edith Wharton had the uncommon chance to put her literary ideas into practical use. During the summer of 1914, from her apartment in the rue de Varenne, she witnessed the traumatic beginnings of what would build over time into the First World War. Not unlike her fictional characters John Amherst and Gerty Ferrish, Wharton herself turned to philanthropic labor in response to the cataclysm, even as she resisted, much as Justine Brent had done, being thought of as a philanthropist. The question for her was how to use wealth and influence to ameliorate the conditions of the war unfolding around her in Paris. In response, she constructed, managed, and supported a network of charities. It is fashion that prompted Wharton's war work. As she looked around Paris, what she noted from her own experience was the plight of seamstresses out of work as some of the couture house in the rue de la Paix closed in an early economic response to the fighting in Europe.

Wharton's charities, built over the long course of the war, came to constitute an enterprise very like the social settlements of the late nineteenth century. Chicago's Hull House, founded in 1889 by Jane Addams and Ellen Gates Starr, organized and supported many Progressive programs to ameliorate urban poverty, including a book club and reading room, college extension courses, a nursery and kindergarten, a working women's housing collaborative, sports teams and urban playgrounds, even an experimental theater, a multiethnic kitchen, a coffeehouse, craft studios, and a museum. The women and men of Hull House supported labor unions, scrutinized the city Health Department, advised the Bureau of Justice, and hosted the Working People's Social Science Club. They called for safety in the workplace, the end of child labor, the creation of juvenile courts, the eight-hour workday, workmen's compensation, social security, and health care. Addams became a founding member of the American Civil Liberties Union and of the Chicago branch of the National Association for the

Advancement of Colored People. In 1912 she became the first woman to speak at a major national political convention; she seconded the Progressive Bull Moose nomination of Wharton's friend Teddy Roosevelt and secured his support for a plank on women's suffrage, a battle that she and other feminists finally won in 1920.

Wharton's philanthropic work in Paris follows the contour of many Progressive Era initiatives. One would not, however, associate Wharton with suffragists, much less with pacifists. In her war novel, *A Son at the Front* (1923), she caricatures the conversion of the superficial pacifist Harvey Mayhew into a rabid militarist. She satirizes, too, a group she calls "The Friends of French Art" who support reading rooms, clubs, recreation centers, and lectures on aesthetics and politics; the group engages, too, in private jealousies and petty retaliations.[8] Other volunteers in her novel, however, do laudable work packing medical supplies, keeping ambulance accounts, and aiding refugees and wounded soldiers. "There was enough misery and confusion at the rear for every civilian volunteer to find his task," she explains in a somber and sincere passage about the human cost of war (*SF* 129).

As the fighting in Europe escalated, Paris became a city of charities supported by elite American families, including the Astors, Vanderbilts, Whitneys, and Roosevelts. Wharton initially responded to a request from the comtesse d'Haussonville to set up an *ouvroir* or sewing room for working-class women. Alan Price in his study of Wharton's war charities notes that she was one of as many as twenty-five thousand American women who volunteered in one way or another in Europe and Asia.[9] It was fashionable to work through the Red Cross by offering shelter for wounded soldiers, and it seems that Wharton wanted to do something closer to her own experience in offering employment to seamstresses out of work. She began her war business with two thousand dollars she was able to raise among her wealthy friends and family in New York in just the first two weeks.

Wharton wrote "a sincere report" of her war work for the *New York Times* in November 1915 in an effort to raise awareness among New Yorkers and convince them to send more money. "At first, my plan was to collect money for the purchase of materials and the payment of the women's wages and board and to give away all the garments we made," she told her readers. "This plan is still in practice in a number of Paris workrooms, but when the hope of a speedy victory disappeared it seemed to me more sensible to sell our garments at a very moderate profit and try to make the work nearly self-supporting." Even as she urged New Yorkers to order their lingerie from her workroom and to send money for her hostels and sanitarium, she questioned the idea of charity or philanthropy. While volunteer labor during time of war would seem like a good idea, she pointed out, it has the unintended consequence of encroaching on the "rights of the un-employed" to earn money for their labor. She prided herself on establishing the first *ouvroir* to pay seamstresses for their labor on a business model. Each woman earned twenty cents a day and received "a good midday meal" in return for six hours of labor. On Thursday, everyone got a paid "half-holiday" which allowed the women to spend time on their other domestic responsibilities. Women worked for two months at a time and were then rotated to piecework and encouraged to look for a steady job. If the female workers had not found another job after a month, however, they could rotate back into a vacant position. Using the furlough system, Wharton was able to employ as many as ninety women in all. Her sister-in-law Margaret Cadwalader "Minnie" Jones reported to the American Hostels committee in New York that the enterprise from February to August 1915 had a budget of $6,725.88.[10]

In appealing for support among New Yorkers, Wharton boasted that although her other war projects for the rescue and succor of Belgian refugees required charity, the sewing rooms supported themselves by charging customers for fine lingerie made of silks and laces. "The whole point is there," she admonished her readers. "If the friends of the Paris workgirl will continue to send me orders as generously as they have hitherto my ninety seamstresses are safe till the war is over and they can take up their normal work."[11] Wharton's initial workroom at 25 rue de l'Université was near her apartment in the rue de Varenne and allowed her to operate much of its business herself. Over the first year of operation, the average of sixty women worked a combined 14,732 days, making 15,200 garments out of $6,000 worth of fabrics with $500 for general expenses and $5,500 in pay for labor (figure 3.3). Wharton's workroom turned a profit that she estimated at $5,000, the distance she calculated between the $17,000 value of the garments and the $12,000 cost for their production. Some of the garments were sold and others given to hospitals, so that the profit was not necessarily money in hand. The successful year was marked with a celebration that included managers and seamstresses. "In honor of the occasion," Wharton told her New York readers, "we had a little teaparty at which were present not only the friends who helped to organize the work, and still direct it with me, but the eight or ten young women—cutters and lingères—who form our permanent staff." The article, as she explained in a letter to her sister-in-law Minnie Jones, was meant to urge her wealthy compatriots to order more garments and to send money to keep her charities running through the war years. "O all you happy peaceful people at home," she begged, "if I could show you what we are seeing and hearing over here every day and every hour, I say again I should not have to beg of you: I should only have to tell you what I need!"

Letters to female friends, among them Sara "Sally" Norton, Daisy Chanler, and Margaret Cadwalader "Minnie" Jones, give a clear portrait of Edith Wharton as an entrepreneur and remind us that she came, after all, from a mercantile family that had made its fortune in business. In her letters, we find her doing such seemingly peripheral chores as ordering a supply of coal, for example, and organizing the purchase of a "big supply" of factory-made shoes for refugee children.[12] Even as she worked to produce lingerie, she kept her eye on the health of her workers and provided medical care when necessary; one young woman, for example, she recommended to the tubercular hospital for care. She lamented to Minnie Jones in January 1916 that she was "on the brink of a complete break-down."[13] In the wake of Henry James's death, she was exhausted by both grief and the physical effort of running the workroom. And yet she performed a considerable feat: "I have had ten days of dreadful bother moving my ouvroir." The French government rented and put at her disposal for the length of the war "a whole floor in a big building of the Boulevard St. Germaine."

Wharton, it comes as no surprise, had trouble delegating work. As she put it to Minnie, "I have not found anyone with imagination enough to get the right groups, & it is quite impossible to find time to do it myself." In hiring Elisina Tyler, she admitted the young woman was "efficient" but lamented, "I can't load her with my whole job besides her own!" She selected a permanent staff of eight or ten seamstresses to manage operations in the workrooms. Wharton herself often organized the ordering of material, asking Minnie to send such things as flannel for hospital sheets and dark blue serge for uniforms, and she even set the prices of items. "The small lingerie orders are very worrying," she wrote to Minnie, "I think hereafter it wd be better to refuse any of less than $20, on the ground that the price of materials is going up so much. We certainly can't make chemises for less than 15–20 fcs, & nightgowns for less than 20–25 fcs." The *New York Times* article generated $1,716.41 in income from New York City and another $1,000 from Boston, but her growing business remained in need of funds. Later in 1917, Edith joked to Minnie about the efforts of her and her daughter Beatrix Cadwalader "Trix" Jones, "I wish you and she could beg all over America for me."[14]

Her American Hostels for Refugees, an undertaking that involved hundreds of people at a time, provided the sorts of amenities that Jane Addams had set up in Chicago at the turn of the century and that Wharton has John Amherst set up for workers in *The Fruit of the Tree*, including a reading room, a nursery school (on the Montessori model), and English classes, along with accommodations for the unemployed and help in securing jobs, together with a sanitorium for the treatment of tuberculosis. She established the sewing rooms as well as a clothing depot in the rue de Boétie and, later, the rue Bossy-d'Anglais. Her Children of Flanders Rescue Committee had grown to five houses by 1915, caring for nearly nine hundred people (including refugee nuns) and some two hundred infirm and aged men and women. The children arrived ill, filthy, and hungry, Wharton told the *Times*. Her charity offered a lace-making school modeled on the Ecole Normale of Bruges (figure 3.4). "We have started schools of lacemaking for the older girls," she explained, "and this will give them the means to make a livelihood." Her philanthropy in establishing the lace-making school arose from the same philosophy as her workrooms: not to give merely but to provide training for female workers to make their own way.

Even as she responded in progressive ways to ameliorate harsh working conditions and promote health and safety among the laboring classes, Wharton remained conservative politically. The idea behind Wharton's philanthropy was to reinforce labor in the sewing industry, not to promote class mobility. Letters from the time, however, reveal her mentorship of young Frenchwomen who were helping her to manage the charities. Gabrielle Landormy, a niece of a music critic, developed considerable skill as "a lingère and dressmaker" as she supervised a workroom for Wharton's Children of Flanders charity, and she requested Wharton's help in establishing a business of her own.[15] Wharton wrote to Minnie that it is "only fair to let her start for herself" as a way of earning a living. "I am told she has very pretty models," Wharton added hopefully, "and she certainly deserves to suc-

*Fig. 3.4.* Edith Wharton, Children of Flanders Rescue Committee, House at St. Ouen, Lace School. *Yale Collection of American Literature, Beinecke Rare Book and Manuscript Library.*

ceed." Wharton continued to help Landormy over the years and would bequeath to her "a moleskin coat and coral necklace."[16]

We see the astonishing results of Edith Wharton's business acumen in a New York City publication called *Heroes of France.* The bulletin reports that the French Heroes Fund had taken over the support of her American Hostels at a cost of fifty thousand francs a month. According to this accounting, Wharton's charities, by 1918, comprised a "cheap" restaurant that served five hundred meals a day, the women's workroom, a day nursery to care for workers' children, a medical dispensary that workers could use three times a week, a dental clinic, five lodging houses with a dispensary for the distribution of foodstuffs (particularly bread), a rest home for women and children, an employment agency, a dispensary for gifts of furniture, and a staff of inspectors.[17]

A question that comes to mind, of course, is, What did philanthropy cost Edith Wharton as a writer? Biographer Hermione Lee reads her war letters, all of them crisply written, and bemoans the loss of time and talent that might have gone into the writing of imaginative literature. To encourage American involvement in the European war, Wharton wrote what she called propaganda in *Fighting France: From Dunkerque to Belfort* and *French Ways and Their Meaning.* She wrote two war novels, perhaps marred by her zeal, *The Marne* and *A Son at the Front.* And yet over the war years, she wrote the Berkshire Mountain novel *Summer,* admittedly a short work but a considerable literary achievement. As the war came to an end in 1919, Edith lamented to

Minnie that she could not write for more than two hours a day and, even then, "always with my tired and constantly interrupted pen."[18] We are reminded that she wrote during the morning hours with a pen and not a typewriter. Yet Wharton held in high regard the letters and reports and essays that forced her to "find the words of persuasion to obtain more help." Her war writing had a practical force and literary elegance that would, together with her entrepreneurial system of charities, earn Edith Wharton the French Legion of Honor.

Wharton's fiction and philanthropy reveal a woman who thought critically and carefully about the literal making of fashion, the "thin shoulders in shapeless gingham" that bent over "the bobbins and carders" to craft the garments she wore. She admired work performed by hand and luxuriated in couture garments made of silks and satins and trimmed in antique laces and intricate embroideries. She eyed the machine with suspicion and bemoaned the uniformity of ready-to-wear clothing, an industrial process that she believed demeaned seamstresses and cheapened the value of labor. The ethical problems she explored in her writing remain at issue and make her critique of fashion relevant to us as readers in the twenty-first century.

# 4

# DESIRE IN THE
# MARKETPLACE

"You're an American, ain't you? What you want is the
home-made article."
—*The Custom of the Country*

There is nothing more American than shopping. By the turn into
the twentieth century, the country was awash in goods, available
to any social class, certainly not restricted by laws of inheritance or
sumptuary laws. Bill Brown asks the prescient question in such an acquisitive culture: "How are things and thingness used to think about
the self?"[1] Buyers bargained for merchandise in dollars and their status accrued from skill in selection and abundance of things, all of them
for sale. In the years leading up to the First World War, Edith Wharton wrote *The Custom of the Country* (1913), a novel essentially about
shopping in vague Midwestern towns like Apex, in the supposed
wilderness of the Dakotas, and in posh resorts like Newport as well as
in major cities such as New York City and Paris and its surrounding
cities including Nice. Both men and women shop for clothes and, as
Wharton's novel makes clear, it is also the custom of the United States
and the countries of Europe as well, for men and women to shop for
each other, marrying and divorcing as whim and pocketbook allow.
Even as individuals collect things, they take on the very quality of
thingness, a quality that enhances their desirability. And the things they
own stand in judgment of their presumed owners. This chapter considers Undine Spragg and Elmer Moffatt as consumers of goods and,
ultimately, as goods themselves. The putative hero schools his heroine
in the ultimate love scene: "You're an American, ain't you? What you
want is the home-made article" (575). The question here is what constitutes homemade goods in an industrialized global marketplace?
How does one make fashion in the United States?

*The Custom of the Country* features a heroine who makes sense of life by chatting with her clothes as she primps before the mirror. Undine Spragg, a young Midwesterner living at the Stentorian Hotel, begins her journey into Old New York society by selecting a dress to wear for a dinner at the Fairfords, the first such invitation she has received during her two years of living near Central Park and working to break into elegant New York society. As the masseuse and nail-polisher Mrs. Heeny has explained, nothing goes quickly in such a rarified world: "If you go too fast, you sometimes have to rip out the whole seam" (*CC* 13). Her sewing metaphor will govern the action of the novel. The heroine will move too quickly, especially on marriages, and will find herself having to "rip out the seam" several times in a string of divorces. To select a gown for the Fairford dinner, Undine calls her French maid Céleste to display the three dinner gowns that have remained in her wardrobe (others she has cast off to Céleste in irritation). The heroine sulks in front of the remaining gowns that hang "like so many derisive points of interrogation" (*CC* 20). Two of the gowns have old-fashioned sleeves and the third suffers from having been worn recently, yet Undine dons this pretty one for primping (*CC* 22).

Undine indulges in "dressing up" and "making up," the two activities that Wharton describes in "Life and I" and *A Backward Glance* as essential to her sense of self. Judith Butler, in defining gender, refers to iterations of behavior as displays that define gender and class identity. Gender, for Butler, is not essence but action, a series that she calls *performativity*, the repetition of the rituals of dressing up and making up. What we see and think of as a coherent pattern of gender is just that, a pattern repeated before our eyes. "In this sense, gender is always a doing, though not a doing by a subject who might be said to preexist the deed," Butler insists.[2] Wharton would, no doubt, take issue with Butler over the question of essence; nonetheless, in this novel performativity comes to define the heroine. Undine Spragg desires to act as a doer even though she can conjure no identity beyond performance. She had discovered as a child that her "chief delight was to 'dress up' in her mother's Sunday skirt and 'play lady' before the wardrobe mirror" (*CC* 22). Much of the novel takes place before the mirror: characters scrutinize garments for possible purchase and construct a sense of self based on the things they buy and especially the clothes they wear.

The leisurely life, as it turns out, requires considerable expenditures of time and money on the art of dressing up, the performance that more than any other—then as now—defines identity in the United States. In the late nineteenth century, leisure-class women, including Carry Astor and Pussy Jones, learned to spend their days selecting and donning as many as nine costumes, moving into and out of garments

throughout the day in a dialogue of skin and fabric. Consuelo Vanderbilt complained about the rigors of dressing up, yet we hear in her tone
the boast: "'First, we put on a dress to dress in. Then we are ready for
breakfast. After that we dress for the beach, then for the bath, then for
dinner, then for the drive, then for the ball, and then for the bed. If
that isn't being put through a regular course of dimity and diamonds,
than I am no judge of such performances.'"[3] A regular course of dimity (a light cotton fabric made heavier by the weight of woven checks
or stripes) and diamonds (the ultimate sign of wealth as "a girl's best
friend") belies the claim of hardship.

Wharton, too, complains and brags about the ritual of dressing up
in the posh resort town of Newport, Rhode Island, where the Vanderbilt summer home, The Breakers, stood on the ocean shore as the
most insistent sign of wealth. She writes in *A Backward Glance* that
New Yorkers summered by spending their days in a series of performances requiring specific costumes (*BG* 845–846). Regularly in the af-
ternoons, matrons and daughters mounted Victorias or barouches or
"new-fangled *vis-à-vis*," a carriage with four seats and a rumble seat
for the footman, and paraded up Bellevue Avenue and out onto
Ocean Drive for a ride up the rocky ocean coastline on Narragansett
Bay. "For this drive," she tells us, "it was customary to dress as elegantly as for a race-meeting at Auteuil or Ascot." A typical dress ensemble included a brocade or satin-striped day dress, cinched in at the
waist gripped by a powerful whaleboned corset, and a flower-trimmed
bonnet secured by a length of tulle tied in a bow under the chin. A
lady's pale skin (even her whiteness signified fashion) was shielded
from the sun by a dotted tulle veil, and her gloved hand grasped the
ivory handle of a fringed silk or velvet sunshade for the daily journey
between "wilderness and waves."

We imagine the ritual of dress for a leisure-class woman at the late
nineteenth century, as shown in an ensemble of undergarments from
the 1880s (figure 4.1). Even on the hot days of summer, the woman
wakes and washes, assisted by the hands of her maid, and slips into cotton or silken stockings gartered above the knee. She steps into high-
cut shoes and fastens the buttons. Over the shoes and stockings, she
pulls on cotton trousers or pantaloons, designed perhaps with an open
crotch to allow ease of access during the day. She draws a knitted or
silk or light cotton chemise over her head, feeling the comfort of soft
fabric against clean skin. And then the heavier weight of a corset curls
around the ribs, another comfort from years of living within its precise form, the muscles of the back and chest and abdomen given
strength from the elegant brace, pulled quickly, neatly, efficiently as the
laces bind the body into the form it has agreed to take and the culture
has come to prize. The young woman, relying early on the bones or

*Fig. 4.1.* Women's under-clothing, 1880s, made in America. Ensemble includes a cotton muslin and lace camisole; a cotton sateen and ribbon corset with metal busks or fasteners and stays; open-crotch cotton batiste pantaloons with embroidered cotton tape and machine-made lace; and a cage bustle of cord-covered steel wire, cotton tape, and cotton broadcloth. *The Mint Museum of Art, Charlotte, North Carolina, Historic Costume and Fashionable Dress Collection.* (Plate 13.)

metal of the corset stays, truly feels strong in it; without it in the evening, she is limp from the atrophy of muscle. After the corset comes a cage bustle of wire and cloth, designed to frame the derriere with perhaps a pad to enlarge the abdomen in order for the body to accept the shape of a dress and cloak. The whole apparatus provides a frame to drape the fabric without spoiling the design that stands erect and molded into the form of beauty and wealth and leisure, the glory of womanhood. On a cold day, a woman might well make her way into the street carrying as much as twenty-five pounds of fabric and bone and fur on her body. To the eye and to the touch, the textures of skin and fabric blur into a single object of desire. The subtle layerings give the viewer only surface contours, like a Monet painting of water lilies, out of sight of the pumps that produced the illusion of his garden, leaving the lovely image of pad in water. Once locked securely into bodice and skirt, a woman might move from carriage to street or from chair to dance floor revealing little about her gown's story. The theater of the gown conceals the constriction of muscle and the restriction of movement, the sacrifices of the woman required to create the surface of her ornament.

In the early wardrobe scene, we find Undine dressing up before a pier-glass mirror, a performance that signifies the ritual of primping as well as shopping and links such activities to sexual desire. The pier-glass mirror may have looked much like the one James Carroll Beckwith (1852–1917) used in his painting *The Old Pier Glass* (c. 1900), which features a well-muscled female figure admiring her body in its reflection (figure 4.2).[4] The tall version of the pier-glass mirror, usually thirty to forty-two inches wide, was typically mounted between windows that provided piers or columns as the structural support for so heavy a load on the wall. The tall mirror included molding in a frame, like the one in the Beckwith painting, and was often covered with gilt in an elaborate design. The Hall of Mirrors at Versailles is made of pier glass, and Wharton links American narcissism to the aristocratic preoccupations and pretensions of the French monarchy.[5] Undine Spragg works to display her clothes and jewels as Marie Antoinette would have done before the mirrors of Versailles (figure 4.3). The tragic French queen stands as the iconic image of luxurious fashion in Western culture, and we see in Wharton's novel Undine's desire to define herself in Marie's image.

Pier-glass mirrors were often mounted in shops and stores to allow women to see themselves in garments and imagine how they might look to others. Reflection of the self in garments has become the central ritual of shopping for clothes. In the couture houses of Paris, the

*Fig. 4.2.* James Carroll Beckwith (1852–1917), *The Old Pier Glass*, c. 1900. Exhibited in New York at the Anderson Galleries, February 1912. *Private collection.* (Plate 14.)

*Fig. 4.3.* Marie Louise Elisabeth Vigée-Lebrun: Queen Marie Antoinette, 1778. *Commons.wikimedia.org.* (Plate 15.)

Worths and Doucets made sure that women would have a variety of imaginative experiences, first seeing the fabrics themselves and then viewing assembled designs on wooden mannequins surrounded by mirrors and cushioned in soft light. Live models became another way to see garments before trying them on, and the lovelier the model, the more inviting the body and the more desirable the clothing. Worth and, especially, Doucet also designed for actresses who performed on- and offstage as a lure for costumers. Jeanne Paquin sent her live models to the racetrack and other public events to entice shoppers and reinforce the idea of couture fashion as necessary costume for leisure-class life. By the time a shopper actually slipped into a design model and stood before the pier-glass mirror, the purchase was often already secured. The final reflection of the garment might, by that time in the sale, be as imaginative as it was real.

As the sale of fashionable clothing made its way into the wider marketplace, plate-glass windows served as mirrors to lure shoppers even as they protected the goods inside stores. Strolling down a city street, a man or woman could experience in a public way a ritual that had been conceived in the privacy of homes and the interiors of small shops. In 1838 Aristide Boucicaut established Le Bon Marché in Paris, an enterprise that would grow over the next twenty years into the first department store, selling an array of goods at fixed prices. By the 1850s, the store employed four thousand people and generated three hundred thousand dollars a day in sales. Department stores opened in European and American cities in the middle of the nineteenth century, including Delany's New Market in Ireland, Bainbridge's in England, Marshall Field's in Chicago, John Wanamaker's in Philadelphia, and Joseph Lowthian Hudson's in Detroit.

The defining department store in New York City was the business of an Irish immigrant, Alexander Turney "A. T." Stewart (1803–1876). What he called a "Marble Palace," the largest retail store in the world, opened at 280 Broadway in 1848 (figure 4.4). Designed to mimic a Renaissance palazzo, the store brought luxury and style associated with European royalty to shoppers in the United States. For the store's signature feature, Stewart used full-length mirrors of pier glass to create a gallery on the second floor where women could try on and view garments and thereby create a fashion show. The building was known, too, for its arched Palladian windows and the use of natural lighting to sell goods. As his income grew during the years of the Civil War, Stewart built an even bigger department store that he called the "Iron Palace" at Broadway and 9th Street; it filled a city block and provided two and a half acres of emporium space along with a background of organ music to lure shoppers. In Wharton's youth—the period of the 1870s that features so frequently in her fiction—the retail section of Old New York was moving uptown from the Marble Palace to a row known as the "Ladies' Mile" that stretched from 8th to 23rd Street and included Lord & Taylor and Macy's. Lord & Taylor equaled A. T. Stewart in the price of goods and perhaps rivaled it in quality of goods and reputation for taste.

Stewart's Iron Palace supported large plate-glass windows shaped like the tall pier-glass mirrors in the private space of the fitting rooms. It had a 60,000 square foot ground-floor salesroom, with space enough for a hundred counters backed by low shelves stuffed with goods.[6] The main floor, punctuated by wooden pens for cashiers, had as its center a rotunda. Various counters set up as separate departments displayed clothing for women and children, and dozens of ushers moved through-

*Fig. 4.4.* A. T. Stewart's Marble Palace, stereopticon slide by L. G. Strand, Worchester, Massachusetts.

out the store directing customers to various counters and departments. The idea was to keep the flow of customers moving across the sea of goods. On the ground floor, seamstresses and tailors were on duty to provide made-to-order clothing, a convenience that competed with privately owned establishments (like the shop the Bunner sisters tried and failed to keep going). Ready-made clothing and upholstery were the provinces of the second floor and vast collections of carpets lay on the third. The building also housed workshops and laundries so that labor could be performed quickly and conveniently on site as customers continued looking at goods.

Much as Walmart does today, Stewart bought in large quantities that allowed him to control prices and drive out smaller businesses that could not compete. His contemporary James McCabe reported in *Lights and Shadows of New York Life; or, The Sights and Sensations of the Great City* that New York salesmen were rude and insolent although shoppers seemed not offended enough to complain. Shopping in America, then as now, requires little civility to accommodate a high volume of transactions. A. T. Stewart's averaged 15,000 purchases a day at a yield of $4 each. McCabe describes the sales floor in a scene that Wharton would have recognized: "Looking down from one of the upper floors, through the rotunda, one can witness as busy and interesting a scene as New York affords. All kinds of people come here, from the poor woman whose scanty garb tells too plainly the story of her poverty, to the wife of the millionaire whose purchases amount to a small fortune, and all classes can be suited."[7]

What defines the custom of the country is the image of the Mall of America. Stewart earned a fortune selling Americans silks, muslins, calicoes, velvets, and laces to make clothing, as well as ready-made suits, shawls, furs, and children's clothing together with carpets and notions for the home. According to McCabe, Stewart's sales averaged $60,000 a day; on good days, however, sales went to $87,000. Patrons, most of them women, shopped between noon and five o'clock in hours when most men worked and children studied. On a typical day, customers would spend $15,000 on silk fabrics, $3,000 on muslins, $2,000 on velvets, and $1,500 on calicoes; most fabrics would be used for sewing projects performed in the home. The female shoppers bought gloves, hosiery, and furs for themselves and their daughters as well as ready-made clothing for their sons. Carpets were also displayed and purchased, bringing in $5,500 a day.

A main feature of the department store was the plate-glass window that allowed the scene in the street to blend with and blur into the supposed comfort and privacy of the inside space. Full-store windows allowed the public to peek into the world of luxury at the same time that the glass reflected the gaze of buyers, inviting an imaginative association with the goods displayed. The plate-glass window, like the pier-glass mirror, became a central icon of shopping in the modern city. Stewart's lavish store featured nineteen departments that made available to working- and middle-class customers delights similar to those offered the upper classes in the couture houses of Paris: bolts of silks and brocades and laces together with patterns and, as the century went on, racks of ready-to-wear garments. Dress goods were being made available and affordable by the industrialization of textiles and, increasingly, the mechanization of sewing.

In 1902, Daniel Burnham designed a store at the site of Stewart's palace for John Wanamaker, who was expanding his Philadelphia business. Wanamaker was a successful businessman and politician, becoming the U.S. postmaster general under President Benjamin Harrison.[8] He started a clothing bazaar in 1876 in Philadelphia and began what he conceived as a consortium of shops on the model of London's Royal Exchange and Paris's Halles Centrales in the converted Pennsylvania Railroad Freight Depot. Advertised as a "New Kind of Store," the Grand Depot housed the "largest space in the world" for retail shopping with a series of concentric counters that featured shows of elegant ball gowns at its hub (figure 4.5). The sorts of gowns designed by French couturiers at the Houses of Worth and Doucet, we note, take center stage in the ritual of American shopping. How many times, we might ask, would a female shopper in New York City attend a ball? In his New York City store, he sold Paris fashions that allowed the do-

*Fig. 4.5.* Wanamaker's Grand Depot, c. 1876, interior with concentric circles of goods.

mestic consumption of couture garments without the need of European travel. Wanamaker wanted to give shoppers a palace of consumption and added electric lights and elevators and even a restaurant.

New York City and Chicago became major cities for the importation of European goods and for the manufacture of American-made apparel. Wharton's novel about shopping suggests, as well, the flow of goods across the United States by way of the railroad. She sends Undine Spragg to the Dakotas for one of her divorces and to Las Vegas for an even easier one. The ability, as Mrs. Heeney metaphorically puts it, "to rip out the whole seam" arose from the increased acceptability of divorce; indeed, the practice grew common over the years of Edith Wharton's life; she would divorce her husband Teddy after she moved to France. Divorce facilitates the plot of *The Custom of the Country* by permitting the heroine to shop again for a yet richer husband. Undine begins as the furtive bride of a young and not yet successful Elmer Moffatt, goes into wealthy New York society as the bride of Ralph Marvell, completes her social rise in a marriage to the French aristocrat Raymond de Chelles, and deliciously ends her purportedly upward struggle by remarrying Moffatt, who has made a fortune in railroads.

Undine's divorce trip to the Badlands of Dakota, however, would not have left her, as we might imagine, outside the limits of fashion and shopping. The Northern Pacific Railroad stretched across the Dakota territory; when Theodore Roosevelt arrived by train in 1883 to hunt bison and "rough it," he was able to bring goods with him to his Elkhorn Ranch, including a bathtub for comfort. The site of his ranch is now a national park outside Medora, North Dakota. The town was named for someone Wharton may well have known, Medora von Hoffman, the daughter of a wealthy New York banker.[9] Traveling in France, Medora met Antoine Amédée-Marie-Vincent Manca de Vallombrosa, titled the marquis de Morès and married him in 1882 (figure 4.6). Theirs was the very sort of marriage that Wharton chronicled in her fiction. What we know about Medora is that when she arrived in the Badlands with her husband who had set up a ranch and meatpacking business, she lived in what the town called "the Chateau de Mores," a twenty-six-room summerhouse full of European-made furniture, oriental carpets, French wines, and gourmet food. The North Dakota Historical Society provides a menu gleaned from receipts found among the Madame de Morès papers. Teddy Roosevelt may well have dined during an evening with the de Morès on raw oysters, mushroom soup, baked salmon, filet of beef, lemon sorbet, wild duck, and chocolate mousse. Medora shopped for dresses at the French couture houses in the rue de la Paix and brought with her to the Badlands twenty-one trunks, each of them carrying a single couture ensemble with compartments for petticoats, corsets, bustles, bodices, skirts, and hats. Teddy

didn't much like the marquis but did like the marquise Medora, an accomplished woman who knew seven languages, played piano, and painted watercolors that display considerable talent. What Teddy adored most, however, was her athleticism as a horsewoman and game shooter, a sporting activity that allowed her to cross-dress in men's clothing. After her husband's death Medora settled her family in Paris, lived out her life as an expatriate, and worked alongside Edith Wharton and other wealthy Americans in providing war relief. The colorfully adorned and brazenly unconventional Medora de Morès is very likely the sort of character Wharton had in mind as she created Undine Spragg and transformed her through multiple marriages into the Marquise de Chelles.

Undine is "fiercely independent and yet passionately imitative" (*CC* 19). That combination of confidence and doubt describes Wharton's notion of the national character. It is the custom of an American, as she put it, to model oneself on the last person met, so that performances mimic observed behavior. Through a reflection in a mirror, or a plot of a novel, or a scene from an opera, or a column in the newspaper, Wharton's women see themselves dressed, already in performance; only then are they able to measure their sartorial worth. *The Custom of the Country* presents the world of fashion as reflected in mirrors and windows, paintings and performances, plots of novels and gossip in newspapers. Undine schools herself in the mysteries of American taste by viewing clothing from various perspectives. She reads the society column "Boudoir Chat," where pigeon-blood notepaper and white ink are presented as "smart" and remains puzzled over "the old-fashioned white sheet, without even a monogram" that invites her to dine with the Old New Yorker Mrs. Laura Fairford (*CC* 18). Popular novels, including *When the Kissing Had to Stop* and *Oolaloo* and *The Soda-Water Fountain*, school Undine in fashion as well as manners and mores (37). And Wharton delights in drawing the caricature in thick lines: just what happens when the kissing has to stop?

As Undine marries into Old New York society, she negotiates to have her portrait painted in the mode of the elite class. She believes— and apparently she is right—that for the price of a painting, she herself can become the iconic image of an Old New Yorker. Claude Walsingham Popple, the painter, is something of a prima dona, "clad in mouse-coloured velveteen" and stationed in a cushion-covered couch next to a tea table flanked by sandwiches and pastries (*CC* 188). His particular expertise is the painting of pearls—and the ones Ralph has given Undine are small, a fashion detail that will return at the novel's end—but Popple highlights instead the glittering diamonds of her new tiara (another detail that will return). She is transformed into the painting itself: a shadowless golden lady seated on a gilded throne of "pseudo-Venetian design" and dressed in a faint and shining gown that accentuates the long curve of her neck and the "dead" whiteness of her skin (*CC* 189). Little wonder that social distinctions seem labyrinthine to Undine as well as to Wharton's readers, and the delight of reading the novel comes in large part from its airtight ironic tone.

The novel shows Undine on shopping trips, most notably during her honeymoon with Ralph Marvell. He hopes to instruct her on the beauty of the European countryside, but Undine insists on going to cities that will provide a background for her clothes. He responds sardonically, "You poor darling! Let us, by all means, go to the place where the clothes will be right: they are too beautiful to be left out of our scheme of life" (*CC* 145). Clothes hold the whip hand, as Ralph will come, even more clearly, to understand. In Paris, Undine makes a "round of the rue de la Paix" and refuses to go with him to classical performances at the Français where, as she derisively notes, "they walk around in bath towels and talk poetry" (*CC* 174). The visual and visceral life of shops and restaurants absorb her attention and imagination. Dresses themselves come to dominate Undine: "Early and late she was closeted with fitters and packers—even the competent Céleste not being trusted to handle the treasures now pouring in—and Ralph cursed his weakness in not restraining her" (*CC* 181). Specific couture houses go unnamed, perhaps because her shopping prowess is strengthened by not naming designers at the Houses of Worth or Doucet or, by this time, Paul Poiret. Undine buys from an unnamed dressmaker,

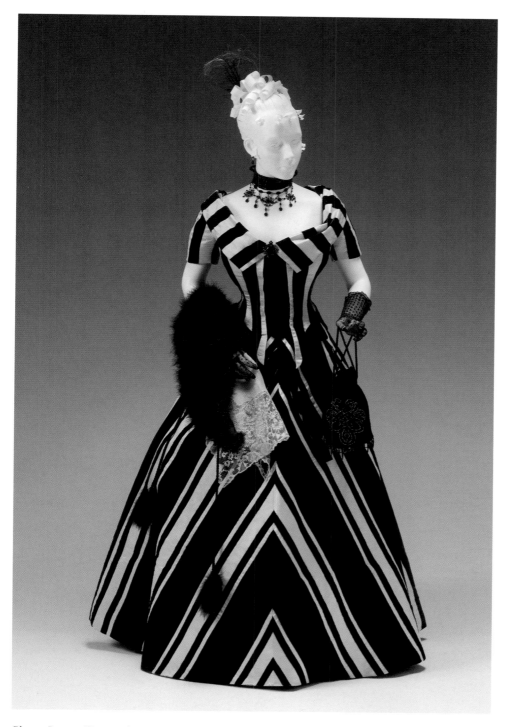

*Plate 1.* Jacques Doucet (1853–1929). Ball Gown, circa 1890s; black silk velvet and white silk satin with black silk velvet ribbon. *The Mint Museum of Art, Charlotte, North Carolina. Historic Costume and Fashionable Dress Collection.*

*Plate 2*. Franz Xaver Winterhalter (German, 1805–1873), The Empress Eugénie (Eugénie de Montijo, 1826–1920, Condesa de Teba), 1854. *Metropolitan Museum of Art*.

*Plate 3.* Charles Frederick Worth (1825–1895), Evening/Reception Gown, 1890; silk chiffon and silk net with Alençon lace appliqués over silk satin. *The Mint Museum of Art, Charlotte, North Carolina. Historic Costume and Fashionable Dress Collection.*

*Plate 4.* Edward Harrison May, painting of the red-headed Edith Wharton at age eight, 1870, in a blue satin dress with sash and fur trim at the neck and cuff. *Yale Collection of American Literature, Beinecke Rare Book and Manuscript Library.*

*Plate 5.* Charles Frederick Worth (born in England, 1826–1895). On left, ball gown of pale green and ivory silk satin and yellow, pink and ivory silk chiffon with embroidered sunburst pattern in silk, glass, and metallic thread, label "Worth, Paris," circa 1887. On right, ball gown of pink damask with crystal embroidery, designed by Jean-Phillip Worth, 1892. *The Metropolitan Museum of Art, Gift of Orme Wilson and R. Thornton Wilson, in memory of their mother, Mrs. Caroline Schermerhorn Astor Wilson, 1949. (49.3.25a,b; 49.3.28a,b). Image copyright The Metropolitan Museum of Art.*

*Plate 6.* Sports Jacket in wool twill and wool flannel with silver commemorative, circa 1895–1905, by Brooks Brothers Company; and American-made wool bloomers, circa 1895. *Mint Museum of Art, Charlotte, North Carolina.*

*Plate 7.* Advertisement for Singer Sewing Machines, "The Cycle of a Century" 1800–1900. *Prints and Photographs Division, Library of Congress, Washington, D.C.*

*Plate 8.* Henri Boutet, *Les modes féminines du XIXe siècle, interprétées en cent pointes sèches aquarellées au pinceau, 1801–1900* (published in 1902). Compare Wharton's tailleur or suit in figure 1.10. *Fashion Plate #99. New York Public Library Digital Gallery.*

*Plate 9.* James Tissot, The Shop Girl, 1883–1885. *The Art Gallery of Ontario. Commons.wikimedia.org.*

*Plate 10.* Henri de Toulouse-Lautrec, Divan Japonais, 1892–1893, color lithograph, featuring feathered hat designed by Mme. Virot, Paris. *Commons.wikimedia.org.*

Plate 11. Madame Virot, Paris. Hat comprising aigrette (the tufted crest of an egret), ostrich plumes, silver embroidery, and pearls, 1896. *Museum of the City of New York. Gift of Mrs. S. Breck Parkman Trowbridge (49.125.2). Ben Fink Photography Inc., New York City.*

Plate 12. Madame Virot, Paris. Hat fabricated of an entire Quetzal (a vividly-colored, long-tailed Central American bird) and silk velvet, circa 1898. Compare Wharton's hat in figure 1.6. *Museum of the City of New York. Gift of Susan Dwight Bliss, 1937 (37.252.4). Ben Fink Photography Inc., New York City.*

*Plate 13.* Women's underclothing, 1880s, made in America. Ensemble includes a cotton muslin and lace camisole; a cotton sateen and ribbon corset with metal busks or fasteners and stays; open-crotch cotton batiste pantaloons with embroidered cotton tape and machine-made lace; and a cage bustle of cord-covered steel wire, cotton tape, and cotton broadcloth. *Mint Museum of Art, Charlotte, North Carolina. Historic Costume and Fashionable Dress Collection.*

*Plate 14.* James Carroll Beckwith (1852–1917), The Old Pier Glass, circa 1900. Exhibited in New York at the Anderson Galleries, February, 1912. *Private collection.*

*Plate 15.* Marie Louise Élisabeth Vigée-Lebrun: Queen Marie Antoinette, 1778. *Commons.wikimedia.org.*

*Plate 16.* Pierre-Paul Prud'hon, Portrait of the Empress Josephine (1763–1814), 1805. *Commons.wikimedia.org.*

*Plate 17.* Two white cotton mull dresses with cotton embroidery, Empire design, circa 1810, made in France. *The Metropolitan Museum of Art, Rogers Fund, 1907, and purchase. Gifts in memory of Elizabeth N. Lawrence, 1983 (07.146.5, 1983.6.1). Image copyright The Metropolitan Museum of Art.*

*Plate 18.* Georges Lepape (French 1887–1971). Pochoir or stenciling illustration of Denise Poiret wearing Paul Poiret's "1811" gown, an Empire style designed in 1907. *The Metropolitan Museum of Art, The Irene Lewisohn Costume Reference Library, Special Collections. Image copyright The Metropolitan Museum of Art.*

*Plate 19.* Jacques Doucet (1853–1929). Red cubist design ensemble dress, 1920–1923. *Costume Institute, Metropolitan Museum of Art. Image at ARTstor.*

*Plate 20.* Paul Poiret (1879–1944). Two-piece afternoon dress of navy-blue silk faille, block printed in red, circa 1920. *The Metropolitan Museum of Art. Gift of Mrs. Muriel Draper, 1943 (C.I.43.85.2a,b). Image copyright The Metropolitan Museum of Art.*

*Plate 21.* Madeleine Vionnet (1876–1975). French evening dress, spring/summer 1938. Pale gray-blue rayon crepe, completed and trimmed with rows of matching fringe in applied scallop design; view of side and back. *The Metropolitan Museum of Art. Gift of Madame Madeleine Vionnet, 1952 (C.I.52.18.4). Image copyright The Metropolitan Museum of Art.*

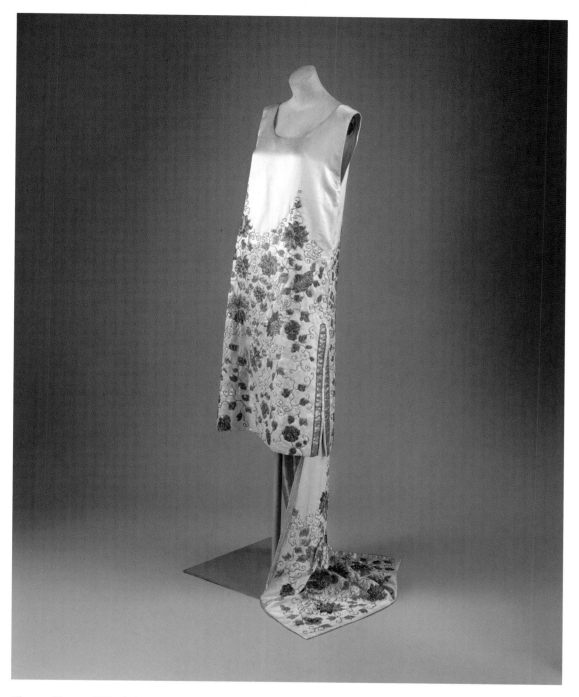

*Plate 22.* House of Worth (1858–1956). French evening dress in cream–colored silk satin, embroidered with glass beads and metallic thread in a meandering floral motif. Worn by the Marquise de Polignac when she was presented at Court, 1925. *The Metropolitan Museum of Art. Gift of Mrs. Harrison Williams, Lady Mendl, and Mrs. Ector Munn, 1946 (C.I.46.4.20a,b). Image copyright The Metropolitan Museum of Art.*

*Plate 23.* Jean Patou (1887–1936). Possibly House of Patou (founded 1919) or House of Lucien LeLong (founded 1923). Black cotton alphabet-motif lace and black silk chiffon; separate rhinestone bow from the late 1930s; view of full back. *The Metropolitan Museum of Art. Gift of Richard Martin and Harold Koda, 1992 (1992.399a,b). Image copyright The Metropolitan Museum of Art.*

lodged in the fashionable rue de la Paix, and prides herself on bargaining for lower prices on labor and materials. Wharton's heroine is, after all, as much a businessman as her father. She pares prices down, evades paying fees, and uses her considerable personal force to "brow-beat" small tradespeople and "wheedle concessions" from "great" ones (181). Even the corners of glazed black boxes stacked in pyramids threaten Ralph as they are delivered by milliners' girls and *vendeuses* or saleswomen. But it is the appearance of "the blond-bearded jeweler" that truly frightens him: the jeweler signals great expense and Undine's desire to remount the family diamonds.

The heroine shops in all her marriages when she is bored; the acquisition of things serves as solace. As she ages in the novel, Undine turns to buying popular gadgets that promise youth. She pages through fashion-papers to find "facial bandaging, electric massage and other processes of renovation," and reverts to an atavistic interest in "faith-healers, mind-readers and their kindred adepts" (521–522). What she seeks is the same ministrations that the masseuse Mrs. Heeny had performed for her as a young woman. Wharton's portrayal of Undine's ambition remarkably evokes our contemporary desires to remain young or at least to look young.

The question that comes to Undine's mind, of course, comes to ours as well: what makes one fashionable in the premier city of the New World? The culture that Undine Spragg finds in New York City is ethnically, economically, and—above all—socially fluid, in part because the mass production and affordability of clothes made sumptuary codes difficult to read. Her beauty and her father's money allow her to move easily and quickly from the picket fence in Midwestern Apex—and her girlhood friend Indiana Frusk will join her—into the rarified and seemingly reified world of American aristocracy, a group of Old New Yorkers that Wharton's mother always told her constituted a middle class because the families had made their fortunes in merchandise and not from royal European lines of descent. Undine judges the Fairford house as small and shabby in faint pools of green-shaded lamplight with wood-fire for heat and rows of books for company. The ethnicity of Wharton's social group was Dutch, a closed and smug clan who called themselves "the old Knickerbockers." Families like the fictional Dagonets, Marvells, and Van Degens come from inherited fortunes and own valuable real estate in the heart of the city, property with fluctuating value, the very sort of shortfalls that required Wharton's parents, during her youth, to live in Europe where the cost of living was significantly lower. James McCabe stereotypes the Dutch as cultivated but stolid: "They make an effort to have their surroundings as clumsy and as old-fashioned as possible, as a mark of their Dutch descent." Wharton's characterizations are not far from McCabe's: Mrs.

Fairford dresses in "dowdy black and antiquated ornaments," and Miss Harriet Ray appears in "last year's 'model,'" even at that, a plain garment (*CC* 33). In a household considered the "stronghold of fashion," only Claire Van Degan seemed "elaborately dressed and jeweled" and yet dark and strangely girlish (*CC* 36).

Wharton tells the story of fashion as the distinctive feature of the financial and upward social struggle in the United States. Details of garments are few in a tale set in the nearly contemporaneous world before the First World War. Those few details, however, are suggestive of character. Mrs. Spragg dresses in black brocade and her hands are heavy with rings, a sign of her husband's money and of her discomfort with ceremonial display. Mrs. Heeny, masseuse, manicurist, and muse to the Spraggs, wears a rusty veil and carries a shabby bag that highlight her comic role in the novel. Mr. Spragg, whose visage is amply drawn, carries a high hat and overcoat; a Masonic emblem dangles from a heavy gold chain across his crumpled black waistcoat and bears the defining hint of his supposed fidelity to his business compatriots. He will eventually betray the fraternal trust in order to find money to invest in Undine's social rise. Undine studies the fashion of a tall girl she spots in an art gallery who is wearing "a tortoise-shell eye-glass adorned with diamonds and hanging from a long pearl chain," much like the Cartier chain that Wharton herself owned (*CC* 49). Ralph Marvell in proposing gives Undine "a band of sapphires," old stones in a quaint setting, much like the band that Edith Jones's mother gave her as a wedding band. Undine slips on the ring and arranges her tangle of lush hair as she appears more and more in the mode of New York fashion: "Her shoulders shone through transparencies of lace and muslin which slipped back as she lifted her arms to draw the tortoise-shell pins from her hair" (*CC* 85).

Undine peers into a hand mirror and Mrs. Heeny reminds her of her image in the *Radiator*, an article that initiates a collection of clippings that report her social performances. She imagines scenes of fashionable society from her experience at the theater and from reading fiction and is astonished to learn that these scenes had little resemblance to the actual world of the Marvells and Fairfords and Van Degens and the Dagonets. At a debut of a fashionable London actress, the newly engaged heroine, who has appeared "in all the papers," is herself the object of anonymous desire: "'There she is—the one white, with the lovely back—' and a man answers: 'Gad! Where did he find anything as good as that?'" (97).

The wardrobe scene repeats toward the novel's close when garments again interrogate Undine, who has supposedly reached the height of American social ambition by marrying into the French aristocracy. Locked away in her chambers at the elegant Saint Désert, Undine as the Marquise de Chelles sulks and considers her fate. All around her, female life in the rarefied world of the French nobility clicks with the sound of knitting needles, "the rise and fall of industrious fingers above embroidery-frames" that are "steadily increasing the provision" of wall hangings and tapestries, a home-made craft that had been going on for generations (CC 513). The idle and bored American-born marquise turns to her chief companions, the gowns that signify her social rank. They hang "like so many unfulfilled promises of pleasure, reminding her of the days at the Stentorian when she had reviewed other finery with the same cheated eyes" (CC 521).

The happy ending of the novel, as ironic as that ending will be, comes about because of Undine's power to sell the rarified goods that mark the de Chelles dynasty in order to finance her escape from Saint Désert. It is Moffatt's new fortune, the billions of dollars that have come into his hands from the railroad industry, that provide money for the purchase transaction. Undine sends for a Mr. Fleischhauer, "a small swarthy man who, in spite of his conspicuously London-made clothes, had an exotic air" that suggests he is Jewish (CC 529). His expertise will set the price of the Boucher tapestries belonging to the de Chelles family for the prospective buyer Elmer Moffatt. Although he barters, we note, he is the only one in the scene who appreciates the value of the tapestries. Undine denies that they are for sale and explains that the men have made the trip for nothing, and Fleischhauer responds, "It is not nothing to have seen such beauty" (533). Wharton makes the point that things themselves, especially things that are usually beyond the sight and monetary means of nearly everyone, have considerable power; they are "not nothing." Moffatt wants to buy the tapestries to furnish his private railway car, a juxtaposition that would be flatly funny if it were not so incongruous.

The novel transforms human interactions, especially the intimacy of sexual desire, into business transactions. The custom of the country becomes a tyranny of things. Elmer Moffatt, more than any character, prizes objects. As he offers Undine the proposal of a second marriage, he sees her as older and stouter and yet more desirable. "'You're not the beauty you were,' he said irrelevantly; 'but you're a lot more fetching'" (568). It is her proximity to the things that mark social class, such as the Boucher tapestries and paintings by Ingres and Van Dyck, that fetch him to her a second time. Her simulation of aristocratic "shades of conduct, turns of speech, tricks of attitude," the performativity that characterizes her sense of self, adds value to Undine as a thing worthy of Moffatt's desire (CC 558). Undine is hypnotized by "all the things she envied" and comes to maturity in the custom of her country through her relationship to the goods she learns to desire and becomes able to buy (CC 561). "She knew her wants so much better now, and was so much more worthy of the things she wanted" (562). Undine turns to the "old warm-toned furniture" and to "her own idle image in the mirror" and marks the things surrounding her by their power to "buy a release" from her financial cares.

As an American (and here is the key to Wharton's sense of fashion in her native country), Undine likes "to see such things about her—without any real sense of their meaning" (*CC* 548). Value resides in ownership, not in culture or history. She plucks and plunders, paying little heed to objects "in situ" and gathering things and repositioning them by right of money. "To have things always seemed to her the first essential of existence" (*CC* 537). Over the course of the novel, Undine learns how to converse with her things, particularly the dresses and jewels in her wardrobe, and becomes in the transaction a more valued thing herself. What Moffatt wants is fashion American-style, the haphazard assemblage of things utterly if not absurdly out of their initial cultural and historical contexts. "I mean to have the best" and "I know it when I see it," Moffatt boasts of his taste and of Undine's (*CC* 538). She gives him entrée to private galleries and watches as he admires each object. The satiric narrative voice notes that "the things he looked at moved him in a way she could not understand, and that the actual touching of rare textures—bronze or marble, or velvets flushed with the bloom of age—gave him sensations like those her own beauty had once roused in him" (*CC* 64). More than the skin of a woman's body, Marvell longs to touch rare bronze or marble or velvet.

It's not about sex but about money. Things rival humans and even transform humans into things. Once Moffatt collects the Boucher tapestries and Van Dyck's *Grey Boy*, he reclaims Undine Spragg Moffatt Marvell de Chelles Moffatt. But Wharton's novel doesn't stop there. She offers a critique of fashion in the American mode from the points of view of Raymond de Chelles and Ralph's son Paul, who has spent his youth in his stepfather's care. Exasperated by Undine's negotiations to sell the Boucher tapestries, Raymond delivers a derisive critique of American fashion in a voice only thinly veiling Wharton's own: "You come among us speaking our language and not knowing what we mean; wanting the things we want, and not knowing why we want them; aping our weaknesses, exaggerating our follies, ignoring or ridiculing all we care about" (545). The stress, and it is shrill, is on things as he adds, "we're fools enough to imagine that because you copy our ways and pick up our slang you understand anything about the things that make life decent and honourable for us!"

We sense Wharton's discomfort in living as an expatriate in Paris as she castigates, perhaps, even her own desire to emulate aristocratic modes of living and to acquire things that mark European status. Edith might well have listened more closely to her mother Lucretia who had warned about social pretension in lecturing her on the middle-class nature of American culture. Wearing haute couture fashions from the rue de la Paix and acquiring an elegant apartment in the rue de Varenne do not make Wharton French and do not even make her upper-class. At the center of Wharton's satire is her aesthetic principle that decoration divorced from structure, in architecture and clothing as well as in the customs of a country, is fraudulent. The acts of making up and dressing up are, after all, both acts of the imagination.

In the end, the very things that Moffatt purchases in Europe turn on him. "The big vulgar writing-table wreathed in bronze was heaped with letters and papers," the narrator tells us and places the vulgar table amid goods Moffatt has collected. "Among them stood a lapis bowl in a Renaissance mounting of enamel and a vase of Phoenician glass that was like a bit of rainbow caught in cobwebs. On a table against the window a little Greek marble lifted its pure lines" (CC 567). The Renaissance bowl made of lapis, the Phoenician vase of rainbow glass, and the Greek marble statue with its pure lines look very like the objects Wharton surrounded herself with in her early publicity photographs. The beautiful things are "not nothing" and have the power to stand in aesthetic judgment: "On every side some rare and sensitive object seemed to be shrinking back from the false colours and crude contours of the hotel furniture." Nine-year-old Paul likewise discerns the incongruity of the American style. He sees his mother's lacy bedroom in "pale silks and velvets, artful mirrors and veiled lamps" and "rows and rows of books, bound in dim browns and golds" locked behind gilt trellises and "the wigged and corseleted heroes" depicted in paintings hanging in the drawing room (CC 579). Most jarring to his sense of where things belong is the placing of the Boucher tapestries, which had always hung in the gallery at Saint Désert, in the "great gilt panels" of the shining ballroom, hanging as the pier-glass mirrors do at Versailles (CC 587).

Reading dress in the novel, we note Wharton's sly reminder of the many fashion details of the novel, tying them neatly together at the end in the image of what constitutes fashion in America. Paul learns about his mother's life through gossip columns read to him by Mrs. Heeny, even as he longs to know about his parents and "not about their things" (CC 584). But there is no difference between thing and person. Undine is indistinguishable from her raiment, a gown of "copper velvet and sables" and "a necklace and tiara of pigeon-blood rubies belonging to Queen Marie Antoinette" (CC 585). Wharton fastens every detail of her satire as even the smartness of the pigeon-blood notepaper returns in the rubies. The last scene places Undine again before the pier-glass mirror, giving "herself a last look in the glass" at "the blaze of her rubies, the glitter of her hair" (CC 594). She stands as Marie Antoinette had stood before the Hall of Mirrors at Versailles and also blazed and glittered. With a million-dollar check in her pocket and a house in New York at 5009 Fifth Avenue, a replica of the Pitti Palace in Florence, Undine stands as "the home-made article," the embodiment of American fashion.

❧ 5

# THE CUT OF A GOWN

"Fashionable? Do you all think so much of that?
Why not make one's own fashions?"
—*The Age of Innocence*

*T*he *Age of Innocence* is full of clothes, music, art, and scenes from
crowded city streets and densely furnished interiors. Writing it
from September 1919 until March 1920 as the First World War came
to an end, Wharton loaded the novel with elaborate details that she
hoped would bring to mind and eye the material culture of her youth,
a culture she and others of her generation believed had been changed
utterly by the events in Europe. It may be her sense of loss was exacerbated by geographic and cultural distance from her homeland; she
would return to America only after the novel's publication to receive
an honorary degree from Yale University. "Everything that used to
form the fabric of our daily life has been torn in shreds, trampled on,
destroyed," she would put it later in the essay "A Little Girl's New
York," "and hundreds of little incidents, habits, traditions which,
when I began to record my past, seemed too insignificant to set down,
have acquired the historical importance of fragments of dress and furniture dug up in a Babylonian tomb."[1] We also hear in the sound of
her voice the urgency of a woman approaching sixty. Her hope was to
reconstruct a lost way of life for a young generation who thought of
themselves as modern in rallying to the cry "make it new." Her goal
was to make the past "new" to twentieth-century readers.

Wharton believed in the meticulousness of her photographic memory. As she reported to Minnie Jones in a 1921 letter about a stage
adaptation of the novel by Zoë Akins: "I am very anxious about the
staging & dressing. I could do every stick of furniture & every rag of
cloth myself, for every detail of that far-off scene was indelibly stamped
on my infant brain."[2] She was a woman used to giving orders, espe-

cially specific orders about clothing, a reminder to us of the charity work she had been doing in the workrooms in Paris. As she visualized the novel for the stage, she worried that the modern imagination would erase such features as a man's curved and twisted moustache, replacing it with a "tooth brush" cut in modern style. She fretted over the details of a man's wardrobe, insisting that a gentleman of the late nineteenth century would have worn by day a dark gray frock coat with violets in the buttonhole together with a tall hat; in the evening a gardenia would have replaced the violets in the buttonhole of a white waistcoat worn with pumps. We sense what it must have been like for Wharton and others of her generation as they accustomed themselves to changing fashions and measured the distance between the centuries in mustaches and buttonholes.

Her novel begins in exacting detail on a January evening in the early 1870s at the Academy of Music in New York City where Christine Nilsson is singing in *Faust*. The "exceptionally brilliant audience" arrives fashionably late in broughams, landaus, and brown coupés in a ritual that the urbane narrator explains was rigidly followed: "what was or was not 'the thing' played a part as important in Newland Archer's New York as the inscrutable totem terrors that had ruled the destinies of his forefathers thousands of years ago" (*AI* 4). Visual, aural, even tactile sensations come to us as Wharton describes the opera and the accompanying performance of the audience. The hero arrives on stage in "a tight purple velvet doublet and plumed cap" (*AI* 5) and Madame Nilsson is costumed "in white cashmere slashed with pale blue satin, a reticule dangling from a blue girdle, and yellow braids carefully disposed on each side of her muslin chemisette" (*AI* 6). The opera glass turns to the audience and records the intensity of color and texture. The would-be heroine of the novel, May Welland, dresses in virginal white down to the fingers of her gloves and shields her body from our gaze with "a modest tulle tucker fastened with a single gardenia." Tulle is a sheer fabric and a tucker is literally a gathering of fabric stuffed into the neckline of a gown to cover any cleavage that may be protruding from the tightly laced corset supporting May's young and slim body. The placement of the tucker suggests to us a love story, one that traditionally ends in marriage.

The plot of the novel will turn, however, on another gown that Wharton slips into the reified world of performances taking place both on- and offstage at the opera. May's cousin Ellen Olenska appears before us crowned in brown curls held in place by a diamond tiara, a sign of the power her beauty has wielded in her marriage to a Polish count. Our eye moves from the glittering headdress to the gown itself, an Empire design: "The suggestion of this headdress, which gave her what was then called a 'Josephine look' was carried out in the cut of the dark blue velvet gown rather theatrically caught up under her bosom by a girdle with a large old-fashioned clasp" (9). Empress Josephine, the wife of Napoléon Bonaparte, dressed in her signature gown depicted here in a painting by Pierre-Paul Prud'hon, governed French fashion after the Revolution in the way that Queen Marie Antoinette had before her demise and the fall, supposedly, of aristocratic style (figure 5.1). We note, too, that in Ellen's pale gloved hand she holds a fan of eagle feathers, an accoutrement of regal fashion—and, of course, the eagle is the American national bird. Wealthy women of the Gilded Age, as we have seen, marked their beauty in elaborately feathered hats and fans, the consumer desire that prompted the Lacey Act to protect wild species, including the eagle.

The men gazing along with us are themselves carefully brushed in white waistcoats. Nothing except the Josephine gown seems out of place to Lawrence Lefferts, the New York authority on form, or to Sillerton Jackson, the historian of elite families. The narrator notes of Lefferts that his knowledge of form "must be congenital in any one who knew how to wear such good clothes so carelessly" (*AI* 18). We are meant, together with Lefferts and Jackson, to gaze on the contrast between May's conventional gown and Ellen's odd ensemble that reveals as she leans forward "a little more shoulder and bosom than New York was accustomed to seeing" (*AI* 15). The gown is shocking to the audience; indeed, Jackson sneers, "I didn't think the Mingotts would

*Fig. 5.1.* Pierre-Paul Prud'hon, portrait of the Empress Josephine (1763–1814), 1805. *Commons.wikimedia.org.* (Plate 16.)

have tried it on" (*AI* 20). Ellen has "tried on" a plunging neckline and, perhaps more shocking to Old New Yorkers, a gown that is clearly out of fashion.

"Fashionable? Do you all think so much of that?" Ellen Olenska asks in the central question of the novel with its heretical corollary: "Why not make one's own fashions?" (*AI* 76). The novel probes a set of ideas. What is the essence of fashion? Is it finally a matter of custom? Or is it possible to dress for the self and to dress as an expression of the self? And even in the most individualized, eccentric designs, aren't there always echoes of past fashions?

Reading dress in the novel, we see how the elaborately detailed world of 1870s New York evokes images of pre-Revolutionary France as well as Paris fashions in 1920. The strength of the novel comes from the weaving together of past and present, a texture that we can see and feel in the dark blue velvet of the Empire gown caught in the large old-fashioned clasp, a gown as anachronistically drawn as the puffed sleeves had been in the novella *Bunner Sisters*. Curiously, Wharton places the Empire gown, perhaps the quintessential style of early twentieth-century France, at the center of a story about nineteenth-century American taste. Ellen establishes over the course of the novel her determination to live according to her own predilection, which turns out to be thoroughly French. Looking closely at the Empire gown, we see how carefully Wharton selected costumes for her novel and moved them into performance. At first blush, it would seem that Ellen wears décolleté to lure the men around her; she is, after all, a woman who has left her husband and may be in the market for another man. Clearly the men turn opera glasses in her direction and move toward the exposed skin. At the same time, the would-be heroine seems oblivious. She does not consciously expose her body, and it is precisely that confusion over fashion that moves the action of the novel.

Writing much in the mode of a cultural anthropologist, Wharton tells a tale that seems almost ethnographic in the precision of detail. As scholars have noted, however, the world of the novel is not a precise historical account. In correspondence between Wharton and Minnie Jones, we find that Nilsson was not singing *Faust* in 1875 at the Academy of Music and *The Shaughraun* was actually being performed at Wallack's Theatre in 1874.[3] In Wharton's letters, we find that breaches of accuracy didn't bother her much. She once defended her craft in a letter to Robert Bridges, a member of the editorial staff at Scribner who had alerted her to historical mistakes in *A Son at the Front* (1923), "As a matter of fact, though I naturally dislike to be inaccurate, I am not much troubled, for I have not been writing history but fiction."[4]

Wharton avidly read scientific texts and especially admired followers of Charles Darwin, including the ethnographer Edward Westermarck who spent his career analyzing human marriage and morals. It may be that Edith Wharton as an ethnographer had in mind Westermarck's analysis of marriage customs and the meaning of dress. We know that she owned a book he published in 1906, *The Origin and Development of Moral Ideas*, and she no doubt had read his seminal study *The History of Human Marriage*, which first appeared in 1891.[5] A contemporary, Westermarck (1862–1939) was educated at the Swedish lyceum and then the University of Helsinki; he spent his teaching career as professor of sociology at the London School of Economics and Political Science. His science is based on Darwin and a belief that there is no absolute standard in morality. In *Christianity and Morals* (1939), he would characterize homosexuality—his own orientation—as psychical and not moral. In *The History of Human Marriage*, Westermarck draws several conclusions about marriage that might well have caught Edith Wharton's eye. On the subject of promiscuity, for example, he deduces that such behavior is more likely to occur among what he called "advanced people" than, as was customarily believed, among the "lowest races." Darwin and his followers looked for proof of human evolution by amassing data on various cultures in the nineteenth century together with earlier studies of human behavior in a synthetic and comparative method of analysis. Studying what they considered to be "primitive" cultures in their own time, they believed also that they were looking backward into time, gathering information about earlier stages of evolutionary human development. Westermarck reports that he had found no "savage people nowadays" who practiced promiscuity. Wharton's fiction is full of the promiscuity of the leisure class. Indeed, a working-class woman like Nettie Struther in *The House of Mirth* becomes pregnant unwittingly and secures a faithful marriage as soon as possible. Bertha Dorset, a woman of wealth and leisure, is bored with her marriage and indulges in sex as sport. Ellen Olenska, a wealthy married woman who is rumored to have had an affair, is the subject of *The Age of Innocence*, and this later novel complicates the relationship between leisure and promiscuity.

Edith Wharton would also have agreed with Westermarck that the late nineteenth century favored the ethic of unfettered individual freedom advocated by the Darwinists. The assertion of individuality as a right and even a duty seemed to Westermarck characteristic of the age. He quotes Lord James Bryce on the dominant pressure, "the desire of each person to do what he or she pleases, to gratify his or her tastes, likings, caprices, to lead a life which shall be uncontrolled by another's will."[6] What Westermarck discovers from his research and Wharton depicts in her fiction is the seemingly counterintuitive notion that freedom breeds discontent, especially in marriage. He notes a strong correlation between divorce and suicide. The problem seems to him more acute among Protestants than Catholics, Teutons more than Celts, and in cities more than in the countryside. The emancipation of women, especially those able to earn a living, seems to increase the instability of marriages. In the United States two-thirds of divorces at the end of the nineteenth century were demanded by the wife. As in her own life, Wharton depicts Ellen Olenska as a woman disenchanted with her husband and a marriage that includes promiscuity.

On fashion, Westermarck had much to say that Wharton would have found useful as she dresses and undresses May and Ellen. Among tribes he calls "primitive," he notes married women cover themselves and unmarried ones remain entirely naked. A husband might insist on his wife's garment as a sign of "moral and physical protection against any attack on his property."[7] Westermarck puzzles over the recorded fact that for many people being naked carries no sense of shame; he quotes Jean de Lery's observation during a voyage to Brazil in 1585 that "the nudity of their women proved to be much less exciting than our women's clothing."[8] Westermarck marvels at contemporary reports among modern-day painters and sculptors that nude female models do not sexually arouse male artists. "Venus herself, as she drops her garments and steps on to the model-throne, leaves behind her on the floor every weapon in her armory by which she can pierce to the grosser passions of men."[9] The image of Venus dropping her garment and stepping onto a throne comes close to the spectacle at the opera as Ellen Olenska bends forward and exposes more breast than Old New Yorkers were accustomed to seeing. Modesty, Westermarck concludes, can hardly be seen as the "mother of clothing." Rather, fashion arises from the desire to embellish through ornamentation, even as a "sexual lure."[10] The less flesh one sees, the more the imagination plays with the image, adding piquancy to desire. What he finds ironic is that clothing, although initially designed as a lure, had become among supposedly civilized society at the turn into the twentieth century a requirement of decency.

Reading May Welland's garments with Westermarck in mind, we see the tulle tucker as an especially effective lure, rather than a sign of decency. The fact that no man at the opera gets a view of May's bosom marks her sexual value in Old New York society. And it is a prize not lost on the hero Newland Archer. From the moment at the opera when he sees May's tucker and Ellen's clasp, we note, he moves to secure his engagement to May. And, after their marriage, he will have sexual relations with that woman, May Welland Archer, exclusively. His fascination with Ellen, the old-fashioned clasp and exposed bosom aside, has more to do with notions of independence: a woman's right to be as free as a man and, even more so, the idea of his *own* independence from the stultifying culture that surrounds and defines him. A central irony in the novel is that both of the women are freer than he is, an idea he never gets quite straight.

Both May Welland and Ellen Olenska dress with comfort and ease of movement in mind. In that way, their garments embody the struggles of dress reformers at the turn into the twentieth century. Patricia Cunningham in her study, *Reforming Women's Fashion, 1850–1920*, notes the underlying tension between the desire to appear fashionable in ways that society dictates and the desire to have a hand in what constitutes fashion. A "dressy woman" is one who selects "her styles from those of past generations and develops them in the *fin de siècle* materials"; that is to say, "new" fashion always contains elements of an "old" style.[11] Then as now, the bind for fashionable women, especially middle- and upper-class women who have time and money for shopping, is how to express individuality in the design of rudimentary garments that are acknowledged as "necessary items of a complete wardrobe."

Dress reformers advocated various styles that brought the unstructured comfort of a nightgown or wrapper, even the soft textures of lingerie, into public spaces. Gowns cut in what was called aesthetic or artistic design, as we have seen, freed a woman from the constricting stays of a corset. Aesthetic dress was often worn by intellectual or artistic women, including Jane Morris, the wife of William Morris, whose ideas defined the Arts and Crafts movement at the end of the nineteenth century. Aesthetic dresses were made in soft, flowing fabrics and in unconventional colors such as reds and ambers and blues. The garments seemed to flow without the support of corsets or bustles or elaborate petticoats as illustrated in *Algaia* (1894), a journal that was influential among artistic women (figure 5.2).[12] Similar in style to tea gowns or house gowns and wrappers or morning gowns, they came into fashion through Parisian couturiers in the 1870s and 1880s. Such styles became available to American shoppers as patterns in popular fashion magazines, among them *Godey's Lady's Book* (1830–1898), *Peterson's Magazine* (1849–1892), and later *The Delineator* (1873–1937), *Harper's Bazar* (*Bazaar*) (1867 to the present), and *Vogue* (1892 to the present).

The reform movement that advocated aesthetic or artistic dress focused attention literally on the movement of a woman's body. Catharine Beecher, who authored such advice books as *Physiology and Calisthenics for Schools and Families* (1856), decried the imposition of tightly laced corsets. Not only did they threaten a woman's health by restricting the body's internal organs, they also bound a woman to the house, making movement into city streets difficult. Amelia Bloomer's feminist journal *Lily* published articles featuring cheeky cross-dressing by Fanny Kemble, who wore male attire in Lenox, Massachusetts, in 1849

*Fig. 5.2.* "Aesthetic Dress" illustration in *Aglaia* magazine, 1894.

and was castigated by the local press. Male-styled ensembles were advocated for reasons of health; clearly they allowed women to move about in the world. Frenchwomen—George Sand especially comes to mind—indulged in manly attire in the nineteenth century in a display of freedom and autonomy. Such reformers as John Harvey Kellogg, a medical doctor and founder of the Battle Creek Sanitarium in Michigan, advocated nutrition (especially cornflakes) and exercise as the way to health. He and others advocated a one-piece undergarment for women called "a union suit." Physical exercise for women required looser clothing, and at fashionable resorts such as Newport, Rhode Island, and Saratoga, New York (both Gilded Age vacation towns), women dressed for activities, including archery, tennis, swimming, and riding. Hygiene, as well as physical strength, militated against constricting clothing for athletic play.

Female beauty, too, became associated with the body's "natural shape" and reformers advocated an unfettered image of the female body, patterned after the draped torsos of Greek and Roman statuary. Ironically, as women adopted the notion of an idealized and supposedly natural female shape, they relied more heavily on underwear to create the illusion of perfect beauty. Corsets in the 1890s molded hips, flattened abdomens, and raised the breasts, all in an effort to appear natural. Writing in the *Pall Mall Gazette* in 1884, Oscar Wilde noted the absurdity: "Indeed all the most ungainly and uncomfortable articles of dress that fashion has ever in her folly prescribed, not the right corset merely, but the farthingale, the *vertugard*, the hoop, the crinoline, the modern monstrosity, the so-called 'dress improver' also, all of them have owed their origin to the same error, the error of not seeing that it is from the shoulders . . . that all garments should be hung."[13] The farthingale, the *vertugard*, the hoop, and crinoline were variations of stiffened or structure petticoats, shaped by wire or wood into contraptions designed to exaggerate the shape and direct the billow of a woman's skirt. Wilde's point is a good one: in what society could such a contrivance be considered an "improver"? Reformers believed that the draping of clothing from the shoulders shifted the burden of weight from the waist and allowed the lines of the bones to determine the shape of a woman's body.

To look into Ellen Olenska's closet is to discover how closely her garments resemble aesthetic dress. They are made of soft fabrics and in rich unconventional shades of red, amber, and blue. Her cloaks and gowns drape the body without the artificial shape of a tight corset or superficial decoration. Wharton dresses Ellen much as she furnished a room, with an eye on the underlying form. Ellen's garments hang from the shoulder and not from the waist. Janey Archer, Newland's sister, who dresses her own virginal body in conventional "brown and purple poplins" describes Ellen's blue velvet opera dress as a tea gown, a style that was only beginning to be respectable in public fashion in the 1870s. "'I wonder if she wears a round hat or a bonnet in the afternoon,' she speculates, 'At the opera I know she had on dark blue velvet, perfectly plain and flat—like a nightgown" (*AI* 39–40). As Mary Haweis explained in *The Art of Dress* (1879) simplicity of line and naturalness of style in the cut of a gown signal the morality of a woman. Edith Wharton would echo such ideas in *The Decoration of Houses*. A room, like a dress, should be shaped and ornamented by its structural integrity. The clothes that Wharton selects for Ellen are simple, flat, and relatively unadorned.

Clothes express Ellen's character and flow naturally from her individual sense of style. Wharton makes that point over and over again in the novel and delights in Newland's bafflement as he works to place her fashion in a context that he knows. When his mother and sister note that Ellen fails to arrive at the party following the opera, Newland bristles, "I don't think it was a question of taste with her. May said she meant to go, and then decided that the dress in question wasn't smart enough" (*AI* 43). The dress occasions gossip and analysis among the Archers, who so rigidly follow custom that Ellen's deviation is a true puzzle. His mother hears in the explanation a confirmation of her suspicions. "'Poor Ellen,' she simply remarked; adding compassionately: 'We must always bear in mind what an eccentric bringing-up Medora Manson gave her'" (*AI* 43). Medora Manson, Ellen's aunt, has shouldered the responsibility of rearing her (she may well be named for Medora de Morès, likewise, as we have seen, a colorful and worldly female). To the Archers, character is expressed clearly in clothing.

"What can you expect of a girl who was allowed to wear black satin at her coming out ball?" (43), Mrs. Archer asks. Black had been traditionally the color of mourning and did not become acceptable for evening wear until the couturiere Jeanne Paquin (1869–1936) made the color fashionable by blending it with vividly colorful linings and embroidered trim (figure 5.3). She had trained as a dressmaker at Rouff and in 1890 opened the Maison Paquin with her husband in the rue de la Paix. Considered the first female couturier, Paquin is especially noted for innovative marketing campaigns; she was the first to display designs on models who appeared at operas and racetracks (figure 5.4). And she was the first to organize a traveling fashion show; the show featured a dozen models who toured cities in the United States. Madame Paquin served as the fashion organizer for the Palace of Costume at the 1900 Exposition in Paris (figure 2.4) and received the French Legion of Honor in 1913 (the honor that Wharton would receive for her war charities). Paquin's tailored suits were distinctively trimmed in lush furs—sable, fox, chinchilla, or even monkey—on collars, cuffs, and hems.

Wharton drops her name into *The House of Mirth* at the Stepney–Van Osburgh wedding, a scene that suggests elaborate finery through specific detail. The bridesmaids wear $300 gowns made by a dressmaker Wharton calls Céleste, and the wedding dress comes from Maison Paquin: "we knew at once, from the fold in the back, that it must have come from Paquin" (173). The fold in the back represents Paquin's borrowings from Japanese kimonos, a fashion detail that Paul Poiret and other modern designers would use in the early years of the twentieth century. Bertha Dorset is thought to be the best-dressed woman at the wedding, but the guests cannot adjust their taste to the combination of sable and *point de Milan* lace in her ensemble: "It seems she goes to a new man in Paris" (174). That man was, no doubt, Poiret.

The influence of bohemianism continues to be a focus of attention throughout *The Age of Innocence*. The narrator explains that after adopting the orphaned niece, Medora Manson brings the child Ellen back for her uncle's funeral dressed in "crimson merino and amber beads, like a gipsy foundling" (*AI* 59). Worse, perhaps, is Medora's crape

mourning veil that measures seven inches shorter than those worn by her in-laws, a conflict of signs marking intensity of loss. Not only did Medora dress her young charge in gaudy clothes, the vivid clothes of aesthetic dress, down to the amber beads; she also gave Ellen an "incoherent education" (*AI* 61). The irony, of course, is that what to Old New York constitutes incoherence is in truth authenticity. Ellen learned to draw from live models, for example, and to play piano in quintets with professional musicians. After her return to New York, as her family allowed her to seek what they call her own level, she moves into a bohemian quarter: "Small dressmakers, bird-stuffers and 'people who wrote' were her nearest neighbors" (66). The Bunner sisters would have been suitable neighbors along the disheveled street with dilapidated wooden houses. Newland Archer puzzles over the writer Ned Winsett's apartment in the neighborhood and wonders "with a little shiver, if the humanities were so meanly housed in other capitals" (66). Wharton delights in detailing such clashes of taste. Once inside Ellen's apartment, Newland is even more bewildered by the "tricks" she used to place her chairs and tables so comfortably. She makes her own fashion in placing two Jacqueminot roses in a slender vase, when anyone else in New York's upper class would have ordered roses by the dozen. He smells Turkish coffee and ambergris and dried roses and has no aes-

*Fig. 5.3.* Jeanne Paquin (1869–1936), gown, 1912. *Prints and Photographs Division, Library of Congress, Washington, D.C.*

*Fig. 5.4.* Jeanne Paquin (1869–1936), race gown, 1914. *Prints and Photographs Division, Library of Congress, Washington, D.C.*

thetic context in which to place her selections of Italian art. Sensing his confusion, Ellen asks, "What does it matter where one lives?" (*AI* 73).

Ellen Olenska dresses for the scene in a little velvet bonnet and a long cloak, both garments that allow her to move comfortably in the street and to see the city around her. The eccentrics in her circle dress much the way she does. The Duke of St. Austrey wears "shabby and baggy" clothes with the appearance of being homespun and sports a "vast beard" (*AI* 63). He pilots the "black-wigged and red-plumed" Mrs. Struthers who wears "overflowing furs" (*AI* 76). Such fashions of *des quartiers excentriques* cause Newland's spine to stiffen as he contemplates the world beyond his small and slippery social pyramid, the "unmapped quarter inhabited by artists, musicians and 'people who wrote'" (*AI* 93). The fashions of aesthetic dress come to mind also as Newland considers drawing rooms where Mérimée and Thackeray, Browning and William Morris "mingled with fervid and dowdy women" (*AI* 95). Ellen reads books that Wharton herself owned by Paul Bourget, Joris-Karl Huysmans, and the Goncourt brothers. The Huysmans novel, *A Rebours* (*Against the grain* [1884]), tells the story of a hero who becomes disgusted with bourgeois materialism and mediocrity. We see why Wharton places such a book in Ellen's bohemian apartment.

In this novel more than any other, Wharton discusses fashion itself: "It was usual for ladies who received in the evenings to wear what were called 'simple dinner dresses': a close-fitting armour of whaleboned silk, slightly open in the neck, with lace ruffles filling in the crack, and tight sleeves with a flounce uncovering just enough wrist to show an Etruscan gold bracelet or a velvet band" (*AI* 97). Not much detail is left to the imagination. Her narrative often reads like a booklet on the history of dress, precise and detailed in ways that she did not find necessary or artful in her earlier fiction. Yet Wharton gives readers only what she thinks they will need as context for Ellen's attire: "Madame Olenska, heedless of tradition, was attired in a long robe of red velvet bordered about the chin and down the front with glossy black fur" (*AI* 97). Following aesthetic dress, the robe flows from the shoulders and the velvet is a rich red. The black fur borders bring to mind creations by Jeanne Paquin, as do others of Ellen's fashions. In the scene at Skuytercliff, she arrives again in a red cloak with a fur muff. And when she visits the Archer women, Janey reports that Ellen wore "a black velvet polonaise with jet buttons, and a tiny green monkey muff" (132). The polonaise gown is a historic design from the eighteenth century with a puffed, looped, and draped skirt as its distinctive feature; we saw Marie Antoinette in a polonaise gown in figure 4.3. What Janey is describing, no doubt, is a black velvet jacket, skirted in the polonaise style of the 1870s. Designed to look like a man's cavalry jacket, Ellen's polonaise is trimmed with jet black buttons (also popular in the 1870s); the monkey fur perhaps suggests Paquin's modern styles. The arrival of Medora Manson on the arm of Dr. Agathon Carver is wonderfully detailed. He wears a "shaggy yellow ulster of 'reach-me-down' cut" and she "a very old and rusty cloak with a cape" or "Macfarlane" (*AI* 135). Carver wears an old ulster or overcoat without sleeves, a style that became popular in the 1830s; the descriptor "reach-me-down" suggests the length of the garment. Medora, too, arrives in an old-fashioned coat, hers a cape of Macfalane tartan that is looped and fringed in an intricate and incoherent pattern of plaids and stripes and bands. In her hair is a Spanish comb and black lace scarf, clashing with the Scottish fabric of her cape; on her hands are silk mittens that have been darned, a sign that they too are old and rusty, even shaggy.

As their dress reveals, Medora and her adopted offspring Ellen shun the materialism of Old New York society. And their independence comes with monetary sanctions. Ellen Olenska, if she agrees to return to her rich but abusive Polish husband, Stanislas Olenski, will be paid in considerable treasure: "Jewels—historic pearls; the Sobieski emeralds—sables—but she cares nothing for these!"[14] These are the sort of goods that Wharton herself left in her will and that clearly mark wealth in Europe and the United States. Ellen lives for art and beauty, however, and refuses to be bought back by her husband. The negotiation with her family will leave her free to live independently, much as Wharton did, in an apartment very near Wharton's in the rue de Varenne in Paris. What she will need in order to purchase her independence is family money, and she will get that from her grandmother.

Juxtaposed with the divorce of Ellen and Stanislas is the marriage of Newland and May. At the wedding ceremony, Wharton refrains from detailed descriptions of dress. Instead, she sketches the scene using objects of fashion that define Old New York wealth. We see "faded sables and yellowing ermine" as a display of old money. The ushers wear "gold and sapphire sleeve-links" and the best man sports a "cat's-eye scarf pin." The groom wears a tall hat and pearl gray gloves with black stitching. Mrs. Archer weeps into her Chantilly veil and clutches her grandmother's ermine muff. Julius Beaufort's wife wraps herself in chinchilla and violets. Mrs. Lovell Mingott arrives in black Chantilly lace over lilac satin with a bonnet of Parma violets. And Medora Manson, it comes as no surprise, drapes herself in "a wild dishevelment of stripes and fringes and floating scarves" (*AI* 159). The bride is described in very little fashion detail, a sign that Clair Hughes would read as indicative of a good marriage. She floats into Newland's consciousness—a man's consciousness is Wharton's preferred way of presenting desirable women—as "the vision of the cloud of tulle and orange-blossom floating nearer and nearer" (*AI* 159). Wharton's readers would need little more than the texture of tulle and the scent of orange blossom to bring a wedding gown vividly to mind; by the 1920s the image had become standard in anyone's thinking about wedding raiment, as we will see later.

May's wedding clothes also signal a desire for dress reform. May Welland Archer leaves for her honeymoon in a dove-colored traveling cloak and with a "glaringly new dressing-bag from London" (*AI* 160). The newness of her dressing bag suggests her resistance to fashion. As it turns out, she is more athlete than shopper: "Her own inclination (after a month with the Paris dressmakers) was for mountaineering in July and swimming in August" (*AI* 166). May, as Ellen does, wears loose-fitting garments, such as "her sky-blue cloak edged with swansdown" (*AI* 168). She appears for an afternoon of archery in a white dress with a green ribbon and matching ivy wreath in her hair, and distinguishes herself as "nymph-like" in her ease of movement. Her gown flows in classical lines that bring to Newland's mind the goddess Diana. Yet she defends what Newland dismisses as "the religious reverence of even the most unworldly American women for the social advantages of dress" (*AI* 168). She retorts, "'I don't want them to think that we dress like savages.'" Newland muses condescendingly on the relationship between women and clothes, "It's their armour . . . their defense against the unknown, and their defiance of it" (*AI* 169). Thus May endures the dressmakers in the rue de la Paix and later dresses seductively to lure her husband to bed, a feat she must accomplish in order to become pregnant and thereby save her marriage. May reluctantly outfits herself in "the low-necked and tightly-laced dinner-dress which the Mingott ceremonial exacted on the most informal occasions, and had built her fair hair into its usual accumulated coils" but she remains wan and faded (*AI* 236). She is not, we note, comfortable in conventional clothing. At the opera performance near the end of the novel, May wears the blue-white satin and old lace wedding dress (and we finally get a better look at it) that reveals a thickening of her body. But she muddies and tears the dress that has served its purpose, signifying the cost of her marriage in psychological terms; May has done what she must do to secure her marriage and produce a family.

There are signs in the novel that Old New York is already changing in the 1870s. Sillerton Jackson's sister, for example, gossips that only one dress at the opera looked like last-year's fashion and even it had been altered. "Yet I know," she reports very much in the mode of her brother, "she got it out from Worth only two years ago, because my seamstress always goes in to make over her Paris dresses before she wears them" (*AI* 212–213). American women in the Gilded Age, as Wharton remembers the custom in Boston, stored Paris gowns for two years to let them "mellow under lock and key." The fear, of course, was that new models mark new money and thereby lessen a gown's social cachet: "Old Mrs. Baxter Pennilow, who did everything handsomely, used to import twelve a year, two velvet, two satin, two silk, and the other six of poplin and the finest cashmere," the usual order of a wealthy woman (*AI* 213). The narrator notes wryly that after Mrs. Pennilow's death and the obligatory period of mourning, her daughters were able to take the House of Worth gowns out of the tissue paper and appear comfortably in fashion. Old New Yorkers, like Mrs. Archer, would wait a year, but Regina Beaufort, married to new money, wore her dresses right away. The system of fashion reticence as a marker of social class was already breaking down in the 1870s.

The breaking down of protocol in the late nineteenth century depicted in Wharton's novel suggests her ambivalent response to the world around her in postwar Paris. In her most sardonic tone, she records the fate of the writer Ned Winsett, a "man of pure letters" who cannot market his "exquisite literary" manuscript and so must turn to editing a women's weekly magazine, "where fashion-plates and paper patterns alternated with New England love-stories and advertisements of temperance drinks" (*AI* 111). Women's magazines, including *The Delineator*, pandered to the taste of middle-class American women, and we hear Wharton's contempt. A woman who delights in New England love stories and thinks that temperance is a good idea can hardly be trusted as an arbiter of fashion. We read her tone in the knowledge that Edith Wharton will market her own stories and series of her novels in such magazines. Even as she sells her writing in these venues, she bristles at the notion that her readers would ever believe that she is one of them. It is poor Ned Winsett who recommends politics to Newland Archer even though the United States "was in possession of the bosses and the emigrant" (*AI* 112). Estranged as Edith Wharton was in 1920 from the country of her birth, she tips her hat to Teddy Roosevelt who becomes the one great acquaintance of Newland's minor life in politics.

Ellen Olenska and her dark-blue opera gown challenge the fashion of Old New York. Cunningham concludes about aesthetic dress: "Women who wore artistic dress at public gatherings may have been snubbing their noses at current hegemony—fashion and status quo" (155). Snubbing her nose is not quite what Wharton had in mind for her heroine although Old New York considered the dress a snub, not thinking that the Mingotts would "dare to try it on." It is true that the Empire design resembled the cut of a negligee, but Ellen had been trained to see such a dress as elegantly comfortable and stylish in Paris. Mingott women, who come also from Spicers, have a bohemian tendency and a desire to establish their own fashion. The Spicer line comes from a great-grandfather who had had an affair with a Cuban dancer and had apparently embezzled the family fortune. The Spicers married into the Mingott family, securing a place in the New York elite, and married their daughters off to an Italian marquis and a London banker. The matriarch of the clan, Catherine Mingott, "put the crowing touch to her audacities by building a large house of pale cream-coloured stone (when brown sandstone seemed as much the only wear as a frock-coat in the afternoon) in an inaccessible wilderness near the Central Park" (*AI* 21–22). In perhaps Wharton's most effective description of dress, she puts the stout Catherine Spicer Mingott in a black silk gown with what appears to be a fichu or shawl secured by a brooch: "A flight of smooth double chins led down to the dizzy depths of a still-snowy bosom veiled in snowy muslins that were held in place by a miniature portrait of the late Mr. Mingott; and around and below, wave after wave of black silk surged away over the edges of a capacious armchair, with two tiny white hands poised like gulls on the surface of the billow" (*AI* 33). The modest muslin covering of snowy bosom reminds readers of May's tulle tucker. Catherine's wealth and age and girth seem to put the question of respectability to rest even as she situates her bedroom on the ground floor—an act of indiscretion that reminds us she is, after all, a Spicer.

The ironic layering of seemingly contradictory social and political ideas can be seen in the very clothes Wharton selects for her characters to wear. Ellen's sense of fashion is eclectic, coming as it does from conflicting ideas about dress, age, and gender in Old New York. What Ellen remembers about fashion in her native country is the "knickerbockers and pantalettes" that all the children, regardless of gender, had worn in their youth. The puzzle for her, as it becomes for Newland Archer, is how to reconcile the styles of childhood that allowed equal movement and play for girls and boys with the elaborate distance between genders defined and imposed by the garments they were expected to wear as adults. Even as Newland moves through the utterly conventional rituals of his culture—having an affair with Mrs. Thorley Rushworth and an infatuation with Ellen Olenska as he engages himself to May Welland—he espouses feminism and advocates reform.[15] In conversation with Sillerton Jackson over a cigar, he avers: "I'm sick of the hypocrisy that would bury alive a woman of her age if her husband prefers to live with harlots" and "Women ought to be free—as free as we are" (*AI* 45). A question at the center of the novel is, How free *is* a man of Newland's social class and generation? He reads naturalist novels and selects Eastlake furniture, even as he fails to defy his culture. The furniture, designed by Charles Locke Eastlake, embodies the Arts and Crafts style of William Morris and reflects the style of aesthetic clothing worn by Ellen Olenska. Through his taste in furniture, we see the reflection of his desire for her. And yet we see, too, that the sturdy oak of his tables and bookshelves remain free of ornament and are, consequently, easy to clean. Newland Archer is not a man able to risk much in the pursuit of his passion.

More can be read into Ellen's selection of the "Josephine" style of opera dress, which has a rich history that Wharton's contemporary readers may well have known but that has faded over time and seems almost without context for readers in the twenty-first century. The Empire or Directoire cut of the gown comes from the Directory and Consulate periods following the French Revolution as Napoléon Bonaparte I and the Empress Josephine set fashion in France and indeed throughout Europe. Neoclassical and Egyptian (gleaned from expeditions to the Middle East) designs influenced furnishings, ornaments and art as well as garments and jewelry fashionable at court. An American woman, Elizabeth Patterson, married a Bonaparte brother in an 1803 Empire-cut gown made in muslin and lace that, according to a contemporary, "would fit easily into a gentleman's pocket." The raised waist and natural flow of the skirt marked the move away from the elaborately hooped polonaise silhouette fashionable in pre-Revolutionary France. The Costume Institute at the Metropolitan Museum includes in its collection a pair of white mull or sheer cotton Empire gowns from around 1810 that they describe as exhibiting an "arcadian 'naturalism'" (figure 5.5). The description notes, as was the case of Ellen Olenska's gown at the opera: "Observers of the period frequently deplored the absence of modesty conveyed by a style that was predicated on the prominence and exposure of the breasts and on the barely veiled body."

*Fig. 5.5.* Two white cotton mull dresses with cotton embroidery, Empire design, c. 1810, made in France. *The Metropolitan Museum of Art, Rogers Fund, 1907, and purchase, gifts in memory of Elizabeth N. Lawrence, 1983 (07.146.5, 1983.6.1). Image © The Metropolitan Museum of Art.* (Plate 17.)

The establishment most associated with aesthetic dress, Liberty & Company, was founded in 1875 by Arthur Lasenby Liberty who began his business by importing goods from Asia and selling Japanese kimonos. He sold soft, drapable fabrics in lively colors. By 1884, Liberty opened a dress department and joined other reformers in arguing for simplicity of line, one that follows the natural contours of a woman's body in styles that became associated with Art Nouveau. Liberty & Company advertised their apparel as the expression of a woman's self-reliance and personal taste. We hear Ellen's questions: "Fashionable? Do you all think so much of that? Why not make one's own fashions?" (AI 76) That was precisely what Liberty fashions promised; indeed, the company by 1920 assured customers that their dresses, especially the distinctive Empire or Directoire cut, would 'never go out of style.[16]

The Empire style was modeled on Greek statuary and, thus, carried the imprimatur of classical beauty. Josephine, the wife of Napoléon, had favored a simple chemise-style gown with a high waistline, and the very cut became associated with the French Revolution and notions of independence and free spirit (figure 5.1). The Empire cut of a gown has been fashionable from time to time over the intervening years. In the 1870s, Charles Frederick Worth created similar gowns in a princess-line cut, inspired by the tea gown and meant to flow easily over a woman's body without requiring elaborate corseting. Elizabeth Coleman in *The Opulent Era* notes that fashion journals record the return of the Empire design during the 1880s and 1890s, although she could find only three such gowns in collections today: two in the Brooklyn Museum and the other in the Musée de la Mode et du Costume in Paris. A variation with an elaborate train survives at the Chicago History Museum. As early as 1893, the Liberty & Co. catalogue featured fashion plates juxtaposing Liberty's contemporary designs and models from the Directoire period. The style appeared again in the early years of the twentieth century, as fashion designers responded to the call of reformers for less restricting women's underwear. And by 1905, Liberty gave the name "Josephine" to an Empire evening dress.[17] The short waist of the Empire line made the structure and support of a corset unnecessary and the popularity of the style marks a significant move away from the hourglass silhouette of conventional women's clothing. In advertising his designs, Liberty stressed self-reliance, discrimination, and regard for individual characteristics—all the qualities that Wharton features in Ellen Olenska's sense of style.

The popularity of the Empire gown was driven by the desire for the reform of undergarments. Fashion reformers in the nineteenth century sought to lighten the load on the body by simplifying the system of undergarments and advocated combinations of union suits, chemises, and drawers together with less structured corsets. For women with large breasts, various forms of "bust supporters" were designed. In 2007 we celebrated the hundredth birthday of the brassiere as a design we would recognize today. In 1907, *Vogue* magazine first used the term "brassière," a French term for a child's vest or the shoulder straps of a knapsack (or, in the military, a soldier's arm guard or shield); by 1911 the word "brassiere" had entered the Oxford English Dictionary. Paul Poiret wanted to be known as the couturier who liberated the female body from the constraints of the corset and, indeed, designed Empire styles and chemises that required little or no underlying support. And yet, as Cunningham points out in her study of dress reform, "Poiret also claimed to have invented the brassiere, but we know, of course, that the reformers of underwear had long been promoting a similar garment, a bust supporter, as a reform undergarment."[18]

Mary Phelps Jacob, who patented a version of the breast supporter in 1914 under the business name Caresse Crosby, is generally considered the inventor of the modern brassiere. She sold the patent to Warner Brothers Corset Company, who began producing "bras" at their factory in Bridgeport, Connecticut (figure 5.6). In 1925, Ida Rosenthal, a Russian immigrant, and Enid Bisset, a dressmaker, founded Maidenform in Bayonne, New Jersey, and designed bras, for the first

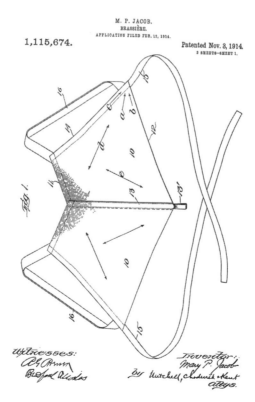

Fig. 5.6. Mary Phelps Jacob (1891–1970), patent for first brassiere, 1914. *Prints and Photographs Division, Library of Congress, Washington, D.C.*

time, in different cup sizes. The Costume Institute at the Metropolitan Museum houses what it calls a "feather-light dream" brassiere from the 1920s made of pink silk and beige lace that is tucked slightly to follow the natural shape of the breast. A large-breasted woman—and that would include Ellen Olenska—depended on a bust supporter and, in the 1920s, on an elastic bandeau to shape the body in the slim prevailing mode. Ellen's opera gown, however, appears to flow without underlying support in an amplitude of flesh. Changes in women's underwear, the literal support for female garments, had everything to do with the modern turn toward freedom of movement for women in social and political life.

In dressing Ellen Olenska, Wharton signals a desire for freedom and the Empire gown she wears, of course, is meant to be out of style, as the characters exclaim. Ellen makes the argument that fashion ought to be a matter of individual taste and desire: exactly the point of Liberty's advertising message. The Empire cut is not a dress that New Yorkers or even Parisians considered the gown à la mode in the 1870s. And yet Ellen's dress is the very sign of modernity in fashion if we consider the time of the novel's composition, the years following the war as couture houses re-established themselves in Paris and women in the United States pushed for victory on universal suffrage. During the years of the First World War, designers had looked toward male-styled attire for models of women's clothing. Few women of that era, Edith Wharton included, favored a return to the demanding stays of a corset once they had been modified and then abandoned.

Although Liberty and Paquin had designed Empire gowns, the French couturier most associated with modern renditions of the Directoire design is Paul Poiret (Figure 5.7). Wharton may well have had him in mind as she was writing *The Age of Innocence*. Poiret had worked for the houses of Worth (with Gaston, Charles Frederick's son) and Jacques Doucet before launching his own establishment in 1906. The signature design of his early years echoed the Empire or Directoire gown of the French Revolutionary period. The recent Metropolitan Museum of Art exhibit of his work, "Poiret, King of Fashion," featured a gown from 1907 that he called "1811," a high-waisted and long-sleeved version of the French style of that time in the patriotic colors of blue and burgundy (see a version of the gown in figure 5.8). The Empire cut literally freed the female body from the corset. Even as he moved couture fashion into modern, even modernist shapes, Poiret criticized the avant-garde for a disregard of history and tradition.

Edith Wharton would have agreed with Poiret about the significance of the past and the desire to shape one's art in traditional designs. During the First World War, as Parisians witnessed the fall of Belgium and feared the fall of France, Poiret's gowns grew somber in color, fea-

turing blacks and browns in nationalistic, even militaristic outline. He served in the war and closed his couture house, along with many other couturiers, as the country used its resources to support the fight. After the war ended, Poiret reopened his bankrupt business with styles that celebrated French history, an allegiance to tradition that placed him out of favor with postwar innovators who were eager to break from the past by making art, including fashion, radically new.

In a similar way, Edith Wharton valorized French history in her postwar novel *The Age of Innocence*, a story ostensibly about the Old New York of her youth. Fashion is the key to understanding the hybrid texture of the novel. Ellen arrives at the opera in a style of dress that Poiret brought back into fashion with his "1811" gown, a style that became widely popular in the 1910s. Wharton places the gown in the 1870s and notes it as an inappropriate design, little admired or understood by a stuffy, introverted American elite class. The Empire gown in its historic design and, even, in its rich blue color, signals Wharton's gratitude to France as her adopted country. In March 1916, the French government had made her a Chevalier de l'Ordre National de la Légion d'honneur. Hermione Lee notes the significance of the Legion of Honor's being awarded to an American woman: "It was a particular honour in 1916, as Wharton told Scribner, because the government had decided not to give out honours to civilians or foreigners during the war."[19] Even the French seamstresses working in her *ouvroir* wrote congratulations to her. Wharton adorned the lapel of her coat with the Legion rosette, designed in the French national colors of red, white, and blue.

We may see, I am arguing, Ellen's opera ensemble as a sartorial salute to France. The gown signals Wharton's patriotism in the wake of the First World War; like the Legion of Honor rosette, it also displays her gratitude to France, her adopted country. And the ensemble includes the feathered folds of her eagle fan: a tribute not only to Napoléon but also to the United States, connoting pride in her countrymen, especially those who had served in the war. The plot of the novel, like the costume itself, is hybrid in nature. Newland Archer marries May Welland and stays at home, a patriotic act in the minds of the Nobel Prize committee who read the ending without irony as a tribute to Newland's morality and manhood. Ellen Olenska flashes her breast, a sign of independence if not sexuality, and moves into an apartment in Paris not far from Wharton's own in the rue de Varenne.

Ellen Olenska's later appearances in the novel seem strikingly modern. Newland searches for her at a party given by Professor Emerson Sillerton, who was a "thorn in the side of Newport society" because he became an archaeologist and a professor. He, like Ellen, is an eccentric whose parties attract "long-haired men and short-haired women" (*AI* 186). The fashions at the party have the look of modern garb. Later Newland mistakes a conventional pink parasol for Ellen's and finds her in Boston carrying "a grey silk sunshade" and a dark hat with long wrinkled gloves. What is modern, here too, is the fact that her long veil leaves her face uncovered" (*AI* 200). In New York City as they tour the Metropolitan, Newland watches her youthful body under heavy furs and her face under a "cleverly planted heron wing in her fur cap"; he admires "the way a dark curl lay like a flattened vine spiral on each check above the ear" (*AI* 247). Such "delicious details" suggest the bobbed hair with its curls across the ear, fashionable in the 1920s. Even in the last scene as Newland declines to mount the stairs, he sees himself as old-fashioned and Ellen's apartment building in Paris as modern. Although the novel sets the ending at the turn into the twentieth century, Newland describes a world very like the one Wharton saw from her window at the end of the First World War. Newland's son sounds like a brash young man of the 1920s, "the spokesman of the new generation which had swept away all the old landmarks, and with them the sign-posts and the danger-signals." Ellen's desire to make her own fashion is a clear sign of Wharton's embrace of Paris in the 1920s even as she situates the novel in Old New York.

## ❧ 6

# DRESSING FOR MIDDLE AGE

"See, I'm growing gray on the temples—don't try to make me
look like a flapper."
—*The Mother's Recompense*

As Wharton moved into her sixties in 1923, she wrote *The Mother's Recompense*, a novel about what it feels like to age and to dress and act the part. The novel is a later work and we might expect Wharton to load it with apparel, except that the story takes place at the beginning of the 1920s and, thus, as was true in *The House of Mirth*, fashion details are meant to suggest styles rather than give a full picture for the reader. She observes the aesthetic "tact of omission" that governs her literary style, giving mere glimpses of fabrics and lines and colors. Contemporary readers would need little more to bring whole garments to mind, the radically modern angular styles that came into fashion at the end of the First World War. Parisian couture houses reopened during and especially after the war as designers vowed to "make it new" and vied to create fashions for women newly empowered in the United States with the vote. The heroine, Kate Clephane, struggles to find raiment appropriate to middle age, even as she desires the youth of her daughter Anne in an oddly incestuous competition for the love of a young man, Chris Fenno. The theater of fashion, here youth versus age, reflects a psychological drama. Although Wharton gives us little detail about clothes, she makes a single gown—as in *The Age of Innocence*—the focal point of the struggle. In shedding the look of a flapper, the very sign of youth in the 1920s, Kate must relinquish as well her claim on one dress she covets: "There, on the bed, in a dazzle of whiteness, lay the wedding-dress."[1] If she is to accept middle age, she must resist the dazzle.

The novel opens with the arrival of a telegram that sets the heroine "into a complicated finger-reckoning" to calculate how old she and her former lover Chris and her daughter Anne must be, and leaves us working with her to do the math: "[I]f Chris were thirty-three, as he certainly was—no, thirty-one, he couldn't be more than thirty-one, because *she*, Kate, was only forty-two . . . yes, forty-two . . . and she'd always acknowledged to herself that there were nine years between them; no, eleven years, if she were really forty-two; yes, but was she?" (*MR* 11). Perhaps she is forty-five. She had moved to a Riviera town in 1916 at the end of her affair with Chris and lived quietly there for three years, setting the story in 1919 or so (after the Armistice). If her memory serves us, we know that Kate was born in the Midwestern town of Meridia in perhaps 1874 and had married a wealthy New Yorker, John Clephane, in 1895, when she was twenty-one. Two years later, she had given birth to Anne, whom she abandoned at the turn of the century. After the war and the deaths of her husband John Clephane and his mother, the prodigal mother is invited back home to New York by a daughter now nearly twenty and in control of the family money and authority.

The plot juxtaposes youth and age in a variety of costumes and disguises. As Wharton's other heroines often do—Undine Spragg especially comes to mind—Kate gauges her age and beauty through reflection in mirrors. After the telegram arrives in the opening scene announcing that her mother-in-law Mrs. Clephane is dead, Kate calls her maid Aline to bring a looking-glass. She sees "the reflection of her radiant irrepressible hair, a new smile on her lips, the first steak of gray on her temples" and responds to the gray hair and harsh lines by calling for Rachel powder (*MR* 12). Rachel powder was a popular make-up in the 1920s, produced by Barbara Gould and marketed in a cream-toned linen box with red trim and a signature red block of wood on the top as an opener.[2] Kate returns to the mirror throughout the novel, checking for traces of an advancing age she cannot quite feel within herself. Considering the distance in age between Chris Fenno and her current suitor Fred Landers, Kate "turned and looked at herself in the glass above the mantel, seeing the gray streaks and the accusing crows'-feet" (*MR* 291). As she fights against the still palpable desire for Chris, she winces at being so clearly Fred's age. In response to the image of his "elderly" movements of mind and body, she shuts her eyes to the vision of aging, noting ruefully that her own body seemed to her "supple, free and imponderable" (*MR* 99). It is the mirror that registers the difference between what she experiences inwardly and what she projects outwardly. "If it had not been for her looking-glass she would never have known she was more than twenty" (*MR* 299). Fred expresses a youthful desire for her, and she thinks with a shiver, "It's I who am old now" (*MR* 302). Wharton uses costume throughout the novel to move the heroine from a fraudulent youth to true middle age. Although she refrains from telling us much about the experience of dress, she uses garments as symbols of emotional transformations.

The paucity of garment detail in the novel reminds us that very rarely in her fiction does Wharton write about the sensation of wearing clothing, the brushing of fabric against the skin or the tightness of a garment as it restricts the body. Perhaps her reticence to tell us what a character senses as she is getting dressed or moving across a room or settling the stomach with food and drink is a matter of social class; it would be unseemly in a woman of her rank and time to dress and undress characters in public or to complain about a tight corset or a prickling petticoat and certainly never indigestion. Nor do her characters luxuriate in the softness of silk or the warmth of wool. Our animal nature comes almost always in Wharton's fiction through reflection in the eye, as in Kate's mirror, and in the mind.

In Wharton's fiction, female garments often come to us through male eyes. In her early story "Souls Belated" at the Hotel Bellosguardo, it is Monsieur Grossart who gazes on Mrs. Linton as she "trailed her Doucet draperies up and down the garden" (*CS* 1:115). What the draperies may have looked like is left to the reader's imagination; our male observer points only to the pedigree of the dress, an haute couture creation of considerable monetary value. And in "The Other Two" our sense of clothes comes from the epiphanies of Waythorn as he weighs the meaning of clothes in imagining his wife's life with her first husband: "it was uppermost in Waythorn's mind that Haskett had worn a made-up tie attached with an elastic" (*CS* 1:389). He ponders what seems to him a central question: "Why should that ridiculous detail symbolize the whole man?" Why, indeed, and yet in his reading of fashion and social class, the ready-made tie with its elastic band signaled every distinction he thought necessary in gauging the man's manners and thereby his morals. Waythorn is chagrined to discover that prêt-à-porter garments do not make the man. In the story "Les Metteurs en Scène," Jean Le Fanois, clothed in an "impeccably tailored frock coat" and looking out on the world with the impertinence of a Parisian aristocrat, eyes Miss Lambert in a "street dress of understated elegance" and reads "a nuance of Parisian refinement—as if a florid complexion had been softened by a film of tulle" (*CS* 1:555). Often we read Wharton's costumes through the male perspective; especially in her short fiction, every discrimination made by the male observer holds meaning.

Some stories hint at what life might be like within clothes. In "The Letters" Lizzie West experiences weather through her inexpensive garments, "sometimes with her umbrella bent against the rain, sometimes with her frail cotton parasol unfurled beneath a fiery sun, sometimes with the snow soaking through her boots or a bitter wind piercing her thin jacket, sometimes with the dust whirling about her and bleaching the flowers of the poor little hat" (*CS* 2:177). Even in the sensual scene, however, it is not Lizzie's body but her parasol that feels the sun and wind, her boots and jacket that are pierced with snow and wind, and her little hat that suffers bleaching. We don't find in Wharton's oeuvre descriptions of how the world feels from the inside out as we do in stories like Kate Chopin's "A Pair of Silk Stocking" or *The Awakening* or Willa Cather's "Paul's Case."

Men come closer than women in Wharton's fiction to a tactile relationship with clothes. Woburn, for example, in the story "A Cup of Cold Water" leaves the "overheated splendor" of the ballroom at three in the morning to discover that the footman had assigned him a "ready-made overcoat with an imitation astrakhan collar" in place of his "unimpeachable Poole garment," and he discerns the difference in warmth that the coat makes in the chilly morning air (*CS* 1:151). Astrakhan fur comes from newborn or fetal Persian or karakul lambs and was fashionable for trim on a man's coat but the ready-made garment that Woburn mistakenly takes is made even more cheaply with imitation fur.[3] He feels at home in his handmade coat from Henry Poole & Co. in London. Even in advertisements today, the tailor promises integrity and substance: "Henry Poole's cut is classically British: the shoulders are moderately padded, the armholes are high, and the waist is subtly shaped. There is hand stitching along almost every seam as well as know-how, which is something that can never be described, but can only be enjoyed—the inexplicable but critical element that experienced hands bring to fine suits."[4] Hence, Wharton provides the shorthand descriptor, "unimpeachable." Mr. Minton in the short story "The Line of Least Resistance" becomes aware of being "hot and grimy in the yachting clothes he had worn since morning" (*CS* 1:222).

At times, men feel the sweat of clothing, but women almost always touch and examine clothes from the outside looking in, either by watching themselves in mirrors or by examining garments after taking them off, as Lily Bart does in the penultimate scene of *The House of Mirth*, gazing and caressing and smelling haute couture gowns, creations of Jacques Doucet and Charles Frederick Worth. Lily measures garments in emotional and intellectual lengths and widths by their "sweep and amplitude" and savors in Proustian fashion the associations lurking in folds, "each fall of lace and gleam of embroidery was like a letter in the record of her past" (*HM* 512). Wharton offers the sensations of smell, sight and sound—"an odour of violets" and a "gleam of light" and "note of laughter"—as triggers of memory.

Even in a story like "The Pretext," which allows the heroine Margaret Ransom to experience sensation from the inside out in the surprising middle-age passion she feels for the young Guy Dawnish, Margaret's sense of self is realized as she views her own blushes in reflection: "She approached the cramped eagle-topped mirror above her plain prim dressing table" (CS 1:632). The mirror, the narrator explains, is "a meager concession to the weakness of the flesh"—a line that makes clear a Puritan suppression of the senses. Remembering their moment on the river bank when "her heart was beating so violently that there was a rush in her ears like the noise of the river after rain," she examines her sensations in the context of French novels and opera plots, and she follows Guy's life only through pages of society news torn from the London *Times* (CS 1:643–644). Through such reflection, Wharton's women see themselves clothed and are thereby able to gauge their sartorial value.

Kate Clephane is a character very much in the mode of Margaret Ransom and Charity Royall, the young heroine of *Summer* who feels the breeze through her blouse and desires the physical experience of sexual contact. In *A Mother's Recompense*, Wharton tells the story from an aging woman's point of view. When she was twenty-four, Kate had followed passion with an illicit lover, Hylton Davies, and again at thirty-nine with Chris Fenno. By the novel's close, when she is forty-six or so, she rejects an offer of marriage from her contemporary Fred Landers, the one she sees as already elderly. Wharton leaves her heroine, much as she did Ellen Olenska, living a comfortable expatriate life in her middle years. Kate Clephane settles back into a desultory life on the Riviera very near Wharton's town of Hyères. She attracts the attentions of Lord Charles, an aging gentleman who likewise lives on the periphery of society. "Marry him?" she muses, "God forbid!" (MR 336). What Kate seeks is male company "simply to fill certain empty hours"; very much an adult at the end of the tale, she admits that "was all she wanted of him; perhaps all he wanted of her" (MR 337).

Kate Clephane, the touch of clothing aside, is a thoroughly sensual creature. She soaks in a slant of late morning sun across the bed of her shabby and cramped room in the Hôtel de Minorque, and the light brings to her mind associations of youth: "the scramble up hill through the whitening gray of the garden, flicked by scented shrubs, caught on perfidious prickles, up to the shuttered villa askew on its heat-soaked rock—and then, at the door, in the laurustinus-shade that smelt of honey, that unexpected kiss" (MR 3). Her reveries are corporeal—garden, shrubs, prickles, rock, and shade—and prepare her for the "unexpected" insistence and pressure of young lips. Memories collect around the affair with Chris, who on a trip into the countryside had sketched by the river bank as Kate "watched the farmyard life waking at dawn" and "dashed her face with cold water and did her hair and touched up her face" (MR 5). Violets arrive in her hotel room, and she luxuriates in the first sensations of her morning, "every touch of the sunshine, as its golden finger-tips pressed her lids open and wound their way through her hair" (*MR* 7).

Kate Clephane inhabits a world very like that of Virginia Woolf's heroine Clarissa Dalloway, as reviewers and critics have noted, and the prose itself often approximates the stream of consciousness technique associated with experimental writers, especially Woolf.[5] This novel, more than any other that Edith Wharton would write, seems modern—even, at times, modernist—in the flow of language and thought. Moving backward and forward in time, Kate's mind waltzes and eddies "like the sunlit dust which the wind kept whirling around the corners in spasmodic gusts" (*MR* 13). She indulges herself in affording to keep her maid Aline and, as she soaks in the morning sunlight, she peers out her window unto "the triangular glimpse of blue wind-bitten sea between the roofs" (*MR* 6). We are reminded that Wharton's first published short story, "Mrs. Manstey's View," features a view from the window as the chief delight of an aging woman's life. Adding to touch and sight and sound, Wharton conjures taste and smell; Kate senses the "hot chocolate coming" and imagines a new hat she has ordered from the milliner.

Shopping for appropriate fashions sets the novel into action and punctuates the plot. Kate begins her day with two appointments, one with the milliner at eleven followed by one with a dressmaker at eleven-thirty. What shopping makes clear to her, in light of her daughter's invitation to return to New York as a mother, is that she has "been dressing all this time like a girl in her teens" (*MR* 20). Kate has been content to dress like a teenager among her expatriate friends and in front of her own mirror. The telegram, with its promise of another audience, forces the aging heroine to reassess her wardrobe. How can Kate construct a middle-aged self through clothing? As Judith Butler has articulated dress, Kate experiments with performance to redefine gender and age and wealth. What ought she to buy and what can she now afford? She demands that the milliner show her a darker hat, "yes, the one with the autumn leaves" (*MR* 20). It is as clear as fashion detail gets that a woman embarking on a journey into middle age must think in autumnal shades. And thinking about a return to wealth in New York, she eyes another hat trimmed in stately blue fox fur, the sort of fashion accessory she would have been wearing had she remained in New York. The ironies of the novel become clear to readers through such purchases.

"See, I'm growing gray on the temples—don't try to make me look like a flapper," Kate sternly cautions her milliner and herself. The flapper line will echo through the novel as Kate works to figure out exactly how she ought to be dressing as a maternal, even matronly, figure. The conflict repeats at the appointment with the dressmaker. Wharton doesn't tell us much about garments but does give us Kate's reflection "with a retrospective shiver, that her way of dressing and her demeanour must have thoroughly fixed in all these people's minds the idea that she was one of the silly vain fools who imagine they look like their own daughters" (*MR* 20–21). This reflection is Kate's struggle: how can she be young if she is old? Kate will return to the child she had abandoned twenty years before and encounter an adult who has desires of her own.

Another fashion irony is that the daughter Anne dresses more conservatively than her mother, who has been "silly" indeed. Kate's dressmaker brings out a "dashing little frock prepared for her" and we see it in garish detail: "an orange silk handkerchief peeping from the breast-pocket on which an anchor was embroidered" (*MR* 21). The orange hue and anchor motif suggest resort apparel in the style of a sailor dress, a popular style following the war. On the Riviera, where everyone is a tourist, Kate has been free to dress on whim. Seeing the frock as her daughter might view it, Kate blushes and orders "instead, something sober but elaborate, and ever so much more expensive." Never again in the novel will our heroine dress cheaply.

In the year after the First World War, as Kate Clephane walks into the shop, she encounters garments very different from those fashionable at the turn into the twentieth century. In place of the corseted S-curve of the hourglass figure of her youth, the modern gowns before her scarcely have a waistline at all, or else one that falls at the hip. In place of the tea gown, she finds a far less structured chemise, the style that will come to define the "flapper girl" of the 1920s. The new garment hangs from the shoulders, following the lines advocated for decades by fashion reformers. The loosened dress associated with flappers gives the illusion of being utterly free of corsetry or petticoat, allowing the female torso to flap and twist on the dance floor as well as on the street. Women with full figures, however, employed longline corsets to achieve the boyish silhouette considered the very mark of a woman's sexuality and freedom of movement.

We know from comments throughout the novel that our heroine has managed to keep a girlish figure over the years of her exile and consequently has been able to wear flapper clothes. Her body is young in an age defined by a youthful body. Kate's sister-in-law Enid Drover delivers the modern credo on the value of a girlish figure: "I do believe it gives one more hold over one's girls to have kept one's figure. One can at least go on wearing the kind of clothes they like" (*MR* 96). And, true enough, Kate's daughter Anne adores her mother's youth and beauty: "And what a beautiful mother you are! And nobody wears their clothes as you do" (*MR* 158). The puzzle for the heroine is exactly what dress to wear to please her daughter and, at the same time, please herself.

It is a mark of Wharton's craft—it is at about the same time that she is working on *The Writing of Fiction* (1925)—that in this novel of youth and age she is abstemious about details of costume. Although the plot moves back and forth across the divide of the war, we note that Wharton spends very little time calling to mind garments and accessories from her heroine's youth in the 1870s or her marriage in the 1890s or even her affair of the prewar teens. In the 1890s affair with Hylton Davies, for example, Wharton dresses him with flourish in "his yachting-clothes" and his subsequent lover "in muslin dresses and white sunshades," a figure as unreal to Kate as "a lady on a 'jacket'" of a racy novel (*MR* 17). Images come to mind of popular ladies' fiction and we all think we know how a racy woman might dress. As Anne meets her mother on her return to New York, she recognizes her from "a funny old photograph, in a dress with puffed sleeves"—the mutton sleeves in style in the middle 1890s date the photograph from the point of her marriage to John Clephane. The dress with the puffed sleeves may well have been her wedding dress.

Fashion details suggest the larger context of change in the design and manufacture of clothing. What Wharton saw around her in Paris at the end of the war was the reopening of the haute couture houses in the rue de la Paix, and the return to work of seamstresses she had employed in her war charities. Designers sought styles and fabrics that would distinguish fashions of modern women from garments that had been worn by their mothers—precisely the drama of dress that is occurring in *The Mother's Recompense*. Jacques Doucet, who had designed the gowns Wharton had used to attract the attention of Henry James and other readers, had failed to exhibit his creations at the 1900 Exposition in Paris. His reluctance to participate in defining the fashions of the twentieth century signals a turn away from his craft. Doucet's prestige as a couturier continued, however, perhaps because his distinguishing use of flowing silks and tulles trimmed in handmade laces and embroideries expressed the organic forms and lines of the Art Nouveau style fashionable at the turn into the twentieth century. And he was a good businessman. The Maison Doucet employed hundred of seamstresses skilled in handmade artistry, even as by 1902 his business included hundreds of ateliers or workrooms dedicated to producing ready-to-wear garments, the mechanized mode of fashion production that would make his signature gowns obsolete in the 1920s. The Costume Institute includes in its collection a striking cubist skirt and blouse by Jacques Doucet, one that the catalogue credits as being avantgarde: "Suturing skirt and top with dynamic crests, Doucet borrowed the energetic emblems of Cubism as devices for fashion" (figure 6.1).

*Fig. 6.1.* Jacques Doucet (1853–1929), red cubist design ensemble dress, 1920–1923. *Costume Institute, The Metropolitan Museum of Art. Image at ARTstor.* (Plate 19.)

As he collected avant-garde art, he clearly worked such designs into women's dresses. Nonetheless, he did not, as Coleman and other fashion historians argue, survive the fashion upheavals as the First World War came to a close. He would die in 1929.

Doucet's contribution to postwar fashion, however, may be seen most forcefully in the work of two of his apprentices who defined modern dress. Doucet hired Paul Poiret in 1898 and became his mentor, so much so that Poiret adopted "Doucet's beard and mirror-polished leather shoes, and . . . put himself in the hands of the same tailor."[6] It was Poiret who worked most closely with the actresses Réjane and Sarah Bernhardt, even taking them with him when he moved to the Maison Worth in 1901 and then to his own establishment in 1903. Poiret called himself "the king of fashion," as he bragged of freeing the female body from the corset into Empire lines in 1907 and the unstructured chemise in 1910, garments perhaps constructed to accommodate his wife Denise's pregnant body. Calling her "the inspiration" of all his fashions, he dressed her lithe body and, in so doing, defined the ideal shape of the female in the era before the First World War. "The sinuous line of her body and the suppleness of her posture preclude the presence of any structural underpinnings," the 2007 exhibit, "Poiret, King of Fashion," at the Metropolitan Museum declares (see figure 5.8).[7] Poiret had not been trained in traditional ways as a tailor or dressmaker and admitted that he was not a seamstress. Perhaps that shortcoming allowed him the freedom to think of coats and gowns as fluid structures achieved by folding and draping long rectangular cuts of fabric into shapes inspired by the Japanese kimono.[8] His simple construction could be made so quickly that it was dubbed "robe de minute." Poiret dressed Denise in shockingly supple and colorful pantaloons and kimonos, and designed turban hats to complement her bobbed hair, much like a gown he designed for Gimbel's department store (figure 6.2). As fashion historians note, his garments freed a woman from the stays of a corset—and consequently the labor of a maid whose job it had been to lace and tighten corsets and lift heavy pads and fabrics to achieve the elaborate structure beneath the belled and then bustled outlines of the late nineteenth century and the hourglass contour of the early twentieth century. It is significant that Poiret, unlike his mentor Jacques Doucet, thought of his garments as pieces of art. He wrote in his memoir *The King of Fashion* (1931): "I have always loved painters, and felt on an equal footing with them. It seems to me that we practice the same craft, and that they are my fellow workers."[9] He sought the expertise of such fellow workers, particularly avant-garde artists Paul Iribe and Georges Lepape, to publish limited-edition albums of his designs, using *pochoir*, a stenciling technique that required hand coloring and, therefore, was considered too elaborate for mere fashion illustration. Poiret made fashion an art that responded to changes in the mode of living that women experienced in the early years of the twentieth century.

Working-class women had often, of course, labored in jobs performed by men. During the war years, middle- and upper-class women, too, took up male tasks, as Wharton did, in charity organizations, providing relief to soldiers and victims of the conflict. As a consequence of war work and mourning, female clothing adopted features of male attire, including uniform designs, tailored styles, and somber colors. The skirt length also continued to shorten, freeing the ankle and allowing greater range of activity to the female torso. It is a fitting consequence of the blurring of gendered fashion that universal suffrage in the United States was accepted finally in 1920. That is not to say that fashion change was necessarily rational or consistent. Reform of women's clothing in the twentieth century came in oddly overlapping impulses; corsets sold well in 1915, even as Poiret experimented with high waists and pantaloons and narrow skirts. One of his signature designs, the hobble skirt, we note, got its very name from the verb "to hobble." Ostensibly a sign of liberated movement, the long narrow design of the skirt, especially in its couture extremities, restrained female mobility, perhaps more so than the cage crinoline or bustle of the past. Although the hourglass corset would all but disappear by the

*Fig. 6.2.* Paul Poiret (1879–1944), Gimbel's model wearing harem pants designed by Poiret. *Prints and Photographs Division, Library of Congress, Washington, D.C.*

time that Wharton is writing *The Mother's Recompense*, the corset would return in the 1930s as women struggled into clinging gowns. And trousers as an acceptable garment for professional women would not arrive until late in the twentieth century. The black pantsuit became a uniform of sorts in the twenty-first century for Hillary Rodham Clinton during her campaign for the U.S. Senate, and vibrantly colored pants and jackets marked her failed bid to become the Democratic nominee for president in 2008.

The end of the First World War heralded significant changes in women's dress, changes that flummoxed supposed fashion innovators. Paul Poiret, who had served in the war, emerged as a figure out of step, much as Wharton was, in an age insistent on uniformity as the basis of mechanized production and androgyny as the basis of female style. Even as he had dressed Denise in outrageously unstructured apparel, Poiret blended classical designs with reprises of eighteenth-century French styles in vivid colors associated with orientalism. Fashions of the past informed what he had considered radical designs. What has come to be called modernism demanded a sharp break with the past as designers turned away from classical draperies and historical dress in order to make fashion "new." Poiret was surprised to discover that his couture house was considered by many to be out of date. He stubbornly continued to salute the achievements of the past in allusive fashions and to argue for individual modes of dress and, especially, artisanal creations. A typical gown in his postwar oeuvre is a patriotically colored navy and red block-printed design in silk faille from 1922 to 1923, the very time that Wharton was writing *The Mother's Recompense* (figure 6.3). Poiret and Wharton would have agreed that the art of the present always rests on the art of the past, as we have seen in the case of Ellen Olenska's Empire gown. Both artists believed in individual artistry over mechanized uniformity and delighted in work performed by human hands. We see them as modern even as they stood in opposition to postwar styles and in anguish at a world eager to abandon tradition. The story of opposition and anguish is the story that Wharton tells in her novel, a narrative that we can trace in the fashion details she gives us.

The other mentee of Jacques Doucet was the young Madeleine Vionnet (1876–1975), a designer who displayed an inclination and talent for innovative, even revolutionary dress and performance that would define Art Deco fashion into the 1930s.[10] Doucet hired her in 1907 and at the first showing of her creations, "thinly veiled, barefooted mannequins . . . sashayed before clients in the coming mode of uncorseted figures."[11] Vionnet's contribution to modern dress—and it is considerable—is the use of bias-cut fabric, that is to say, cloth cut on the diagonal so that it stretches easily. Her signature designs are fluid and encourage the contours of a woman's body to graze the surface and mold the shape of a gown. The Metropolitan has examples of her gowns from the 1930s worn by such celebrities as the Duchess of Windsor. One stunning example, Vionnet's gift to the Metropolitan, features an embroidery "of individual graduated lengths of silk thread passed through the fabric, with each thread forming two drops of fringe" (figure 6.4). The gown clings to the body with an exactness that Edith Wharton might have appreciated in the slimness of her youth; the effect, however, would have been difficult for an aging woman to carry off. The return of a curvaceous figure in the 1930s required a reprise of the corset, and *Harper's Bazaar* admonished its readers in 1933, "You cannot have a roll of flesh about the midriff. An uncontrolled derriere is vulgar in a slinky dress."[12] Vionnet's ideal of the slinky gown survived through the wars and the Depression of the twentieth century; truth is, her gowns are fashionable even today.

Wharton's most enduring patronage of couturiers, however, was at the House of Worth. She lets us know in novel after novel that her characters—Bertha Dorset and May Welland Archer come especially to mind—likewise shopped at Worth. Actually, Charles Frederick

Worth had died in 1895, and it was his sons Gaston-Lucien (1853–1924) and Jean-Philippe (1856–1926), both Wharton's contemporaries, who brought the Maison Worth into the twentieth century by adopting simple, minimalist lines as illustrated in this gown from the Metropolitan collection (figure 6.5). The elaborate glass beadwork and metallic embroidery evoke the ornament of Worth gowns from the nineteenth century. The chemise dress, the garment that defined what it meant to "dress like a flapper," had the unstructured comfort and sleek texture of an undergarment. As was true of the tea gown at the turn of the century, the chemise marked the movement into the public square of garments that had been considered appropriate only for wear within the privacy of the home. The flapper-style dress released the female body from the corset and erased the hourglass waist in favor of a smooth articulation from breast to hip, giving the female body a boyish silhouette.

The couturiere who attracted the patronage of women in the 1920s more than designers at Doucet and Worth or the prewar innovators Vionnet and Poiret was Gabrielle Chanel (1883–1971). With the flair of the Jazz Age, she called herself "Coco," a stage name she later used

*Fig. 6.5.* House of Worth (1858–1956), French evening dress in cream-colored silk satin, embroidered with glass beads and metallic thread in a meandering floral motif. Worn by the marquise de Polignac when she was presented at court, 1925. *The Metropolitan Museum of Art, gift of Mrs. Harrison Williams, Lady Mendl, and Mrs. Ector Munn, 1946 (C.I.46.4.20a,b). Image © The Metropolitan Museum of Art.* (Plate 22.)

when she apprenticed as a milliner and then a dressmaker (figure 6.6). Designing from a woman's point of view, Chanel simplified the line of dresses and made them more functional and youthful, the sorts of styles that Wharton's characters wear in *The Mother's Recompense*. The homogeneous style and standard black color of Chanel's dresses perplexed Poiret; when first seeing her wearing one of them, he supposedly asked sardonically whom she was mourning. "You," she quipped in a witty response that proved prophetic.[13] She was often photographed in her little black dress draped in furs and strings of pearls, an image that strikes us as contemporary in the twenty-first century. Unlike Poiret and the couturiers at Maison Worth, Chanel abandoned allegiance to historical costume and established a simple and discreet style of dressing as she opened her Paris house in 1913. She began working in jersey, a thin stretchy fabric associated with men's clothing, and continued to use it during the war years because it was inexpensive and available. And she opened boutiques in the towns of Deauville and Biarritz, giving shoppers places to patronize as the war threatened big cities. She later moved her Paris shop to 31 rue Cambon, where

*Fig. 6.6.* Adolph de Meyer (American, born in France, 1868–1949), Gabrielle "Coco" Chanel in the 1930s. *The Metropolitan Museum of Art, Rogers Fund, 1974 (1974.529). Copy photograph at The Metropolitan Museum of Art.*

the House of Chanel stands today. *Vogue* magazine called the little black dress a "Ford," the very sign of the assembly-line uniformity of design and efficiency of production associated with American culture in the twentieth century.

Coco Chanel's angular body and bobbed hair seem the image Wharton had in mind as she dressed Lilla Drover Gates, the flapper who captivates and appalls Kate Clephane in *The Mother's Recompense*. Lilla is the modern equivalent of the rebel that Kate had been in her youth, and Wharton uses costume to establish and emphasize the connection. We wince along with Kate as she recognizes the "impudent stripped version of herself, with dyed hair, dyed lashes, drugged eyes and unintelligible dialect" (*MR* 64). The very tone of the description grates on eye and ear. Lilla comes dyed and drugged and "dressed with a kind of savage soberness" (*MR* 89). Kate judges the "heavy lusterless beauty, bored but triumphant" (*MR* 89). Later we see Lilla "tawny and staring, in white furs and big pendulous earrings," smelling of cigarettes and Houbigant (*MR* 99). The white furs and big earrings suggest luxury, as does the dropping of the name Jean-François Houbigant (1752–1807), who opened a shop called A la Corbeille de Fleurs in 1775 in the rue du Faubourg Saint-Honoré.[14] His perfume gained the favor of the queens of Europe, including Marie Antoinette, and it is ironic that Lilla, the sultry flapper, smells of his scent and cigarettes. As Wharton works to catch a whiff, so does she work to find the erratic rhythm of flapper speech: "'Well—I chucked something bang-up for you,' Lilla explains coolly to Anne as she agrees to view her art studio. "'Mercy—you *have* cleared the decks!' . . . 'Ain't there going to be any more furniture than this?'" (*MR* 99). The first section of the novel ends with a ghostly confluence of the two wayward women: "The sight of Lilla lingering in that deserted path had called up old associations. [Kate] remembered meetings of the same kind—but was it her own young figure she saw fading down those far-off perspectives" (*MR* 106).

At the end of the war, Wharton moved to the Riviera, refurbishing a former convent, Sainte-Claire du Château, in the town of Hyères and saw around her the sorts of characters who frequented resort hotels. It is a town like the one Ellen Olenska had in mind as she chills Newland Archer's desire to find a place where words like "adultery" don't exist, and it is exactly the hotel clientele featured in the short story "Souls Belated." The clothes are gaudy and, as Kate's are, often youthful, suggesting more than sartorial fraudulence. "Everyone in Kate's circle had a past," Wharton explains, "and had escaped to Europe as an exile" (*MR* 32). The fashion accessories symbolize the point. Marcia Betterly, for example, enters "clanking her jeweled bangles, twisting one heavy hand through her pearls, and clutching with the other the platinum-and-diamond wrist-bag" (*MR* 32). The women come laden with booty from their questionable encounters in the world.

It is through fashion decisions in the novel that the ironies of changing manners are most vividly portrayed. We do know that Kate is old-fashioned in preferring "to slip into a tea-gown and go down to a quiet dinner," the tea gown being the appropriate and elegant garment for a quiet evening at home in the 1890s (*MR* 59). Wharton details costumes and customs of mourning in Old New York: "three crape-walled years for a parent, two for sister or brother, at least twelve solid months of black for grand-parent or aunt, and half a year (to the full) for cousins" and "the weeds of widowhood" yet more exacting (*MR* 62). Kate weighs subtle distinctions between hypocrisy and harmony when replacing "the coloured finery bought on the Riviera by a few dresses of unnoticeable black, which, without suggesting the hypocrisy of her wearing mourning for old Mrs. Clephane, yet kept her appearance in harmony with her daughter's" (*MR* 61). The dresses of "unnoticable black" are kin to Chanel's little black dress, garments that carry no sign and can therefore be used anywhere. The young society surrounding Anne questions the constricting conventions that Kate had questioned in her own youth. Why wear black for mourning? Why mourn at all? "Much as Kate Clephane had suffered under the old dispensation, she felt a slight recoil from the indifference that had succeeded it" (*MR* 62). What happens to a culture when tolerance applies to everything? Good question.

Wharton returned to New York as she was writing the novel, her first visit home since before the war in 1913. When her heroine Kate Clephane rushes through "the vivid air" of the city, she records sensations that Wharton herself experienced: "the spectacle of the new sumptuous city; of the long reaches above the Hudson with their showy architecture and towering 'Institutions'; of the smooth Boulevards flowing out to cared-for prosperous suburbs; the vista of Fifth Avenue." The new city acted "like champagne on Kate Clephane's brain, making the world reel about her in a headlong dance that challenged her to join it" (*MR* 61). Twentieth-century New York, vivid and sumptuous, is the world that Kate thought she had wanted. And yet she finds here a complacent and shadowless culture with a "fresh blunt face . . . as inexpressive as a foot-ball" (83). Her early indiscretion, the very sin that she carried with her to Europe, is as irrelevant as the black dress she selects. Kate "no longer thought of herself as an object of curiosity to any of these careless self-engrossed young people" (*MR* 89–90). The very garments of the flapper signal the considerable cultural change over her years in exile. Wharton's voice is thinly veiled in Kate's musing: "Again the sameness of the American Face encompassed her with its innocent uniformity" (*MR* 90).

A second set of costumes, symbols of the tension between youth and age, link mother and daughter. Kate remembers an opera night in the 1890s and the cunning fingers of her maid who divides and coils the ripples of her hair into "nests of curls" (*MR* 77). Her lush long hair is crowned in a diamond coronet and her neck is cradled in a ruby sunburst and triple strands of pearls selected by her husband John Clephane to display his wealth. All we know of her gown is that it is fashioned of splendid brocade. Her reverie is broken by the sight of her current garments, an "evening dress and opera-cloak on the bed, and . . . Beatrice Cenci looking down on them through her perpetual sniffle" (79). Beatrice Cenci had, according to legend, suffered incest at her father's hand and then execution by beheading for his murder. (Wharton will give the name Beatrice to the heroine of her pornographic tale of incest, a fragment, "Beatrice Palmato," found among the Beinecke papers by Cynthia Griffin Wolff and first published by R. W. B. Lewis in his biography.) The reference titillates in a tale of ghostly incest as Kate desires Chris Fenno who desires her daughter Anne.[15] All we know is that the dress is black, and we are reminded again of Coco Chanel. To ornament the gown, Anne has surprised her mother by returning the jewels she had abandoned along with her family. The family pearls have an incestuous luster. Kate imagines "the orient of the pearl" merging in the young skin of her daughter; and Anne turns "with a childish pleasure to the pearls hanging down over her mother's black dress" (*MR* 78 and 81). The black dress and orient of pearls signify the psychological drama blurring youth and age.

Likewise, each scene of confusion is marked by jarring juxtapositions of fashion. The intrusion of Chris Fenno sends Kate to the comfort of fashion magazines. "She dragged herself back to her own room, switched on the light, and sat hunched over the pages of a fashion-paper she had picked up on her sitting-room table" (*MR* 118–119). The style change that catches her eye is that the narrow skirt will be the spring fashion, and we think of the hobbling effect the narrowness suggests. As Kate comes to understand the nature of Anne's attraction to Chris, she sits between them "hugging her new self in her anxious arms," and turns a "smooth face toward them" in a furtive regulation of gestures and sounds (*MR* 136). She struggles to dress the part as well as to mimic the composure of her daughter's generation. New Yorkers, like Enid Drover, surround themselves with art that would not chip or fade and furniture that "would welcome her back to domesticity" (*MR* 142). Anne's next gift to her mother is the Clephane house, "one of the few surviving from the time when Fifth Avenue had been New York's fashionable quarter" (*MR* 154). Kate recoils, "This is what I ran away from." And yet even as she resists the spectacle, she imagines herself in sables and pearls: "Mrs. Clephane, sables and pearls, with a great house at her orders, was evidently a more considerable person than the stray tenant of the little third-floor room at the Hôtel de Minorque, and no one was more competent to measure the distance between them than Aline" (*MR* 179). Kate challenges Chris by visiting his home in a "Quakerish quarter" where "an elderly negress with gray hair" ushers her into a dull sitting-room with "funny tufted arm-chairs" and a "rosewood 'what-not'" table, both defining styles of the working class. At home, reconsidering her power over Chris, she forgets to undress, sitting "in her traveling dress and hat, as she had stepped from the train" (*MR* 178). Her forgetfulness and the ensemble itself reinforce the state of her mind and the transient nature of her social and emotional condition.

Anne's fashions convey not only her youth but also her decisiveness and tenacity. She does not have her mother's sense of irony. Anne stands before Kate in her dark braids, looking "as firm and young as a Greek marble," the embodiment of New York blandness and rigidity. Kate sees her daughter as "tall and ghostly in her white linen riding habit, the dark hair damp on her forehead" (*MR* 189). The mother has visions of her past, dressed in "an elaborately looped gown," a garment that embodies her psychological dilemma. Viewing herself against images of her daughter, Kate feels isolated and bewildered: "Yet her real self was not in it at all, but blown about on a lonely wind of anguish, outside in the night"; she "felt like a dizzy moth battering itself to death against that implacable blaze" (*MR* 209 and 225).

A comedy of manners typically ends in marriage, and *The Mother's Recompense* will wind its way toward a wedding ceremony. Wharton plays with the theme of marriage and its many variations: the divorced Kate had married into wealthy New York society and fled the stultifying culture; Chris will, by novel's end, marry into the same wealth but only because he does not tell the truth about his past; Anne will marry the man she thinks she wants; and Kate will relinquish a chance to marry money a second time. The first wedding in the novel is Lilla's to a wealthy and learned older man, Horace Maclew, who pays a price for marrying a younger woman in that he sacrifices his library to provide the space for her ballroom. At the family house on Long Island, "laden with golf-sticks, tennis racquets, and homespun garments," Lilla reigns with a "bolder dash of peroxide on her hair, the glint of jewels on her dusky skin . . . looking like a tall bronze statue with traces of gilding on it" (*MR* 226). Kate notes with chagrin that she did not have the will to turn her early marriage to John Clephane to such advantage, nor does she have the monetary power that Maclew has to lure a younger mate. Rather, she finds herself out of fashion and out of sorts. As the young friends pour out of motor cars, "all ruddy, prosperous, clamouring for food," Kate feels "tenuous and spectral" (*MR* 229). Society in the 1920s seems to her like "a huge sliding stairway," the image of a department store escalator (*MR* 230).

One dress will focus Kate's mind: "There, on the bed, in a dazzle of whiteness, lay the wedding-dress" (*MR* 261). What could be more familiar to us than the wedding dress? Clair Hughes places the history of the wedding gown in the history of the novel of manners, noting that the wedding ceremony, legal and religious in nature, came into law in 1753 with the Marriage Act in England. Samuel Richardson in *Pamela* dresses his heroine in a "suit of white, flowered with silver, a rich head-dress, and the diamond necklace" and earrings given as a bridal gift by the groom, the wealthy Mr. B. as the couple enters church after the wedding ceremony.[16] According to Aileen Ribeiro, brides and grooms from the upper classes wore white and silver clothing by the end of the eighteenth century, and bridal garments, while selected to mark the special occasion, were meant to be worn again.[17] Jane Austen dresses her heroines without much regard to detail in Empire-cut gowns of silk or muslin together with veils of lace. The Mint Museum's exhibit "To Have and To Hold: 135 Years of Wedding Fashion" (2000), featured fifty bridal gowns housed in their collection dating from the 1850s to the 1980s and illustrated that the idea of a dazzlingly white gown, to be worn once, is relatively new. Queen Victoria had selected a white gown for her marriage to Prince Albert in 1840 and the image of her dazzling dress became iconic for Victorians. According to historians, the modern ritual of a Western wedding comes into place over the late nineteenth century: the white wedding, the virgin bride, the veil and orange blossoms, diaphanous fabrics of tulle, silk, muslin, and lace, and a crowded church.[18] By all accounts, the wedding ceremony as we know it was in place by the 1920s, the time that Wharton was writing *The Mother's Recompense*. "In fact," Hughes reports "the wedding dress has fossilized into near-uniform, nostalgically retaining key attributes of 'romance'—veils, long skirts, tight bodices and orange blossom."[19]

The wedding dress that defined the garment at the turn into the twentieth century may well have been the gown worn by Consuelo Vanderbilt in her marriage to the duke of Marlborough in New York City in 1895.[20] One would expect the Vanderbilts to shop at the couture houses in the rue de la Paix as a clear mark of their elegance and wealth. Instead, Consuelo worked with a well-known dressmaker in New York City. It was, no doubt, Jacques Doucet who had designed the gown although it was Mrs. Donovan who had constructed it from his model. The elaborate gown of ivory satin that had draped the eighteen-year-old body in yards of fabric came with trademark signs of Doucet's style, including a "full, widely belted waist and an abundance of lace."[21] The gown that has become the icon for weddings of all sorts was reputed to have cost $6,720. Mrs. Donovan created lace garnishes that were copies of *point d'Angleterre* laces that had been worn by Consuelo's maternal ancestors.

Wharton had in mind the trademark design of Jeanne Paquin as she wrote *The House of Mirth* and staged the marriage of Jack Stepney and Miss Van Osburgh. We see the dress first through Lily Bart's eyes and she sees only "the mystically veiled figure" and notes that Percy Gryce carries "something almost bridal in his own aspect" (*HM* 140). More than garments, Lily fixes on the bride's jewels, which represent the true exchange of ceremonial goods. She eyes "the milky gleam of perfectly matched pearls" and "the flash of rubies" and the "intense blue rays of sapphires kindled into light by surrounding diamonds" (*HM* 144). Gerty Ferrish, whose sense of style is not discerning, notes the showy gift from Simon Rosedale of a "diamond pendant—it's as big as a dinner-plate," but Lily lingers on the "exquisite white sapphire" from Percy Gryce. Wharton uses every flash and ray to measure money and status. Molly Van Alstyne gossips with her mother, who gossips with Mrs. Peniston, who consequently although not at the ceremony confidently describes the wedding finery to Lily: "we knew at once, from the fold in the back, that it must have come from Paquin'" (*HM* 173).

The marriage of May Welland and Newland Archer in *The Age of Innocence*, as we have seen, casts the gown as a blur in the groom's consciousness: "the vision of the cloud of tulle and orange-blossoms floating nearer and nearer" (*AI* 159). The family worries over exposing the bride to "the mob of dressmakers and newspaper reporters" who will describe the private ceremony to an eager audience. Wharton tells us that the wedding finery included "faded sables and yellowing ermine," signs of old money, and it is among the wedding party that she sharpens the fashion detail. The eight ushers wear "gold and sapphire sleeve-links" and the best man glitters in a "cat's-eye scarf pin" (*AI* 155). The groom is traditionally attired in a dark-gray waistcoat and carries on his head a tall hat and on his hands "pearl-grey gloves with black stitchings." His mother softly weeps "under her Chantilly veil" with her hands together "in her grandmother's ermine muff" (*AI* 156). Beaufort's wife is "all silvery chinchilla and violets" and set against Mrs. Lovell Mingott who arrives in "black Chantilly over lilac satin, with a bonnet of Parma violets" (*AI* 158). It is Medora Manson who most disrupts Old New York splendor "in a wild dishevelment of stripes and fringes and floating scarves." May, by contrast, leaves in her "dove-coloured traveling cloak" and takes "her sky-blue cloak edged with swansdown" (*AI* 168).

In the same way, Wharton uses shifting perspectives rather than what she called "Kodak" realism to describe the wedding gown in *The Mother's Recompense*. Kate spies the white dress lying across Anne's narrow bed, a sign of virginity. And later she gazes upon Anne and Chris as they gaze upon the gown: "All their faculties were absorbed in each other. One of his hands reached about her shoulder and, making a cup for her chin, pressed her face closer. They were looking at the dress; but the curves of their lips, hardly detached, were like those of a fruit that has burst apart of its own ripeness" (*MR* 277). The fact that Chris sees the dress before the ceremony connotes the consummation of their sexual union, and as that idea makes its way into Kate's consciousness, she senses the incestuous nature of the triangle: "in every cell of her body she felt the same embrace, felt the very texture of her lover's cheek against her own, burned with the heat of his palm as it clasped Anne's chin to press her closer" (*MR* 279).

The wedding dress carries symbolic and psychological weight in

*Fig.* 6.7. Edith Wharton on the patio of Ste. Claire with two of her dogs and Catherine Gross. *Yale Collection of American Literature, Beinecke Rare Book and Manuscript Library.*

the novel as it releases Kate's desire for youth and leaves her free to be middle-aged. The dazzle of the gown breaks the spell and she emerges fully fleshed, no longer spectral. Relinquishing youth, sexuality, and motherhood, Kate is free to return to the desultory life she had been living on the Riviera. "This sense of unsubstantiality had eased Kate Clephane's taut nerves, and helped her to sink back almost unaware into her old way of life," the narrator assures the reader (*MR* 330). Only her maid Aline is miffed about losing a prestigious house in New York City, even as they settle into a posher hotel, the Petit Palace, and more spacious rooms. Her friends of middle age remain "pleasantly incurious" (*MR* 330). The comfort of the resort with its evenings of cocktails and mah-jongg and flirtations with other castoffs is precisely the world that Wharton's aging heroine prefers. It is a life much like the one Wharton enjoyed living in Hyères, albeit in grander fashion. We see Wharton here at her home Sainte-Claire du Château, elegantly dressed in modern and matronly fashion. Her skirt is short enough to reveal stylish shoes and her body is comfortably draped in a knit jacket, the style she preferred to wear in her sixties. In her hands, we see the lorgnette tethered on the Cartier chain. She seems at ease with her lap-dogs as she converses with her companion and housekeeper Catherine Gross (figure 6.7). *The Mother's Recompense* measures success in terms of fashion. Kate resists the impulse to dress in youthful clothes and comes to understand the meaning of her own admonition to the dressmaker, "don't try to make me look like a flapper." She returns to middle age and the obscurity of the Riviera "evidently a more considerable person than the stray tenant of the little third-floor room at the Hôtel de Minorque." Her friends read her success in her clothes: "handsomer, better dressed—yes, my dear, actually *sables!*" (*MR* 329).

## 7

# DEMOCRACY AND DRESS

Seeing them through the eyes of the new young men
Mrs. St George felt their collective grace with a vividness
almost exempt from envy. To her, as to those two foreigners,
they embodied "the American girl," the world's highest
achievement. . . .
—*The Buccaneers*

As a septuagenarian Wharton loaded her writing with clothes. The
later the book or essay and the earlier the setting, the more she
elaborates the drama of costume. It is a matter of aesthetics and, perhaps too, the tendency of an aging mind to rely on memory, the early
fund of costume and props provided by the experiences of youth.

The novel she was working on as she died, *The Buccaneers* (incom-
plete manuscript, published posthumously in 1938), is a costume drama
set in Old New York. Yet, by reading dress closely, we see an underlying drama about the modern world. The plot that she left behind
and the considerable manuscript, rough in sections but assuredly full
in many scenes, tells a complicated tale of marriage and culture, much
in the tradition of Jane Austen but with decidedly modern twists. It is
a novel of manners that relies on divorce as the central device. American girls, beautiful and rich, mate with British aristocrats, handsome
and not so rich, in marriages fraught with cultural misunderstanding.
For the tale to end happily, the women must divorce and elope with
mates more suited to their souls. The clothes Wharton uses to dress
characters, especially the women, suggest the democratization of fashion, a process under way in the 1870s and well established by the time
she is writing in the 1930s.

In essays and books she wrote in her seventies, Wharton used memory and research to construct the stage and dress her characters. In her
memoir *A Backward Glance*, she delights in being the "eager-eyed little
girl" who had watched the costumes arrayed around her in Old New

York and Newport, Rhode Island. The memoir begins, as we have discussed, in the bright sun of midwinter as the young Pussy Jones dresses in an elegant coat and Valentine bonnet. As Wharton says of her youthful self, "The episode is literally the first thing I can remember about her, and therefore I date the birth of her identity from that day" (*BG* 777). The memoir features, too, the young woman Edith Wharton in the Doucet dress, "a tea-rose pink, embroidered with iridescent beads" she had worn to catch the eye of Henry James (*BG* 913). Wharton embraces the garments of her youth and delights in the fashions of the 1870s. As she looks back, she sees fashionable Newport women, as we have seen, dressed in heavy layers of fabric as they parade in carriages down Ocean Drive: "A brocaded or satin-striped dress, powerfully whale-boned, a small flower-trimmed bonnet tied with a large tulle bow under the chin, a dotted tulle veil and a fringed silk or velvet sunshade, sometimes with a jointed handle of elaborately carved ivory, composed what was thought a suitable toilet for this daily circuit between wilderness and waves" (*BG* 845–856). Not content with a single scene of fashion, two pages later she dresses her brother Harry in "a frock-coat, a tall hat and pearl-gray trousers" with a damsel in "a heavy white silk dress with a broad black satin stripe, and a huge hat wreathed with crimson roses and draped with a green veil against the sun" (*BG* 847). The *Ladies' Home Journal* serialized her memoir in 1933 and 1934, placing the text alongside illustrations of opera gowns from the 1890s, a strange spectacle of wealth during the hardest years of the Great Depression.

Looking back on her autobiography only four years later, Wharton calls herself "a sentimentalist watching the slow downward flutter of the first autumn leaves."[1] The stock market crash of 1929 devastated the finances of everyone, including a woman as wealthy as Edith Wharton. Recent biographers Benstock and Lee detail the effects of the Depression on Wharton's household money and her writing. Although she had funds to maintain two sumptuous houses, the Pavilion Colombe in St. Brice-sous-forêt and Sainte-Claire du Château in Hyères, and to retain servants, and even enough money to continue traveling, her income from New York rental properties and the family trust were greatly reduced by the financial upheaval. For the first time, Wharton relied on her writing to pay her bills. She wrote to her niece Beatrix Ferrand in 1934, "My income has been so much reduced in the last few years that, in the years when I don't publish a novel, I have very little superfluous cash."[2] Her income fell seventy-five percent from 1932 to 1934, and she worried over her ability to pay taxes in the United States on her literary earnings and in France on her properties.

In marking the distance between Old New York and New Deal

America, she catalogues the things that constituted her early life. As she put it in "A Little Girl's New York," "the fabric of our daily life has been torn in shreds"[3] And she uses a literal example. Denouncing museums as cemeteries, she prides herself on wearing out pieces of her mother's collection of old laces even as she recollects the details of "many and many a yard of noble *point de Milan*, of stately Venetian point, of shadowy Mechlin, and exquisite flowered *point de Paris*, not to speak of the delicate Valenciennes which ruffled the tiny handkerchiefs and incrusted and edged the elaborate *lingerie* of my youth." It is in her writing that the laces are preserved, the textile becomes text, and Wharton uses an eager mind's eye to fill the page with vivid memories.

With the same eager eye, she wrote The *Buccaneers* (1938) as a costume drama, laden with apparel. Cynthia Griffin Wolff calls the novel "a delicious romp—an ungrudging tribute to the high spirits of youth, to laughter and happiness and love."[4] And Hermione Lee cautions that beneath the gay costumes lies a somber view of marriage. Both of them are right. The scene opens at Saratoga, New York, during the racing season, as the young women begin their search for mates. Wharton worked on the novel over the last five years of her life; remarkably she experimented with location and movement as a way of widening the stage and filling it with garments. Saratoga is a resort town without the cachet of Newport; the young women come from families on the way up socially and with much to learn about fashion. Their mothers, Mrs. St George, Mrs. Elmsworth, and Mrs. Closson, find the new fashions incoherent. Mrs. St George begins the novel in nostalgia for the dresses of her own youth in the 1850s and 1860s when the crinoline petticoat marked the belled shape of "a black alpaca skirt looped up like a window-drapery above a scarlet serge underskirt" (4). It was the era, as we have seen, when Empress Eugénie at the French court defined fashion as the haute couture houses of Worth and Doucet opened in the rue de la Paix. The daughters of Saratoga wear "tight perpendicular polonaises bunched up at the back" that are the new fashion design of Parisian dressmakers who were moving the female silhouette toward the bustle. The young Saratoga ladies also prefer the décolleté neckline, the brazenly low-cut style made popular by actresses (and favored by Wharton herself). Mrs. St George discovered at the opera in New York that she "could hardly tell a lady now from an actress, or—or the other kind of women." The manners of youthful Americans seem as "mixed and confusing as the fashions."

In this novel, Wharton finally describes the discomforts of dress, particularly those experienced by older women whose bodies have become what we call matronly. Mrs. St George, perhaps her blood a little sluggish, shivers "under her dotted muslin ruffled with Valenciennes," light, gauzy layers of handmade finery that do little to keep her arms warm. She draws around them "a tippet edged with swans-down," the old-fashioned cape marking her age. Her daughter Virginia, who judges garments by fashion alone, gazes on her mother's antiquated boots and tippet, rolling her eyes, perhaps, as modern teenagers do and quipping, "I should think you'd roast with that thing on" (B 10). The old women, in truth, *are* weighted down by the layers of garments that custom has imposed on their generation. Mrs. Closson, the aging Brazilian beauty with a "usual somnambulist's walk, and thick-lashed stare" prefers her sitting-room attire, house gowns and robes, to street clothes that necessitate "encasing her soft frame in stays and a heavily whale-boned dress" (B 33 and 69). She lounges in bed all day "smoking enormous cigars" (B 83). When she is not invited to accompany her daughter in New York City, she is relieved rather than insulted. "First I was afraid I'd have to take Conchita—just imagine it! Get up out of my warm bed in the middle of the night, and rig myself up in satin and whale-bones, and feathers on my head—they say I'd have had to wear feathers!" (B 73). Likewise, the ample matron Mrs. Elmsworth has difficulty getting around in formal dress. Ascending the hotel stairs, she breathes heavily and has to restrain "the impulse to undo the upper buttons of her strongly whale-boned Paris dress" (B 149). Even the aging spinster Jacqueline March explains to Mrs. Elmsworth that "going to a Drawing-room didn't really amount to anything; it just gave the girls a chance to dress up and see a fine show" (B 150). The mothers learn about new styles of dress from the hairdresser and the dressmaker Mrs. Connelly and come to rely on the middle-aged governess Laura Testvalley who becomes, ironies aside, "apparently their guide in the fashion world" (B 255).

Ostensibly set in the Gilded Age, this novel carries anachronistic traces of the 1930s just as other Wharton novels have done. Scholars, especially Dale Bauer and Janet Beer, read this last work as a "novel of assimilation" and one that takes up questions of bloodlines and social identity that reflect the racial and cultural strains during the 1930s.[5] Wharton's "American" girl is an amazing assemblage of races and cultures. The governess Laura Testvalley is a British citizen who works in the United States but comes from an Italian family and is described as "small and brown with burning black eyes" (B 95). An immigrant and a migrant worker herself, she identifies with outcasts. The most forceful female among the young Americans is a redhead, Conchita Closson, who has a Brazilian mother and is characterized as a "wild gipsy" (B 103). Her red hair, like Wharton's own, suggests how bloodlines have merged, the Viking gene having made its way into Brazil. The British aristocrat, Lady Brightlingsea, after learning that her son Richard Marable intends to marry Conchita, cryptically telegraphs Laura

Testvalley to ask, "'Is she black his anguished mother Selina Bright-lingsea'" (B 91). The lady had never consulted the globes in her library but rather drew her image of the American girl from a family tapestry entitled "The Spanish Main and the Americas," where she saw "in the foreground . . . a shapely young Negress flanked by ruddy savages and attended by parakeets and monkeys . . . offering a tribute of tropical fruits to a lolling divinity" (B 92). Wharton is having fun here with British ignorance of the Americas even as they live on the spoils of their empire. Conchita seems to them in their ignorance and fear to be vaguely "some sort of West Indian octoroon" (B 114).

The fear, of course, is the possible taint of blood, the sort of anxiety Adolf Hitler and eugenicists stirred among Europeans in the 1930s. Sir Helmsley Thwarte admits to hating Americans, "the whole spitting tobacco-chewing crew" and their "dressed up women" (B 113). He eyes the flashy young women of Saratoga as a "barbarian invasion" led by Conchita, who succeeds in marrying the Marques of Bright-lingsea's son Lord Richard Marable. The plot as Wharton planned it turns on Sir Helmsley's loathing of Americans and his pledge never to allow his son, Guy Thwarte, to mix with the blood of American "heathens." Helmsley comes to desire Laura Testvalley, a woman younger than he and of a common origin with Italian blood, but British nevertheless. What gets in the way of their union is a conflict over another romance. His son Guy falls in love with the American Annette St George who has already married Ushant, the son of the Duke of Tintagel. When Sir Helmsley discovers that Laura has aided Annette in eloping with his son, he abandons her. The strength of American blood wills out, however, and bloodlines mingle in the assimilation that scholars have noted. The problem for British aristocrats of the 1870s is want of money, the most pressing tension of the 1930s. The Duke of Tintagel explains to Ushant that he must marry money to keep up the family estates—Tintagel, Longlands, and Folyat House in London. Exasperated by his father's desire to marry him off to a rich woman, he priggishly retorts, "[W]hy not marry me to a Jewess?" (B 171). Such references to the multiracial American mix and its threat to British bloodlines make it especially clear that Wharton is writing, in veiled ways, about Europe in the years leading up to the Second World War, especially in the anti-Semitic jibe. The scarcity of money to run aristocratic households echoes the plight even of moneyed families during the early years of the Depression years, and Wharton's last novel struggles to string together the anxieties of the age.

Reading dress in the novel, we find Wharton also looking at fashion in suggestively modern ways. The heroines of the novel—and Wharton had not quite settled on the main one—Annette "Nan" St George and Laura Testvalley dress in simple, even somber clothes.

Wharton gives us few details of their garments and makes clear that neither woman gives much value to clothing. It reminds us that she was under considerable criticism in the 1930s for writing stories about the mishaps of wealthy Americans at a time when poverty was the plight of most people. Perhaps to please her contemporary publishers and readers, Wharton created these two heroines who stand at odds with the fashions of the 1870s, women whose fashions seem more at home in the 1930s. The governess arrives at the train station dressed as a servant with an "old black beaded 'dolman' over her arm" and carrying a "modest horse-hair box" as the young women pour out of the hack in "a torrent of muslins, sash-ends, and bright cheeks under swaying hat-brims" (B 41–42). Social class couldn't be clearer. Laura Testvalley is the culmination of the working women in Wharton's fiction, the seamstress Ann Eliza Bunner, the social worker Gerty Ferrish in *The House of Mirth*, and the nurse Justine Brent in *The Fruit of the Tree*. She carries a dolman, a loose garment with capelike sleeves patterned after a Turkish robe; that single coat brings to mind aesthetic dress and the modern styles of Poiret. Laura situates herself into a narrow and dull room in the American hotel, a place that Wharton often lampooned for its semblance of luxury. The truth is that the gilt fixtures are reserved for the public spaces, and not for the private room that Laura can afford, one that reminds her of her own humble home and her mother dressed in "a widow's cap of white crape" (B 53–54). Wharton is specific about Laura's "thick hair re-braided and glossed with brilliantine" and her change of dress from the black merino into "a plum-colored silk with a crocket lace collar, and lace mittens on her small worn hands" (B 54). Laura's plain visage and raiment stand in contrast to the style of 'the American girl.'

Mrs. St George sees her American girls as "the world's highest achievement" (B 35). Virginia St George stands in a "shimmer of ruffled white drooping away from her young throat and shoulder" (B 54). Her class is marked by "a wreath of cornflowers" and "a black velvet ribbon with a locket." What the mothers don't know is that at night the young people smoke and look for sex. Hearing nighttime voices, Laura draws "an austere purple flannel garment over her night-dress" to see what's happening, and then retreats to her room, sitting before the mirror and crimping her hair in pins. Her experience with sex had been of a different order, albeit with the same player. She listens for the footsteps of Richard Marable, who had as a young man entered the bedroom where she been employed by Lady Brightlingsea as a "small brown governess ten years his elder" (B 60–61). The seduction and betrayal had not, Laura thought, damaged her: "her Italian blood had saved her from ever, then or after, regarding it as a moral issue" (B 75). Yet class lines are clear when it comes to dress. Laura Testvalley "had never been invited to a ball, had never worn white tulle [that is to say, never been a bride]; and now, at nearly forty, and scarred by hardships and disappointments, she still felt that early pang, still wondered what, in life, *ought* to be classed as trifling, and what as grave" (*B* 79). She arranges for the Saratoga girls to be invited to parties in New York and then squires them to London in search of wealthier quarry. In London, too, she arrives "small and brown with burning black eyes which did not seem to go with her stiff purple poplin and old-fashioned beaded dolman" (*B* 95).

Her charge, Nan St George, likewise resists ornamental raiment. She never dresses "with the elegance her rank demanded" and manages in the novel "to be considered unfashionable among the unfashionable" in marrying Ushant and becoming the Duchess of Tintagel (*B* 329 and 244). The family had come to prominence in serving the queen; their property and rank were rewards for vestmentary service. Nan knows little about British aristocratic manners; in truth, she seeks a world beyond class distinctions. She blunders, for example, by enlisting "one of the under house-maids to lace up her dinner-dress" (*B* 247). In gaining Nan as a wife, Ushant assumed that he had purchased her, and Laura has to remind him, "But you can hardly regard her as a rare piece for your collection" (*B* 227). Even her soul mate Guy, we note, has the momentary sense that she was "the finest instrument he had ever had in his hand" (*B* 273). Her sister Virginia, gauging the world by fashion, explains that Nan must understand the necessity of dressing up, living up, and playing up to the standards of her wealthy social set. When Nan appeals to Ushant for five hundred pounds to give Conchita, he assumes she must be in hock to her dressmaker. What other expense could a woman possibly have? Worse yet, he tries to trade the money he grants her for sexual favor, a reminder, as Lee reads the novel, that aristocratic marriage may well be simply prostitution of a high order.

What is most striking in Wharton's dressing of her heroines, however, is a single scene about the making of fashion. Having worn in her youth cast-off organdy dresses, Nan consults Laura about a design for her first ball gown, one she imagines as being "pale blue velvet, embroidered all over with seed pearls" (*B* 88). Laura gives a surprising suggestion: "My dear, if you want to talk about ball-dresses, I should advise you to go to the sewing-room and get the maid's copy of *Butterick's Magazine*" (*B* 89). The dropping of the name Butterick into her last novel signals considerable shifts in fashion during the late nineteenth century that had come to predominate in the twentieth. By the 1870s, fashions were available even for a maid, and it is in her sewing room that heroines look for ideas about how to design and construct ball gowns, supposedly the garments of the very rich. The ball gown had by the late nineteenth century become the central garment in John Wanamaker's Grand Depot, the palace of consumption. Still much sewing took place in the home, as well as in factories, and was done on the sewing machine, a technology that promised a democratization of dress.[6] The mass production and distribution of paper patterns for men and especially by the 1870s for women spread the news of fashion across the United States in the surprisingly lucrative pattern business that became a major industry in the late nineteenth century. Wealthy American women such as Wharton traveled to Paris and patronized the couture houses of Worth and Doucet; at home they patronized dressmakers, like the fictitious Mrs. Connelly, who copied French styles. The Bunner sisters and Miss Mellins in Wharton's early seamstress tale use sharp and knowing eyes to translate the fashions of their customers into facsimile garments; when Ann Eliza is unable to imagine the new design worn by the lady with the puffed sleeve, the reader knows that her business is doomed.

A way of achieving fashion for middle-class shoppers in the late nineteenth century was through the perusal of women's magazines such as *Godey's* or *Peterson's* and using what were called "fashion plates" and instructions to reproduce the designs at home. Although rough patterns were available through magazines as early as the 1850s, women struggled to transfer rudimentary information into practical dresses that actually fit individual bodies. The problem of drafting the design and cutting pieces that could be sewn into sleeves, especially, was difficult for anyone not trained as a dressmaker or tailor. Two businesses emerged to standardize designs and draft patterns that would fit different sizes of women. In the middle of the nineteenth century, Ellen Louise Curtis, a milliner by training, married William Jennings Demorest, a dry goods merchant; together they built a fashion establishment that, by 1860, included the magazine *Madame Demorest's Quarterly Mirror of Fashions*. The publication included fashion-plate illustrations of garments and articles about Paris and New York fashions for the market of middle-class women eager to sew clothing that advertisers proclaimed to be the latest in fashion. The pattern-maker that Wharton names in the novel is Ebenezer Butterick. He apprenticed as a tailor in Massachusetts and by the 1860s had crafted rudimentary patterns for men's shirts, a standardized design that did not change much from year to year or from one social class to another. He moved to New York where men's garments—especially for soldiers during the Civil War—were especially in demand.

Turning his eye to women's fashions, Butterick built a considerable business producing and marketing patterns for female consumption (I would use Butterick patterns myself to make prom dresses a hundred years later). His company employed twelve people at its start in 1867;

three years later it had grown to a hundred and forty workers who produced 23,000 patterns a day.[7] He opened what he called a "Fashion House" on Broadway meant to lure middle-class female shoppers with the promise of glamour. As women entered the doors of Butterick's, they were shown a display of fashionable patterns, all cut to size on colored tissue paper. After selecting a dress pattern, they were given catalogues that listed sizes and prices and then ushered into a salesroom where assistants retrieved specific pattern sizes from bins arranged along the walls and then collected their money. The shopping ritual, one that would remain constant well into the twentieth century, echoed the finery of Parisian couture houses but stripped the shopping ritual to its bone.

In mentioning Butterick, Wharton places her heroines in a world that middle-class readers would recognize. Too, she drops the name *Butterick's Magazine* that her readers would know from various associations. In 1867, Butterick began publishing what he called *Ladies' Report of New York Fashions*; the next year, he began a periodical called *Metropolitan Monthly*. The magazine that Wharton no doubt had in mind was *The Delineator, A Journal of Fashion, Culture and Fine Arts* published by the Butterick Company from 1873 to 1937; the journal's last years overlap the time that Wharton was writing *The Buccaneers*. The magazine suffered financially (as everyone did) during the Depression and would become the *Pictorial Review* in 1937. Not so popular as *Harper's Bazar* or even *Godey's* or *Peterson's* during the 1870s, *The Delineator* grew in reputation during the 1880s; by the turn of the century, it had the reputation of being the most fashionable of ladies' magazines.

The seemingly simple line about the maid's fashion magazine resonates in *The Buccaneers*. Wharton would have known that Butterick had invaded London at the time of the novel, setting up a branch of his business at 177 Regent Street in 1874. Indeed, by the 1870s, America had established itself as a fashion center that, especially for middle-class shoppers, rivaled France. Just as Edith Wharton details the "barbarian invasion" of American women into the British aristocracy, so Ebenezer Butterick as a "buccaneer" was making money selling affordable American fashion to English ladies. He made fashion a democratic enterprise, available to middle- and working-class women who could afford the relatively inexpensive paper patterns and recommended fabrics (and who had retained, perhaps through economic necessity, the traditionally female craft of sewing).

*The Delineator* and its editor Oscar Graeve were very much on her mind as Edith Wharton was working on her last novels. She sold manuscripts first to magazines for serialization, as novelists have always done, and then to presses for book publication. During the 1920s and

1930s, she discovered that her plots disturbed, even scandalized the editors of women's magazines, who balked at the frank depictions of sexual encounters and repercussions in Wharton's fiction. She had had trouble publishing "The Old Maid" and "New Year's Day" during the 1920s. Her twin novels *Hudson River Bracketed* and *The Gods Arrive* had been rejected by magazine editors because the plot centered on a pregnancy conceived out of wedlock. That is why Rutger Jewett, her publisher at D. Appleton, had negotiated with Graeve for the serialization of *Hudson River Bracketed* in *The Delineator* before the book's publication in 1929. The sequel, *The Gods Arrive*, was likewise to be published in the magazine before the book came out in 1932. Wharton had been surprised and rattled when Graeve started the series early, before she had crafted the ending of the first novel. Miffed by his treatment of her, she permitted Appleton to publish the book *Hudson River Bracketed* before *The Delineator* had completed the serial. And she continued wrangling with Graeve over the handling of *The Gods Arrive*. He was distressed over the idea that a man and woman would live together, even in fiction, without benefit of marriage. We get a strong sense of vexation in a letter she wrote to Jewett: "When I consider what the *Delineator* is, and what the poorest of my work is in comparison, I confess that I feel indignant at such a tone."[8]

In 1933, Edith wrote to Minnie about the pressures in doing business with magazines. "The fact is that I am afraid that I cannot write down to the present standard of the American picture magazine," she moaned. "I am in as much need of money as everybody else at this moment and if I could turn out a series of potboilers for magazine consumption I should be only too glad to do so; but I really have difficulty in imagining what they want."[9] The *Woman's Home Companion* admonished her for planning the elopement of a married woman at the end of *The Buccaneers*. Outraged, Wharton snapped in a letter to Minnie Jones, "Brains & culture seem non-existent from one end of the social scale to the other, & half the morons yell for filth, & the other half continue to put pants on the piano-legs."[10] It is that stultifying American crowd Wharton had in mind as she plotted her last novels.

Reading dress in *The Buccaneers* we note that even the aristocratic families of England had acquired their money and position as reward for the labor of earlier generations. The Dowager Duchess of Tintagel stresses her role as mistress of the robes to the queen. In a scene full of the accoutrements of social rank, she reviews the things she has come to own or the things that have come to own her: "the treasures, the possessions, the heirlooms: the pictures, the jewels—Raphaels, Correggios, Ruysdaels, Vandykes, and Hobbemas, the Folyat rubies, the tiaras, the legendary Ushant diamond, the plate, the great gold service for royal dinners, the priceless porcelain, the gigantic ranges of hot-houses at Longlands" (*B* 214). We are reminded that Wharton herself had crafted such a list as she willed her possessions to friends and family. The list—and here we think too of the poverty in the 1930s—includes property for the poor, including coal and blankets and charities. The Duchess's satisfaction is that Queen Victoria would never allow her title, mistress of the robes, to fall to a naïve and inexperienced American, her daughter-in-law Nan. Wharton warns about the excesses of wealth and the reliance on things to mark achievement and satisfaction. Yet the novel is not reproachful and not even sharply satirical.

At the end of her life, Edith Wharton indulges in the drama of costume, outfitting her barbarians in fabulous clothes. New York society, she tells us, was in her youth "a nursery of young beauties" and her novel reprises the costumes she had woven throughout her fiction. Her gentlemen are stately dressed in tall hats and frock coats in the afternoon, and don a "light racing suit and gray top hat" at the race-track (*B* 47). Conchita, the most colorful of the American women, is "crowned by a flapping Leghorn hat with a rose under the brim" and carries as ornamental and "reluctant poodle" (*B* 12). Saratoga as a resort town allows reformed dress, loosened corsets, and sporting clothes. For dancing, American girls wear "a red rose in the fold of a *fichu*, a loose curl on a white shoulder, a pair of new satin slippers, a fresh *moiré* ribbon" (*B* 35). Twirling across the dance floor, they seem to their mothers and to Wharton's readers the embodiment of the "American girl" (*B* 35). A fichu is a scarf or shawl worn around the neck for modesty's sake, much as a tucker was used to drape a young woman's cleavage and fresh moiré or watered silk ribbon accentuated a slim young waist. Laura Testvalley, who had begun by working at the stuffy home of the New York Parmores, "had suspected from the first that the real America was elsewhere" (*B* 41); she seems more at home in the freshness of Saratoga society, among the "social as well as the political outcasts" (*B* 68).

The American invaders have little sense of history and, consequently, no regard for the accumulation of goods associated with nobility. Conchita, as Lady Dick, dresses "in a crumpled but picturesque yellow muslin and flapping garden hat" and Honoria Brightlingsea comes to dinner "in a faded dinner-dress." The American girl Virginia, whose "survey of the world was limited to people, the clothes they wore, and the carriages they drove in" finds aristocratic British fashion wanting (*B* 132). As she sardonically put it, "'I guess our clothes aren't half dressy enough'" (*B* 119). When she arrives at the queen's drawing-room party, the girls not invited imagine that she "looks like a queen herself—a queen going to her wedding, with that tulle veil and the feathers" (B 143). American beauty itself, like the beauty of Virginia and Lizzie Elmsworth, "had been known to raise a girl almost to the throne" (B 153). The question at the heart of the novel is, What happens after ascending the throne? What is the fate of beauty after marrying into the aristocracy?

Wharton, as we have seen, often uses a man as arbiter of taste, and in this novel the young man is the fastidious Hector Robinson, whose middle-class family money had come from the cotton industries of Lancashire. He declares candidacy for Parliament as a Conservative, just as he notes with chagrin that fashion had turned toward the Liberals. Gazing at himself in the mirror—and Wharton is having fun with him—he decides to shave his whiskers to stay on the edge of style. He looks around him at the American invasion of Britain, however, and accurately observes, "Everything that happened seemed to be improvised" (B 194). And we see the mating season through Robinson's eyes with "the young women in their starched dresses and spreading hats, the young men in flannel boating suits" (B 197).

Two remarkable scenes are well costumed in the novel fragment. In one, Virginia St George is courting and being courted by Lord Seadown at the country house of Lady Idina Churt, who has had an affair with the young man and arrives to reclaim her property. The American girls cavort with the British young men in scenes of smoking and drinking and poker playing, high-stakes gambling that Wharton depicted in *The House of Mirth* as Lily Bart fell into debt. The scene, in truth, is stiffly dramatic as the women vie for the absurd British lord. Lady Churt demands that he leave with her, but she is no match for the American "girls." Lizzy Elmsworth announces Seadown's engagement to Virginia St George in front of the group and Virginia wins her man. Wharton explains the victory: "Fashionable London had assimilated with surprising rapidity the lovely transatlantic invaders" (B 243). The invasion took the form of poker parties and intoxicating drinks, even banjo playing and dancing the Virginia reel. Fashions conform to the American style of entertainment. "Girls, and even young matrons, pinned up their skirts to compete with the young men in the new game of lawn-tennis on lordly lawns" (B 243). The resort fashions of Saratoga had made their way to the lordly lawns of English estates. In addition, the American love of smoking cigarettes and cigars made its way into dining rooms and libraries and had even invaded the bedroom.

The liveliest scene of the novel is an entertainment given by Conchita that climaxes in a line dance of the Virginia reel—thought by the British onlookers to be proof that Americans behaved, in truth, like the "wild Indians" of the tapestry. Purportedly a staging of a country dance, the scene in curious ways depicts the revelries of the Jazz Age.

The young women dressed in dramatic décolletage gowns dance indelicately from room to room. The matrons of England watch and worry. The Dowager Tintagel notes in alarm, "When crinolines were worn the movements were not as—as visible as now. These tight skirts, with the gathers up the middle of the front—of course one can't contend against the fashion" (B 281). The bustle, to her mind, heralded freer movement of the body and, with it, license to dance provocatively. And Lady Brightlingsea agrees that everything in America, the dance as well as the dress, seems exaggerated. The rows of dancers, originally separated by gender, formed a "giant caterpillar" and "were spinning off down the double-cube saloon and all the length of the Waterloo room and adjoining it, and the Raphael drawing-room beyond, in the direction of the Classical Sculpture gallery" (B 281–282). Conchita led the "wild train" to the "rhythmic chant" that "spun the accelerated reel, song and laughter" in a "rollicking chorus" until door after door "was flung open, whirled through, and passed out of again" in a turbulent and, to the old ladies watching, seemingly pagan rite of youth. In fact, the scene seems to come from the manners and mores of 1920s America.

When Conchita arrives in Nan's boudoir after the romp to borrow money to finance her divorce, she looks much like a beauty from the 1930s. We see her in "a rosy dressing-gown festooned with swansdown" and in "tumbled auburn curls, red-heeled slippers, and a pink dishabille with a marked tendency to drop off the shoulders" (B 297). Wharton tells us that Conchita shops at dressmakers in Paris and offers to buy fashions for Nan in return for the favor of money. "Darling, why don't you strike, and let me order your clothes for you—and especially your underclothes," she offers, looking at Nan's somber attire. Yet her dressing gown, the swansdown trim aside, looks much like the bias-cut creations of Vionnet, Paquin, Chanel, or the young designer Jean Patou (1887–1936), whose sleek gowns defined style in the 1930s. The bias-cut evening gown in alphabet-motif lace covered in black silk chiffon and ornamented with a rhinestone bow, shown in figure 7.1, may well have been designed by Patou. His dresses and sportwear enhanced female freedom of movement, and his models, often imported from the United States, reinforced modern ideas about newly enfranchised American women as fashion buccaneers, much as Wharton's novel illustrates. Conchita's hairdo resembles the waves and curls that lengthen in the styles of the late 1930s; the dramatic tresses of Katharine Hepburn come to mind as do those of Jean Harlow, Greta Garbo, and Joan Crawford. The high-heeled slippers complete the picture. Patou's fashions are, in fact, chic even today. Reading dress in this last novel, we see Wharton situated comfortably in the modern era.

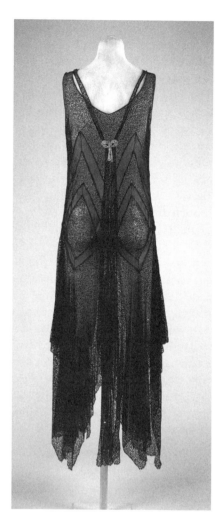

*Fig. 7.1.* Jean Patou (1887–1936), possibly House of Patou (founded 1919) or House of Lucien LeLong (founded 1923), Black cotton alphabet-motif lace and black silk chiffon; separate rhinestone bow from the late 1930s; view of full back. *The Metropolitan Museum of Art, gift of Richard Martin and Harold Koda, 1992 (1992.399 a,b). Image © The Metropolitan Museum of Art.* (Plate 23.)

She relaxes at the novel's end, the writing of which would mark the end of her own life. As her friend Elisina Tyler noted, the novelist had indulged all her life in the "fetish of dressing" and stood by the custom of dressing for dinner as "an absolute sign of civilization." It is fitting that Wharton leaves her heroines and her readers in the costume drama of dinner. As the guest of Lady Glenloe, a comfortably British woman whose free-spirited husband owns a ranch in Canada, Laura and Nan gather to talk again about clothes. The governess, who has served as fashion consultant and social equal in the novel, is planning to wed the father and Nan hopes to elope with the son. They chat about fashion and dress as social equals. Laura wears a "breastplate of brown cashmere" and uses a "new hair-lotion" that gives a puff and even curl to her thick braids (*B* 335). Laura gazes on Nan as she gazes on herself in the mirror. Both women search for anything in Nan's closet that might be promising for the evening. And Nan admits "she owed it to herself to dress her hair more becomingly, and to wear her jewels as if she hadn't merely hired them for a fancy-ball" (*B* 339). The Tintagel jewels, "ponderous coronets and tiaras, massive necklaces and bracelets hung with stones like rocs' eggs," give her a chill. What she wants as an ornament is not the treasure of aristocratic European wealth but rather the democratic simplicity of the American style, more in the mode of a governess than an aristocrat. Nan fastens a "diamond briar-rose on the shoulder of her coral pink *poult-de-soie*" (*B* 340). That brooch had been her father's gift to her mother, "a diamond brooch formed of a spray of briar-roses" (*B* 21). Her coral gown of grained taffeta comes without clear reference to time. The costume reveals the drama of the American empire, the story of the twentieth century. Robinson puzzles over the change in fashion in one of the last paragraphs Wharton would write. With a relaxed frown, he concedes, "The free and easy Americanism of this little band of invaders had taken the world of fashion by storm." He has in mind the Gilded Age garments of the young ladies of Saratoga. Wharton's novel about the moneyed classes at the end of the nineteenth century, however, makes a claim for a modern democratization of fashion. The true American girl, the new mistress of the robes, dresses as Nan and Laura do: in garments and ornaments that follow the simple lines of a woman's body, the straightforward style of dress popular in the twentieth century.

# CONCLUSION
## The Costume Side

... & the rest of the public—the small rest!—will, I think,
be interested in the "costume" side, the pictures,
the Old New York stories, & so on.
—*Edith Wharton, 1921*

Over the last decade of Wharton's life, American audiences saw
her characters dressed for several costume dramas. After *The Age
of Innocence* won the Pulitzer Prize in 1921, it looked as though Zoë
Atkins would write a play version, and Wharton wrote to Minnie in
full-throated anxiety about how her culture should be staged, particularly the material aspects: "I could do every stick of furniture & every
rag of clothing myself."[1] She frets especially about how men are mus-
tachioed and clothed. "I am so much afraid that the young actors will
be "Summit Collar" athletes, with stern jaws & shaven lips, instead of
gentlemen." The tailor Austin Reed on Regent's Street in London
specialized in the "summit collar," a crisply angled white cotton design that looks much like a dress collar does today. Characters playing
the gentlemen of her generation, she instructed, were to wear tall hats
and frock coats during the day with violets in their buttonholes; by
night, they were to wear white waistcoats and pumps with gardenias.
On the topic of female raiment, we would expect more detail, but instead she fussed over the use of slang and scolded that "*no* girl went to
a school." What she meant was that no women of her social class went
to universities; surprisingly, that was the custom even though they
lived among the first generation of college-educated women in America. The ladies of Old New York were distinguished from middle-class
women through private educations provided by governesses and tu-
tors in the home. Edith's letter to Minnie turns to women's clothes in

a cryptic footnote: "older women did not wear pince-nez & white false fronts." We know that Wharton herself carried a lorgnette. Her admonition against a false shirt front, an insert sometimes called a "dickey," seems more symbolic than literal. A wealthy woman would not, in her opinion, opt for the illusion of a garment when she had the money to afford the whole thing. What the letter to Minnie reminds us of more than anything is how visual Edith Wharton was as a chronicler of culture.

Edith insisted to Minnie that others of her novels "have a play" in them "all ready to be pulled out!" And she was right. A dramatization of *The Age of Innocence* opened on Broadway in 1928 with Katharine Cornell as Ellen Olenska. Zoë Atkins wrote the script of *The Old Maid*, which opened in New York City in January 1935 and won the Pulitzer Prize for drama that year. And *Ethan Frome*, written for the stage by Owen and Donald Davis, opened in New York City in 1936 with Raymond Massey as Ethan, Pauline Lord as Zeena, and Ruth Gordon as Mattie Silver; it continued on a road tour and earned $130,000, money that did much to replenish Wharton's bank account.[2] She negotiated on three silent-film versions of her work, *The House of Mirth* (1918), *The Glimpses of the Moon* (1923), and *The Age of Innocence* (1924), produced by Warner Bros. and directed by Wesley Ruggles.[3] In 1930, Lothar Mendes directed *The Marriage Playground*, a movie based on Wharton's novel *The Children* with her sexually suggestive plot smoothed into a toothsome comedy. RKO produced a 1934 film of *The Age of Innocence* directed by Philip Moeller that starred John Boles as Newland Archer and Irene Dunne as Ellen Olenska, and in 1939 Edmund Goulding directed the Warner Bros. production of *The Old Maid*, starring Bette Davis and Miriam Hopkins. The costumes in the stage performances and the films, in spite of Edith's insistent costume directions, came more from popular fashion than from her novels, because theatrical versions of literature are always adaptations. Yet the visual dimensions of Wharton's fiction, as these plays and films attest, attracted audiences.

Ironically, even as her novels were re-created in plays and films, she had increasing trouble in the 1920s and 1930s selling her writing and was especially disappointed in the poor reception of her memoir, *A Backward Glance*. Columbia University sought to honor her with a degree of doctor of letters in 1934, and Rutger Jewett urged her to take the offer because he thought it would spur sale of the memoir. In a fit of pique, Edith quipped to Minnie, "The Western morons to whom he wishes to sell the book wd not be much affected by my Academic distinction," and then her tone softens as she added, "& the rest of the public—the small rest!—will, I think, be interested in the 'costume' side, the pictures, the Old New York stories, & so on."[4] By "Western morons," one supposes she had in mind moralistic readers and skittish publishers in the United States who resisted the darkness of her social realism and sought to bowdlerize references to sexual complexities. The "small rest" of us who have grown in the decades since her death continue to read her books with the "costume side" vividly in mind.

While scholars over the years have considered her work as a cultural anthropologist, we have only recently begun to think about her with an archeologist's trowel in her hand. The tale that Edith Wharton tells in fiction and nonfiction over her long writing career—from the first published story "Mrs. Manstey's View" to the posthumously published novel fragment *The Buccaneers*—comes to us loaded with "things." Bill Brown contends that literary scholars are only beginning to use "things" and "thingness" as ways of refreshing our reading of literary texts. Biographers and scholars, especially since Cynthia Wolff's biography of Wharton, have examined Wharton's depiction of material culture in individual stories and novels. And recently, Gary Totten argues, in *Memorial Boxes and Guarded Interiors: Edith Wharton and Material Culture* (2007), that Wharton made deliberate use of objects in her writing to signal cultural patterns of belief and value. The essays in his collection offer twenty-first-century reconsiderations of "things" in Wharton's oeuvre, such as body art, modern technology and built environments. Two other new books on Wharton, Emily J. Orlando's *Edith Wharton and the Visual Arts* (2007) and Parley Ann Boswell's *Edith Wharton on Film* (2007) focus attention on the visual and costume side of her work.

This book has examined remnants of material culture in Wharton's life and work, especially details of garments worn by women at the turn into the twentieth century. In *Bunner Sisters*, *The House of Mirth*, *The Fruit of the Tree*, *The Custom of the Country*, and the postwar novels *The Age of Innocence*, *The Mother's Recompense*, and *The Buccaneer*, Wharton dressed characters in clothes that suggest her own struggle to become modern, to think and dress and write in modern modes. A dress designed by Jacques Doucet or Charles Frederick Worth or Paul Poiret or Coco Chanel is the sort of literary detail that in the past may have prompted savvy textual scholars to offer information, if at all, in a well-research footnote that a reader may peruse, or not, at leisure. The goal of this book has been to pull the seemingly peripheral story of fashion to the center of study.

Looking closely at the "costume side," we see more fully the woman and her art. Just as Edith Wharton dressed in the conventions of French couture fashion, so did she write in the conventions of French realist fiction. In *The Writing of Fiction* she credits the French realist Honoré de Balzac (1799–1850) with being the first writer "to draw his dramatic action as much from the relation of his characters to their houses, streets, towns, professions, inherited habits and opinions, as from their fortuitous contacts with each other" (*WF* 5). In her fiction, Wharton also places clothes in their dramatic relations. She was a woman who delighted in the art of "dressing up" even as she devoted her life to the art of "making up." As we have seen, she selected each fabric and design of clothing for its sartorial implications and used the same shrewd eye for fashion to dress characters in apparel and ornament that reveal integrity or lack thereof. Articles of dress in a work of literature, she cautioned, should enhance the aesthetic beauty of the text and not merely offer Kodak snapshots of clothing and other goods. She admonished herself and other realist writers to observe tact by omitting details that prize "things" in and of themselves. Yet everywhere in her writing is a strong regard for "things," especially the gowns that adorned women over the course of her long life—from the tightly corseted and belled silhouettes of the 1860s and the narrower bustled lines of the 1870s and 1880s to the sleek uncorseted and unbustled modes of the 1920s and the 1930s. Wharton willed the things she valued most as gifts to friends, and many of those pieces of jewelry and fabric appear in publicity photographs and literary texts. Her favorite "dog collar" necklace—the sapphire and diamond medallion clasping strands of pearls—comes to mind, as does the Cartier chain of diamonds and pearls that she often holds in her hand and places in the restless hands of her characters. The purpose of this discussion has been to place such "things" in the foreground of literary study.

Edith Wharton's life spanned seventy-five years of costume history. She was born into a fashion world very different from our own, yet most of us would feel comfortable and even glamorous today in the couture designs of the 1930s. Wharton's wardrobe and the way she dressed characters chronicle the upheavals in fashion at the turn into the twentieth century. In striking ways, her novels tell the story of the rise of the couture industry in Paris in the 1850s and the struggle of designers, dressmakers, tailors, and milliners to survive. Over those years, the rarified gowns of the Belle Epoque lost sartorial significance as prêt-a-porter copies and printed patterns made fashions available to middle- and working-class women. The literal weight of frame and fabric lightened as the design of female garments responded to changes in women's activities and social reform. In early novels, Wharton imagined the labor of those who work on the "underside of fashion," and during the war years she created, managed, and financed workrooms for seamstresses. Wearing fashionable clothing did not preclude her understanding of the craft of sewing and the art of design; indeed, it enhanced her appreciation of both.

Reading dress closely, we have seen the overlapping of fashion in her novels. Often in writing about the past, she referenced current styles in Paris and New York. Anachronisms are signs of her engagement in current culture even as she ostensibly wrote about the past. The lady with the puffed sleeves who observes the decline of the Bunner seamstress shop in the 1870s seems to be dressed in a tailleur with leg-of-mutton sleeves—not popular until the 1890s, when the novella was written. The Empire style of Ellen Olenska's gown belongs more to the second decade of the twentieth century (even to the second decade of the nineteenth century) than to the story's setting in the 1870s; it thus salutes French history. The costumes in later novels signal a response to those critics during the years of the Depression who regarded the lavish designs and fabrics of the Gilded Age as incongruous, if not merely antiquated and irrelevant, to readers experiencing economic hardship and political anxiety. Perhaps mindful of the clash, she dressed her last heroines, a wealthy wife and a governess, for dinner in simple, seemingly modern raiment.

In the photograph that serves as the frontispiece for this book, Edith Wharton sits upright in a wicker chair beside a wooden bench on the floral shaded patio of Sainte-Claire. Many photographs from the 1920s and 1930s show her together with friends on the bench. With a hand on her cheek, she poses for the camera and smiles openly, genially familiar. Clad in what looks like a wool jersey suit trimmed with lace cuffs and lapel, her body sits comfortably free of corset and bustle. The woman no longer strains to accentuate a wasp waist or eyes the camera pensively. She grasps a string of wooden beads that is free of cigarette case and lorgnette, and she wears, as always, stylishly heeled pumps. Her thinning hair is tucked under a hat that perhaps more than the line of her suit or the point of her shoe, signals modernity. Caroline Reboux opened a Paris shop in 1865, calling herself the "queen of milliners" as she moved fashion away from the bonnet; perhaps, however, she is best known as the creator of the cloche hat, the bell-shaped felt design that became the iconic frame of the modern female face.[5] Wharton's brimmed cloche, viewed against the valentine bonnet she wore as a child dressed in her mother's mode, marks the dramatic change in dress over the course of her long life. The woman in the cloche hat, beckoning us to join her on the bench, is discerningly modern.

# Notes

*Introduction: Remnant and Meaning (pages 1–13)*

1. Edith Wharton, *The House of Mirth* (New York: Scribner, 1905), 512. Pagination will follow the first edition, and other quotations will be cited in the text.

2. The parlor game "tableaux vivants" stages living versions of well-known pieces of art; in this example, Lily Bart portrays the character Mrs. Richard Bennett Lloyd in the painting by Joshua Reynolds (1775–1776). The historic dress that Lily Bart wears in the tableau turns out to be an example of the type of drapery advocated by dress reformers throughout the nineteenth century (see 1907 "Delphos Gown" by Mariano Fortuny, figure 2.14). The loose, diaphanous fabric, featured in the painting, hangs from the shoulders and sweeps across the body in neoclassical fashion. The male characters are titillated by the exposure of the lines of Lily's body (a treat that the parlor game often allows). Gerty and Selden, however, see Lily's true self emerging from the costume. Lily Bart's desire throughout the novel is to get someplace "beyond" the conventions and constrictions of her social class, and the gown itself embodies her desire. It is the Mrs. Lloyd gown that Lily savors at the novel's close, as though she too sees the garment as an expression of her essential identity. The reader is left to wonder what sort of heroine Lily might have been if she had been allowed to dress with comfort and freedom of movement in mind rather than the pressures of gender and social class.

3. Edith Wharton left two wills, one in France and other in the United States. Elisina Tyler was named executrix and residuary legatee of both wills and worked to settle the accounts in France before authorities there discovered the American properties and asked for additional taxes. Benstock, *No Gifts from Chance,* 456–459, and Lee, *Edith Wharton,* 752–755, detail the controversies over the wills. Specific bequests in the French will, listed here, offer a clear accounting of Wharton's actual property and give us her sense of what "things" are valuable after death. Her dresses and other garments, as she notes the custom, were given to her maid. Cast-off clothing was especially valuable to women who worked as servants because the resale price of such garments was considerable. Note that the most valuable items of apparel, handmade laces and linens as well as furs, were bequeathed to close friends.

4. Margaret "Daisy" Chanler was one of "Pussy" Wharton's epistolary female friends, a group that included Sara "Sally" Norton. Wharton's letters

to women differ markedly from her letters to men in that she felt freer to chat in the letters to women about what she was reading and thinking about. Reading their letters, we note that the women rarely talked about fashion, almost never about clothes. Wharton did talk to her sister-in-law Margaret "Minnie" Jones about apparel, especially garments being crafted in Paris workshops as part of her relief and charity work during the First World War. And in later letters to Minnie, Wharton stressed a desire to get the details of history, including costume, straight in her fiction and insisted that theatrical and movie adaptations get the costumes straight also.

5. Bill Brown, *A Sense of Things*, 17. My work owes much to Brown's observation that literature can be read through a study of "things," the material culture that surrounds and penetrates a literary text. Wharton is often talked about as a cultural anthropologist, with a sharp understanding of how groups of people live together, but she was, too, an archeologist, a writer who described specific "things" in precise detail and physical context.

6. Elizabeth Ann Coleman, *The Opulent Era*. My work on clothing and literature relies on the considerable work done by fashion scholars and historians, especially Coleman's research on the haute couture houses of Charles Frederick Worth and Jacques Doucet. Coleman's study, originally an exhibition catalogue for a show at the Brooklyn Museum, features drawings and fashion plates from the nineteenth and early twentieth century as well as lush color photographs of garments in the Brooklyn Museum and the Metropolitan Museum of Art. I am arguing that the meaning of literary texts is enhanced by cross-disciplinary modes of observation and analysis.

7. My work began in 2006 with research in New York City at the Costume Institute in the Metropolitan Museum of Art. I met with Elizabeth Q. Bryan, research associate and collections manager of the Costume Institute. She and her assistant Marci Morimoto selected representative gowns from the late nineteenth century and helped me examine gowns, ensembles, coats, capes and hats. The garments come wrapped in muslin and are stacked on shelves. Marci Morimoto with her hands in gloves unfolded each package and arranged garments on the table for inspection. She opened and turned garments for me as I scrutinized the fabrics and stitches and ornaments. Ms. Morimoto answered my questions about the history of fashion and posed new ones as I struggled to learn how to "read" the dresses as "texts." She knew Edith Wharton's novels well and was alert to literary details of dress. I also talked with Phyllis Magidson, curator of costumes and textiles at the Costume Collection in the Museum of the City of New York, where I was able to examine dresses and capes designed by Worth and Doucet, as well as spectacular hats by Madame Virot. I am grateful to Elizabeth Bryan, Phillis Magidson, and Marci Morimoto for schooling me in the details of their costume collections. Over the course of my study, I visited fashion exhibits in New York that featured the designs of Worth, Doucet, and Paul Poiret. The fall 2007 exhibit, "Paul Poiret: King of Fashion," at the Metropolitan changed my way of reading Wharton's novel *The Age of Innocence* by placing her in the historical context of Paris fashion during the war years. The exhibit illustrated changes in fashion as Western culture turned toward modernism, and I could see how Wharton's fiction moved in response.

8. In 2007, I visited the Mint Museum of Art in Charlotte, North Carolina, to see the exhibit "Dressed to Impress: 18th and 19th Century Fashions from the Historic Costume Collection." The Mint Museum, the first branch of the United States Mint, opened in 1936 as North Carolina's first art museum; it published a lushly illustrated catalogue, *Experiencing Art at The Mint Museum: A Look at the Collections*. The Historic Costume and Fashionable Dress Collection was founded in 1974 and has grown to about ten thousand items from three centuries, including designs by Worth, Doucet, Fortuny, Chanel, Dior, Givenchy, Blass, Versace, and others that "illustrate not only fashion trends and social history but also design elements, fabric selection and construction techniques" (57). The "Dressed to Impress" exhibit showcased female and male attire together with undergarments illustrating the considerable reform in dress over the nineteenth century that allowed freer movement of the body, especially the female body. Items in the exhibit demonstate various modes of design and construction, including garments made at home, in factories, and in the more rarified workrooms of the rue de la Paix in Paris. The director of costumes, Charles Mo, talked with me about the history of the collection and generously allowed me to use images in this book (see figs. 1.2, 1.3, 2.7, and 4.1). I thank him and Andrea Collins, the photographic services assistant, for advice and help in selecting images and arranging permission.

9. Cynthia Wolff, *A Feast of Words*, 27. Wolff's psychobiography, following in the wake of R. W. B. Lewis's less personal, more scholarly *Edith Wharton*, is the first biography to read Wharton's life as closely attached to material culture.

10. Elisina Tyler letter, 5 February 1930, in the Wharton Manuscripts, Lilly Library, Indiana University, quoted in Lee, *Edith Wharton*, 698. Hermione Lee's recent biography of Edith Wharton is impressive in its knowledge of the details of Wharton's life and unequaled in its depth and breadth of understanding. I am grateful to Lee for the care she has taken to place elements of material culture into the story she tells about Wharton's life.

11. Leon Edel first visited Edith Wharton in 1931. The meeting is reported in R. W. B. Lewis, *Edith Wharton*, 501.

12. Martha Banta, "Wharton's Women: In Fashion, In History, Out of Time," in *A Historical Guide to Edith Wharton*, 55. Before earning her Ph.D., Banta worked as copyeditor of *Harper's Bazaar*; she offers scholars detailed and lively discussions of clothes in Wharton's fiction.

13. Cavallaro and Warwick, *Fashioning the Frame*, xvi. The publisher, Berg, an international and independent enterprise, specializes in books on fashion and design, and since 1997 has been publishing *Fashion Theory: The Journal of Dress, Body & Culture*, edited by Valerie Steele.

14. Edith Wharton, *The Age of Innocence* (1920); New Riverside Edition, edited by Carol Singley (New York: Houghton Mifflin, 2000), 47. Pagination will follow this edition, and other quotations will be cited in the text.

15. Margy Kinmonth, *The Secret World of Haute Couture*, documentary film, Tracy Jeune, executive producer, BBC (2006). This is a film worth seeing for its interviews with designers and patrons of haute couture and its footage of garments as they are made and sold. Kinmonth talks with Karl Lagerfeld and

films the making of one of his designs, and also interviews John Galliano, Valentino, Christian Lacroix, and Ralph Rucci. She reveals, too, the other side of the exchange by interviewing "collectors" of haute couture "art," including Betsy Bloomingdale and Carol Petrie (whose wedding dress was designed for her by Christian Dior himself), Becca Cason Thrash (wife of a Texan oilman), Susan Gutfreund (wife of a bond dealer), and Daphne Guinness. All of these women, we note, seem kin to the characters Edith Wharton created a century ago.

16. The essay, which began as "Further Memories," remained uncompleted, perhaps because Wharton had trouble finding a publisher. The final version of the essay, "A Little Girl's New York," was published posthumously by *Harper's Magazine* in March 1938. The essay is included in Wegener, *Edith Wharton: The Uncollected Critical Writings*, 274–288.


*Chapter 1. Dressing Up (pages 14–50)*

1. Hermione Lee reports Wharton's shopping in the rue de Rivoli and Au Bon Marché and then makes a curious judgment: "But she was not interested in fashion" (*Edith Wharton,* 303). As proof, Lee provides a glimpse of Wharton and her corset maker though a conversation Henry James had with Marie Belloc Lowndes in 1913: "[James] said that when [Wharton] was lately at her stay-maker's the latter said to her: '*Cela n'est pas tout à fait cela.*' Mrs. Wharton replied: 'But I feel very comfortable.' The other observed, '*Oui, et ces corsets donnent à Madame de jolies hanches, mais ce ne sont pas les hanches de cette année.*'" Yet early photographs of Wharton display a young woman very much invested in tightly corseted fashions with stylish "jolies hanches." We note, too, that the conversation between Wharton and her stay-maker takes place in 1913 when Wharton was in her fifties and styles were moving away from the tight corset and toward the angular drapery of gowns designed by Paul Poiret and other modern couturiers. She was not alone in desiring a corset that feels "very comfortable."

2. Edith Wharton, *A Backward Glance,* 1934, in *Wharton: Novellas and Other Writings*, with notes by Cynthia Griffin Wolff (New York: Library of America, 1990), 810. Pagination will follow this edition, and other quotations will be cited in the text.

3. I am grateful to Elizabeth Q. Bryan, research associate and collections manager, of the Costume Institute, for this observation about how to identity garments. Part of my initial research was to determine precisely who had designed the gowns Wharton had worn for her publicity photographs, and Bryan's caution was among the first things I learned about the limits of the project. Without a particular gown in hand, it is impossible to say for sure who the designer was.

4. Patricia A. Cunningham, *Reforming Women's Fashion, 1850–1920,* 208. My work on changes of dress in Wharton's fiction owes much to the research Cunningham has done on fashion reform over the same years. Her finely detailed book places women's clothing in the historical context of politics and women's health, the two reform movements working toward similar and

often overlapping goals at the turn into the twentieth century. Cunningham has an eye, too, on fashion as art. Her research on material culture dovetails with the work I am doing on Wharton's fictional costumes over the same period of time, and I am grateful for what I have learned from her research. For photographs of fashion reform styles, see the online exhibition, "The Trouble with Fashion," written by Cunningham and presented by the Historic Costume Collection, Geraldine Schottenstein Wing, Ohio State University.

5. François Baudot, *Mode du Siècle*, 38.

6. Shari Benstock, *No Gifts from Chance*, 180.

7. *The Delineator*, December 1904, pattern 8286, 556. I have also worked in the Irene Lewisohn Costume Reference Library at the Costume Institute in the Metropolitan Museum of Art, home to approximately 30,000 noncirculating monographs, rare books, and periodicals, as well as design archives, sketchbooks, photographs, drawings, prints, and extensive files of clippings pertaining to the history and study of the arts of adornment throughout the world. The library maintains fifty current fashion periodical subscriptions, including a wide range of international magazines and scholarly journals. I am grateful to Tatyana Pakhladzhyan, head of the collection, for help in locating specific garments in contemporary journals. The patterns available in 1905–1907 reveal how fashionable Wharton's selection of dress would have been in the publicity photograph. The tea gown was associated with comfort in the home but had become by 1905 an acceptable and even conservative choice of gown for the public image of a literary woman at her desk.

8. *Femina* no. 146, (1 April 1907), cover; for other photographs of female writers at their desks in similar clothes and poses, see pages 10 and 410 of the same issue.

9. For a discussion of Gibson, see Diana Crane, *Fashion and Its Social Agendas*, 105.

10. I looked through photographs of Edith Wharton in the Yale Collection of American Literature, Beinecke Rare Book and Manuscript Library, and am grateful to the staff for help in locating images for the book. These two photographs in the Beinecke are listed with different dates, 1900 for the image in an evening gown and c. 1907 for the image in coat and fur muff. The background in the photographs, however, suggests that they come from the same angle in the same room and therefore probably on the same day. Note particularly the column in the background and the ornate wooden frame; the difference in the background comes only from the fact that she is standing in the coated image and seated in the gown.

11. Photograph of Réjane, the Parisian actress who was "Jacques Doucet's muse" and who ran her own theatre from 1906 to 1918, is included in Baudot, *Mode du Siècle*, 38.

12. Wharton's bustled gown may be the creation of Charles Frederick Worth, who is credited with the reform design of the caged bustle. The billowing skirt framed by the cage crinoline fashionable in the 1850s and 1860s proved to be a fire hazard for women as they walked past a fireplace. Worth responded to the danger by designing skirts that lay flat across the front with fabrics swept up dramatically on the sides and gathered to form a bustle across the derriere. The idea behind the bustle was to enhance visibility and mobility.

13. For detail on the various dogs Wharton owned, see Lee, *Edith Wharton,* 152.

14. Ibid., 303.

15. Edith Wharton and Odgen Codman, Jr., *The Decoration of Houses* (New York: Scribner, 1897), xix. Pagination will follow the first edition, and other quotations will be cited in the text.

16. Edith Wharton, *French Ways and Their Meaning* (New York: Appleton, 1919), 1. Pagination will follow the first edition, and other quotations will be cited in the text.

17. Edith Wharton, *The Writing of Fiction* (New York: Scribner, 1925), 5. Pagination will follow the first edition, and other quotations will be cited in the text.

18. Edith Wharton, *The Touchstone* (New York, Scribner, 1900), 63. Pagination will follow the first edition, and other quotations will be cited in the text.

19. Edith Wharton, *Sanctuary* (New York: Scribner, 1903), 8 and 139. Pagination will follow the first edition, and other quotations will be cited in the text.

20. Edith Wharton, *Madame de Treymes,* 1906, in *Edith Wharton: Novellas and Other Writings* (New York: Library of America, 1990), 3. Pagination will follow this edition, and other quotations will be cited in the text.

21. Edith Thornton, "*Beyond* the Page: Visual Literacy and the Interpretations of Lily Bart," in *Edith Wharton's The House of Mirth,* edited by Janet Beer, Pamela Knights, and Elizabeth Nolan, 84–96; see esp. 85. Thornton's fine work on Wharton and material culture displays the promise of a young scholar; with her death this past year, the Wharton community has lost a considerable talent and a good friend.

22. Edith Wharton, *The Letters of Edith Wharton,* ed. R. W. B. Lewis and Nancy Lewis (New York: Scribner, 1988), 439. Pagination will follow the first edition, and other quotations will be cited in the text.

23. Edith Wharton, *Old New York,* 1924 (New York: Scribner, 1952), 6. Pagination will follow this edition, and other quotations will be cited in the text.

24. Edith Wharton, *The Buccaneers* (New York: D. Appleton-Century, 1938), 4. Pagination will follow the first edition, and other quotations will be cited in the text.

25. Edith Wharton, "Life and I," appendix to *Wharton: Novellas and Other Writings,* with notes by Cynthia Griffin Wolff (New York: Library of America, 1990), 1071. Pagination will follow this edition, and other quotations will be cited in the text.

26. Coleman, *The Opulent Era,* 18.

27. Valerie Steele, *Paris Fashion,* 141–142.

28. Chapon, *Jacques Doucet; ou, L'art du mécénat, 1853–1929,* 35.

29. See http://www.nypl.org/press/artdecobindings.cfm for examples of exquisite bookbindings in Doucet's collection, offering an astonishing variety of shapes, colors, and textures. It is easy to see why Doucet, a fashion designer, would be attracted to the craft of bookbinding.

30. Quoted in Lewis, *Edith Wharton,* 125.

1. *The Collected Short Stories of Edith Wharton*, ed. R. W. B. Lewis, 2 vols. (New York: Scribner, 1968, 2:39). Pagination will follow this edition, and other quotations will be cited in the text.

2. My research at the Costume Institute, Metropolitan Museum of Art, included garments that had belonged to Caroline "Carrie" Schermerhorn Astor Wilson, a contemporary of Edith "Pussy" Jones Wharton. The ball gowns, opera cloaks, hats and day ensembles from the 1880s and 1890s were designed by Charles Frederick Worth, Jacques Doucet, and Madame Virot. Carrie Astor's clothes are the sorts of gowns Wharton would have had in mind as she created costumes for her characters. Reading descriptions and seeing photographs gave me a sense of color and shape; seeing the garments close up, however, and opening them to view the needlework revealed textures and hues and subtleties of design only available in direct contact with the material objects. I found that examining a garment is a fresh experience for a literary scholar who has been trained to read by text and not by textile.

3. Homberger, *Mrs. Astor's New York*, 4.

4. "A WEDDING AMID FLOWERS: The Marriage of Miss Astor and Mr. Wilson. Many princely presents—A Necklace that cost $75,000—Beautiful Examples of Worth's Art," *New York Times*, 9 November 1894. The article is rich in detail of fabrics and jewels and also lists members of Wharton's Old New York elite.

5. The Wilson mansion today houses the Indian American Center for Political Awareness. For photographs and a history, see *News India Times*, December 2006; see Web site of IACFPA, "An Interior of a Gilded Age: The Marchall Orme Wilson Residence, 3 East 64th Street" at http://www.iacfpa .org.

6. See Diana DeMarly, *Worth: Father of Haute Couture*, 101–102.

7. Nancy L. Green, "Art and Industry," 723.

8. Nancy L. Green, *Ready-to-Wear and Ready-to-Work*, 163–165.

9. Wendy Gamber, "A Gendered Enterprise," 189.

10. Nancy Dye, "Feminism or Unionism?" 111.

11. Veblen, *The Theory of the Leisure Class*, 92.

12. For details of Bloomer's involvement in reform issues, see *Women's Rights: Special History Study*, chap. 4, "Amelia Bloomer," at http://www.nps .gov/history/history/online_books/wori/shs4.htm.

13. For pictures of early models of Singer sewing machines, see http:// website.lineone.net/~linave/singer.htm.

14. Edith Wharton, *Bunner Sisters*, in *Edith Wharton: Madame de Treymes and Three Novellas*, introd. Susan Mary Alsop (New York: Collier Books, Macmillan), 1970, 293. Pagination will follow this edition, and other quotations will be cited in the text.

15. Crane, *Fashion and Its Social Agendas*, 104 and fig. 24.

16. François Baudot, *Mode du Siècle*, page 31; Crane, *Fashion and Its Social Agendas*, 104.

17. Crane, *Fashion and Its Social Agendas*.

18. For discussion of sexual or "white" slavery, see Joslin, introduction to

*A New Conscience and an Ancient Evil* by Jane Addams; see also Margit Stange, *Personal Property*.

19. Clair Hughes, *Dressed in Fiction*, 9.

20. For a detailed description of hat processing in the eighteenth and into the nineteenth century, see *www.whiteoak.org/learning/furhat.htm*. The Web site is organized by the White Oak Society, Deer River, Minnesota.

21. See *Audubon Magazine* Web site, www.audubonmagazine.org/features 0412/hats.html, for a discussion of the damage to birdlife during the late nineteenth century before the Lacey Act of 1904 and of the participation of women's clubs in the reform of feather consumption.

22. Addams, *The Spirit of Youth and the City Streets*, 8.

23. For background on the Spanish designer Mariano Fortuny and dress reform, see Cunningham, *Reforming Women's Fashion,* 212–214.

24. Quoted in Cunningham, *Reforming Women's Fashion,* 214; see Guillermo De Osma, *Mariano Fortuny: His Life and Work*.

*Chapter 3. Philanthropy and Progress (pages 82–98)*

1. See Brown and Tager, *Massachusetts: A Concise History*.

2. "Ball in New Cotton Mill. Dedication of an Addition to the Berkshire Company's Plant," *Special to The New York Times*, 31 December 1899.

3. Edith Wharton, *The Fruit of the Tree* (New York: Scribner, 1907), 56. Pagination will follow the first edition, and other quotations will be cited in the text.

4. See Joslin, "Architectonic or Episodic?" in *A Forward Glance*.

5. Jane Addams, *Democracy and Social Ethics*, 144.

6. See the Guide to the International Ladies' Garment Workers' Union Records, 1906–1985, at http://rmc.library.cornell.edu/EAD/htmldocs/KCL 05780.html. For details of the strikes and the quote from Rose Schneiderman following the Triangle fire, see Wikipedia.

7. See Kimberly Chrisman's detailed discussion of Wharton and fashion in "'The Upholstery of Life': Clothing and Character in the Novels of Edith Wharton." Chrisman compares Justine's desire to be fashionably dressed to Wharton's own desire for clothes. "Wharton never successfully reconciled her dual role as a woman of letters and a woman of fashion, indeed, society wouldn't let her," Chrisman wisely notes.

8. Edith Wharton, *A Son at the Front* (New York: Scribner, 1923), 416. Pagination will follow the first edition, and other quotations will be cited in the text.

9. Alan Price, *The End of the Age of Innocence: Edith Wharton and the First World War*, ix.

10. Margaret Cadwalader Jones, *American Hostels Report*, 1915. Yale Collection of American Literature, Beinecke Rare Book and Manuscript Library.

11. Edith Wharton, "My Work Among the Women Workers of Paris," *New York Times*, 28 November 1915. Available online and in the Yale Collection of American Literature, Beinecke Rare Book and Manuscript Library.

12. Letters, EW to Alice [Meynell?], 2 May 1917; EW to Sara Norton,

5 May 1917; and EW to Margaret Cadwalader Jones, 27 March 1919. Yale Collection of American Literature, Beinecke Rare Book and Manuscript Library.

13. Letter, EW to Margaret Cadwalader Jones, 7 January 1916, in *Letters*, 366–368. See Lee's discussion, *Edith Wharton,* 470.

14. Letter, EW to Margaret Cadwalader Jones, 11 May 1917. Yale Collection of American Literature, Beinecke Rare Book and Manuscript Library.

15. Letter, EW to Margaret Cadwalader Jones, 4 March 1919. Yale Collection of American Literature, Beinecke Rare Book and Manuscript Library.

16. See Lee, *Edith Wharton,* 754.

17. *Heroes of France: A Fortnightly Bulletin Issued by the French Heroes Lafayette Memorial Fund, Inc,* 2 West Forty-Fifth Street, New York City. Yale Collection of American Literature, Beinecke Rare Book and Manuscript Library.

18. Letter, EW to Margaret Cadwalader Jones, 19 February 1919. Yale Collection of American Literature, Beinecke Rare Book and Manuscript Library.


*Chapter 4. Desire in the Marketplace (pages 99–116)*

1. Brown, *A Sense of Things,* 18.

2. Butler, *Gender Trouble,* 33.

3. See Consuelo Vanderbilt Balsan, *The Glitter and the Gold,* 20–21.

4. Beckwith had studied art in Chicago and exhibited in New York and Paris and shared a studio with John Singer Sargent.

5. William Orphen's *The Signing of Peace in the Hall of Mirrors, Versailles* can be found at Wikimedia Commons.

6. For details on the store, see Elias, *Alexander T. Stewart.*

7. McCabe, *The Project Gutenberg: Lights and Shadows of New York Life,* offers a contemporary critique of the store.

8. For background on Wanamaker, see the PBS documentary series, "Who Made America?" at http://www.wgbh/theymadeamerica/whomade/wanamaker_hi.html.

9. Wharton will use the actual name Medora for a colorful character in *The Age of Innocence,* Medora Manson. During my research, I traveled to Medora, North Dakota, and the Theodore Roosevelt National Park. *Medora Magazine: A Visitor's Guide to Historic Medora, North Dakota* (2007) details the history of the town and lists several tours of the area. The "Chateau de Mores," built in 1883, is a site operated by the State Historical Society of North Dakota, and the tour is a wonderful value for six dollars. The summerhouse offers all the amenities of such houses in New England, including a living room, dining room with a kitchen, a pantry, a scullery, and servant's room, together with bedrooms, dressing rooms, bathrooms and studies for the marquis and the marquise, and even a hunting room and a porch—eight rooms in all on the first floor together with a second floor of bedrooms for servants, children, and guests. Medora's trunks are on display along with several of her Parisian couture ensembles; but the fashion that everyone on the tour I took preferred to see was her ammunition belt.

*Chapter 5. The Cut of a Gown (pages 117–138)*

1. Wharton, "A Little Girl's New York," 274.
2. Wharton, Letter to Mary "Minnie" Cadwalader Jones, 17 February 1921, in *The Letters of Edith Wharton*, 439.
3. See Lee, *Edith Wharton*, 568–569.
4. Wharton, letter to Robert Bridges, 11 February 1923, in *The Letters of Edith Wharton*, 463.
5. Lee, *Edith Wharton*, 70.
6. Westermarck, *The History of Human Marriage*, 3:chap. 33, p. 372.
7. Ibid., 1:chap. 16, p. 538.
8. Ibid., 1:chap. 16, p. 547.
9. Ibid., 1:chap. 16, p. 548.
10. Ibid., 1:chap. 16, p. 553.
11. Cunningham, *Reforming Women's Fashion*, 7.
12. Ibid., 125.
13. Quoted in ibid., 92.
14. Sobieski was King John III of Poland from 1624 to 1696.
15. See Joslin, "The Bohemian Peril," in *Edith Wharton*, 89–107.
16. Quoted in Cunningham, *Reforming Women's Fashion*, 126–128, together with an illustration from *Liberty & Co.* catalogue that compares a new Liberty design and a gown from the Empire period.
17. See photograph of "Josephine" from *Liberty & Co.* catalogue, no. 98, (1905), in Cunningham, *Reforming Women's Fashion*, 129.
18. Cunningham, *Reforming Women's Fashion*, 211.
19. Lee, *Edith Wharton*, 503.

*Chapter 6. Dressing for Middle Age (pages 139–161)*

1. Edith Wharton, *The Mother's Recompense* (New York: D. Appleton, 1925), 261. Pagination will follow the first edition, and other quotations will be cited in the text.
2. I found a box of Gould's Rachel Powder no. 2 at Needful Things: Antiques and Collectibles, online at http://www.tias.com/195/PictPage/14999 81.html; this seems to be what Wharton had in mind, suggesting that she herself used the makeup.
3. The Humane Society complained in August 2005 that runway shows in Milan and Paris featured Astrakhan fur on coats designed by Gucci, Dolce & Gabbana, and even Burberry. Such fur detail on haute couture garments can cost "up to $24,150." See http://www.hsus.org/wildlife/wildlife_news/astrakhan_hot_new_fashion.html.
4. For the Poole & Co. advertisement, see http://www.hauteliving.com/ny/aprilmay-2008-sharp/a-hand-tailored-weekend-in-london/.
5. See Joslin, "'Embattled Tendencies': Wharton, Woolf and the Nature of Modernism," in *Special Relationships*, 202–223; see also Lee, *Edith Wharton*, 632.
6. Coleman, *Opulent Era*, 147.

7. See the Metropolitan Web site for "Poirêt, King of Fashion" exhibit, fall 2007, at http://www.metmuseum.org/special/se_event.asp?OccurrenceId= {0DC3D00F-4611-4F91-8DC2-CC3C1A5C48D5}.

8. See the video animation of a Poiret design, RealPlayer: 2:22 minutes, at http://www.metmuseum.org/special/se_event.asp?OccurrenceId={0DC3 D00F-4611-4F91-8DC2-CC3C1A5C48D5}.

9. Quoted in the 2007 Metropolitan Museum of Art exhibition, "Poiret: King of Fashion," at http://www.metmuseum.org/special/se_event.asp? OccurrenceId={0DC3D00F-4611-4F91-8DC2-CC3C1A5C48D5}.

10. See Kirke, *Madeleine Vionnet.*

11. Coleman, *Opulent Era,* 148.

12. Quoted in the Metropolitan Museum of Art's description of the Vionnet gown at http://www.metmuseum.org/toah/hd/20sil/ho_C.I.52.18.4 .htm.

13. See story, perhaps apocryphal, in the Metropolitan Museum of Art exhibition, "Poiret: King of Fashion."

14. See Wikipedia for details on Houbigant and his various perfumes.

15. See Joslin, "Spectral Desire," in *Edith Wharton,* 108–128.

16. Quoted in Hughes, *Dressed in Fiction,* 160.

17. Aileen Ribeiro, *Dress in Eighteenth-century Europe,* 168.

18. See Hughes, *Dressed in Fiction,* 162; Madeleine Ginsburg, *Wedding Dress: 1740–1970,* 2; and Ann Monsarrat, *And the Bride Wore . . . ,* 108.

19. Hughes, *Dressed in Fiction,* 175.

20. In *Harper's Bazar,* 9 November 1895.

21. Coleman, *Opulent Era,* 146.


## Chapter 7. Democracy and Dress (pages 162–176)

1. In Frederick Wegener, *Edith Wharton: The Uncollected Critical Writings,* 274.

2. Quoted in Lee, *Edith Wharton,* 689; see also 690.

3. Wegener, *Edith Wharton,* 274.

4. Wolff, *Feast of Words,* 399, and Lee, *Edith Wharton,* 727.

5. See Bauer, *Edith Wharton's Brave New Politics,* 181–182; and Beer Goodwyn, *Edith Wharton,* 150.

6. See Walsh, "The Democratization of Fashion."

7. Ibid., 304.

8. Quoted in Lee, *Edith Wharton,* 688.

9. Letter, EW to Margaret Cadwalader Jones, 16 October 1933. In *Letters,* 570.

10. Quoted in Lee, *Edith Wharton,* 694.


## Conclusion. The Costume Side (pages 177–181)

1. Edith Wharton, *Letters,* 440.

2. Ibid., 624.

3. For details, see Parley Ann Boswell, *Edith Wharton on Film*.

4. Letter, EW to Mary Cadwalader Jones, 10 April 1934. In *Letters*, 577.

5. See Valerie Steele, *Encyclopedia of Clothing and Fashion* (New York: Scribner, 2005). Wallis Warfield Simpson, the duchess of Windsor, wore a Reboux hat at her wedding to Edward VIII; the Costume Institute at the Metropolitan Museum has the hat in its collection.

# Bibliography

*Image Websites*

http://beinecke.library.yale.edu/dl_crosscollex/SearchExecXC.asp?srchtype
   =CNO
http://commons.wikimedia.org
http://costume.osu.edu/Reforming_Fashion
http://dept.kent.edu/museum/costume
http://digitalgallery.nypl.org/nypldigital/explore/dgexplore.cfm?topic
   =culture&collection _list=DressFashionDesignMa&col_id=215
http://www.metmuseum.org
http://www.mintmuseum.org/collections.html


*Works Cited*

Addams, Jane. *Democracy and Social Ethics*. New York: Macmillan, 1902.
———. *A New Conscience and an Ancient Evil*. 1913. Introduction by Kather-
   ine Joslin. Champaign: University of Illinois Press, 2002.
———. *The Spirit of Youth and the City Streets*. 1909. New York: Macmillian,
   1912.
Auchincloss, Louis. *Edith Wharton: A Woman in Her Time*. New York: Viking,
   1971.
Balsan, Consuelo Vanderbilt. *The Glitter and the Gold*. London: Heinemann,
   1953.
Banta, Martha. "Wharton's Women: In Fashion, In History, Out of Time."
   In *A Historical Guide to Edith Wharton,* edited by Carol Singley, 51–88. Ox-
   ford: Oxford University Press, 2003.
Baudot, François. *Mode du Siècle*. Translated by Jane Brenton as *A Century of
   Fashion*. New York: Universe, 1999.
Bauer, Dale M. *Edith Wharton's Brave New Politics*. Madison: University of
   Wisconsin Press, 1994.
Blandchard, Mary Warner. *Oscar Wilde's America: Counterculture in the Gilded
   Age*. New Haven, Conn.: Yale University Press, 1998.
Beer Goodwyn, Janet. *Edith Wharton: Traveller in a Land of Letters*. London:
   Palgrave Macmillan, 1989.

Benstock, Shari. *No Gifts from Chance: A Biography of Edith Wharton*. New York: Scribner, 1994.

Boswell, Parley Ann. *Edith Wharton on Film*. Carbondale: Southern Illinois University Press, 2007.

Brown, Bill. *A Sense of Things: The Object Matter of American Literature*. Chicago: University of Chicago Press, 2003.

Brown, Richard, and Jack Tager. *Massachusetts: A Concise History*. Amherst: University of Massachusetts Press, 2000.

Butler, Judith. *Gender Trouble: Feminism and the Subversion of Identity*. New York: Routledge, 1989; new edition, 1999.

Cavallaro, Dani, and Alexandra Warwick. *Fashioning the Frame: Boundaries, Dress, and Body*. New York: Berg, 1998.

Chapon, François. *Jacques Doucet: ou, L'art du mécénat, 1853–1929*. Paris: Perrin; new edition with corrections, 1996.

Chrisman, Kimberly. "'The Upholstery of Life': Clothing and Character in the Novels of Edith Wharton." *Dress* 25 (1998): 17–32.

Coleman, Elizabeth Ann. *The Opulent Era: Fashions of Worth, Doucet and Pingat*. Exhibition catalogue, Brooklyn Museum, 1989. New York: Thames and Hudson, 1992.

Coogan, Timothy. *The Forging of a New Mill Town: North and South Adams, Massachusetts, 1780–1860*. Ann Arbor, Mich.: University Microfilms, 1993.

Crane, Diana. *Fashion and Its Social Agendas: Class, Gender, and Identity in Clothing*. Chicago: University of Chicago Press, 2000.

Cunningham, Patricia A. *Reforming Women's Fashion, 1850–1920*. Kent, Ohio: Kent State University Press, 2003.

De Marly, Diana. *Worth: Father of Haute Couture*. London: Elm Tree, 1980; 2d. ed., New York: Holmes and Meier, 1990.

De Osma, Guillermo. *Mariano Fortuny: His Life and Work*. New York: Rizzoli, 1980.

Dye, Nancy Schrom. "Feminism or Unionism? The New York Women's Trade Union League and the Labor Movement." *Feminist Studies* 3, nos. 1–2 (1975): 111–125.

Elias, Stephen. *Alexander T. Stewart: The Forgotten Merchant Prince*. Westport, Conn.: Praeger, 1992.

Flanner, Janet. "Profiles: Those Were the Days." *New Yorker* (20 January 1934), 17–20.

Gamber, Wendy. "A Gendered Enterprise: Placing Nineteenth-Century Businesswomen in History." *Business History Review* 72, no. 2 (1998): 188–191.

Garber, Margarie. *Vested Interests: Cross-Dressing and Cultural Anxiety*. New York: Routledge, 1992.

Ginsburg, Madeleine. *Wedding Dress: 1740–1970*. London: HMSO, 1981.

Green, Nancy L. "Art and Industry: The Language of Modernization in the Production of Fashion, *French Historical Studies* 18, no. 3 (Spring 1994): 722–748.

———. *Ready-to-Wear and Ready-to-Work: A Century of Industry and Immigrants in Paris and New York*. Durham, N.C.: Duke University Press, 1997.

Homberger, Eric. *Mrs. Astor's New York: Money and Social Power in a Gilded Age.* New Haven, Conn.: Yale University Press, 2002.

Hughes, Clair. *Dressed in Fiction.* New York: Berg, 2006.

Joslin, Katherine. "Architectonic or Episodic? Gender and *The Fruit of the Tree.*" In *A Forward Glance: New Essays on Edith Wharton,* edited by Clare Colquitt, Susan Goodman, and Candace Waid, 62–76. Newark: University of Delaware Press, 1999.

———. *Edith Wharton.* Women Writers Series. London: Macmillan, 1991.

———. "'Embattled Tendencies': Wharton, Woolf and the Nature of Modernism." In *Special Relationships: Anglo-American Affinities and Antagonisms, 1854–1936,* edited by Janet Beer and Bridget Bennett, 202–223. Manchester: Manchester University Press, 2002.

Kinmonth, Margy. *The Secret World of Haute Couture.* Documentary film. Tracy Jeune, executive producer, BBC, 2006.

Kirke, Betty. *Madeleine Vionnet.* With a foreword by Issye Miyake. San Francisco, Calif.: Chronicle Books, 1998.

Koda, Harold, and Andrew Bolton. *Poiret.* Introduction by Nancy J. Troy. Exhibition catalogue, Metropolitan Museum of Art, 2007. New Haven: Yale University Press, 2007.

Lee, Hermione. *Edith Wharton.* New York: Knopf, 2007.

Lewis, R. W. B. *Edith Wharton: A Biography.* New York: Fromm, 1985.

Lubbock, Percy. *Edith Wharton: A Woman in Her Time.* New York: Viking, 1971.

McCabe, James D. *The Project Gutenberg: Lights and Shadows of New York Life; or, The Sights and Sensations of the Great City by James D. McCabe.* Release Date: October 27, 2006 [eBook 19642] Language: English Character set encoding: ISO-646-US (US-ASCII). This e-book was transcribed by Les Bowler.

Mint Museum. *Experiencing Art at The Mint Museum: A Look at the Collections.* Charlotte, N.C.: The Mint Museum, 2005.

Monsarrat, Ann. *And the Bride Wore . . .* London: Gentry Books, 1973.

Nenadic, Stana. "The Social Shaping of Business Behaviour in the Nineteenth Century Women's Garment Trades." *Journal of Social History* 31, no. 3 (1998): 625–645.

Orlando, Emily J. *Edith Wharton and the Visual Arts.* Tuscaloosa: University of Alabama Press, 2007.

Price, Alan. *The End of the Age of Innocence: Edith Wharton and the First World War,* New York: St. Martin's, 1996.

Ribeiro, Aileen. *Dress in Eighteenth-century Europe.* New Haven, Conn.: Yale University Press, 2002.

Showalter, Elaine. "The Death of the Lady (Novelist): Wharton's *House of Mirth.*" *Representations* 9 (Winter 1985): 133–149.

Stange, Margit. *Personal Property: Wives, White Slaves, and the Market in Women.* Baltimore, Md.: Johns Hopkins University Press, 1998.

Steele, Valerie. *Encyclopedia of Clothing and Fashion.* New York: Scribner, 2005.

———. *Paris Fashion: A Cultural History.* New York: Oxford University Press, 1985.

Thornton, Edith. "Beyond the Page: Visual Literacy and the Interpretation of Lily Bart." In *Edith Wharton's House of Mirth*, edited by Janet Beer, Pamela Knights and Elizabeth Nolan, 84–96. New York: Routledge, 2007.

Totten, Gary, ed. *Memorial Boxes and Guarded Interiors: Edith Wharton and Material Culture*. American Literary Realism and Naturalism Series. Tuscaloosa: University of Alabama Press, 2007.

Veblen, Thorstein. *The Theory of the Leisure Class*. 1899. Penguin edition. Introduction by Robert Leckachman. New York, Penguin Books, 1981.

Walsh, Margaret. "The Democratization of Fashion: The Emergence of the Women's Dress Pattern Industry." *Journal of American History* 66, no. 2 (September 1979): 299–313.

Welters, Linda, and Patricia A. Cunningham, eds. *Twentieth-Century American Fashion*. New York: Berg, 2005.

Westermarck, Edvard. *The History of Human Marriage*. 3 vols. London: Macmillan, 1925.

Wharton, Edith. *The Age of Innocence*. 1920. New Riverside Edition. Edited by Carol Singley. New York: Houghton Mifflin, 2000.

——. *A Backward Glance*. 1934. In *Wharton: Novellas and Other Writings*, with notes by Cynthia Griffin Wolff, 767–1064. New York: Library of America, 1990.

——. *The Buccaneers*. New York: Appleton, 1938.

——. *Bunner Sisters*. Written 1892, published 1916. In *Edith Wharton: Madame de Treymes and Three Novellas*, 279–388. Introduction by Susan Mary Alsop. New York: Collier Books, Macmillan, 1970.

——. *The Collected Stories*. Edited by R. W. B. Lewis. New York: Scribner, 1968.

——. *The Custom of the Country*. New York: Scribner, 1913.

——. *The Decoration of Houses*. With Ogden Codman. New York: Scribner, 1897.

——. *Edith Wharton: The Uncollected Critical Writings*. Edited by Frederick Wegener. Princeton, N.J.: Princeton University Press, 1996.

——. *French Ways and Their Meaning*. New York: Appleton, 1919.

——. *The Fruit of the Tree*. New York: Scribner, 1907.

——. *The House of Mirth*. New York: Scribner, 1905.

——. *The Letters of Edith Wharton*. Edited by R. W. B. Lewis and Nancy Lewis. New York: Simon and Schuster, 1988.

——. "Life and I." In *Wharton: Novellas and Other Writings*, 1067–1096. New York: Library of America, 1990.

——. "A Little Girl's New York." In *Edith Wharton: The Uncollected Critical Writings,* edited by Frederick Wegener, 274–288. Princeton, N.J.: Princeton University Press, 1996.

——. *Madame de Treymes*. 1906. In *Wharton: Novellas and Other Writings*, with notes by Cynthia Griffin Wolff, 1–60. New York: Library of America, 1990.

——. *The Mother's Recompense*. New York: Appleton, 1925.

——. *Old New York*. New York: Appleton, 1924.

——. *Sanctuary*. New York: Scribner, 1903.

————. *A Son at the Front*. New York: Scribner, 1923.

————. *The Touchstone*. New York, Scribner, 1900.

————. *The Writing of Fiction*. New York: Scribner, 1925.

Wolff, Cynthia Griffin. *A Feast of Words: The Triumph of Edith Wharton*. New York: Oxford University Press, 1977.

# Index

Jones, Lucretia (née Rhinelander) (mother), 8, 41–42, *43,* 44, 61
Josephine, Empress of France, 44, 119, 134

Kellog, John Harvey, 124
Kemble, Fanny, 123–24
*The King of Fashion* (Poiret), 148
Kinmonth, Margy, 7

labor in garment production: alienation in mass production, 65, 69–70, 82–83; and cost of luxury, 5–6, 90; and gender blurring in clothing, 148; gendered division of, 59–60, 61; milliner's life, 51–52, 75, 76, 77–78; and rue de la Paix couture houses, 57–58; seamstress's life, 57; sewing machine's impact on, 64–65; and social status of women, 59–60, 76, 78–79; textile mills, 83–88; underside of garment as indicator of, 56–57; union movement, 91; Wharton's literary perspective, 51–52, 66; and Wharton's WWI charity work, 6, 94–96; working conditions, 84
lace in Gilded Age fashion, 54–55
lace-making school, 96
Lacey Act (1904), 75, 119
Lapape, George, 137, 148
Ladies' Garment Workers' Union, 91
*Ladies' Home Journal,* 163
Le Bon Marché, 104
Lee, Hermione, 70, 97, 164
leg-of-mutton sleeve, 24, 66–67
leisure class: boredom of French women's lives, 113; criticism of Wharton's focus on, 167; and dressing up in front of mirrors, 103–4; European shopping of, 41–43; marriage in, 157–58; private tutoring for educating, 177–78; symbols of, 110. *See also* Haute couture; Old New York
"The Letters" (Wharton), 141–42
Liberty, Arthur Lasenby, 134
Liberty & Company, 134
"Life and I" (Wharton), 37–38
*Lights and Shadows of New York Life* (McCabe), 106
*The Lily,* 63, 123–24
literature and social history, 5. *See also individual works*
little black dress, 152, 153
"A Little Girl's New York" (Wharton), 164

machine as metaphor, 85–86
*Madam Demorest's Quarterly Mirror of Fashion,* 169
*Madame de Treynes* (Wharton), 34
*Maggie, A Girl of the Streets* (Crane), 70
Maidenform, 135–36
Maison Doucet, 8, 9–11, 104
Maison Paquin, 126
Maison Worth. *See* House of Worth
Marable, Richard (character), 166, 167, 168
Marble Palace, 105
Marie Antoinette, Queen of France, *104*
marriage: as economic protection for women, 71, 72, 173; individualism's impact on, 121–22; leisure class customs, 157–58; as sexual outlet for women, 71; wedding gowns, 53, 71, 129–30, 157–59, 161; Westermarck on, 121; Wharton's, 24, 72, 108; in Wharton's work, 157–59, 164; women's emancipation effect on, 122
Marvell, Ralph (character), 110
mass production of garments, social fallout of, 65, 69–70, 82–83
material culture: American style, 113–15; as class definer, 12, 113–14; in literature, 2–3, 117, 179; shopping, 99–116; thingness, 12, 113, 114–15, 179, 180; and women's role in economy, 51–52. *See also* Fashion
McCabe, James, 106
*Memorial Boxes and Guarded Interiors* (Totten), 179
men: as arbiters of fashion, 173; clothing of, 60–61, 87–89, 123–24, 141, 148, 169; as observers of women's clothing, 141–42; tactile relationship to clothing, 142
"Les Metteurs en Scène" (Wharton), 141
middle class: access to fashion, 11, 31, 169–70; as basis of American culture, 115; fashion sense of, 131; sewing machine's impact on, 64; and Wharton's ancestors' dress, 41
Migratory Bird Act (1913), 75–76
millinery, 51–52, 69, 72–79
mirrors, fashion and self-assessment through, 103–4, 105, 140, 142, 176

modern styles: chemise, 44, 134, 135, 145, 151; and class markers in dress, 7, 64, 166–68; corsets in, 149, 150, 186n1; couture adoption of, 146, 151, *152*; cubist, *49*, 146, *147*; development of, 145–53; draping change, 48, 79; flapper, 144–45, 151; freedom for women in, 17, 61, 79; gender blurring in, 64, 67, 148; little black dress, 152, 153; pre-WWI, 79, *80*; and production, 146; and ready-made sewing patterns, 170; turn-of-century advent of, 58; Wharton's adoption of, 14, 48, *49, 160,* 179, 181; in Wharton's work, 130–31, 138, 144, 162, 163–64, 173–75. *See also* Aesthetic dress

Moffatt, Elmer (character), 99, 108, 113, 115

morality: and euthanasia, 89, 91; fashion as indicator of, 88–90, 125, 164, 180; irony of fashion and, 167; and rejection of Wharton's sexual themes, 171; Wharton's focus on, 121. *See also* Labor in garment production

Morés, Marquis de, 108

Morés, Marquise de (née Medora Hoffman), 108–9

Morris, Jane, 123

Morris, William, 123

*The Mother's Recompense* (Wharton), 139–41, 143–46, 153–57, 159, 161

The Mount, 83

mourning dress, 154–55

"Mrs. Manstey's View" (Wharton), 144

museum collections of fashion, 3, 51, 52–53

naturalism, literary: in sexual slavery narratives, 70; Wharton's use of, 12, 52, 68, 71–72, 84–86

New York City: fashionability in, 111–12; as garment production center, 65, 108; late 19th-century growth of, 68–69; Triangle Shirtwaist Factory fire, 91; Wharton's chronicles of changes in, 66; Wharton's post-WWI return visit, 155. *See also* Old New York

nonfiction writing, 29–31

*The Old Maid* (Wharton), 178

Old New York: classic vs. bohemian ironies, 127, 128–29; culture of, 111–12; in *The Custom of the Country,* 100, 110; fashion as social code, 7; leisure class's shopping in Europe, 41–43; mourning customs, 154–55; need to describe for post-WWI audience, 37; Wharton's and James's fashion sensibility, 47; as Wharton's social heritage, 45

*Old New York* (Wharton), 37

*The Old Pier Glass* (Beckwith), 103

Olenska, Ellen (character), 118–20, 122–23, 125–29, 132–33, 138. See also *The Age of Innocence*

*The Opulent Era* (Coleman), 134

orientalism, 149

*The Origin and Development of Moral Ideas* (Westermarck), 121

Orlando, Emily J., 179

ownership of garment production and gender, 59–60

Paquin, Jeanne, 104, 126, *127,* 128–29, 158

Paris, France, Wharton's charity work in, 92–96. *See also* Rue de la Paix couture houses

Paris Exposition (1900), 58–59, 126

Patou, Jean, *175*

patterns, sewing, 11, 123, 168–70

performativity, 100

perfumes, Wharton's descriptions of, 35

*Peterson's Magazine,* 123, 169, 170

petticoats, 125

philanthropy, Wharton's, 92–96

*Physiology and Calisthenics for Schools and Families* (Beecher), 123

piecework production of clothing, 64–65, 69

pier-glass mirror, 103–4, 105

plate-glass windows, and dressing up ritual, 104, 106–7

Plunkett, W. B., 83

Poiret, Paul, 126, 135, 136–37, *147*–48, 149–50, *151, 152*

politics, Wharton's, 93, 96–97

"The Pretext" (Wharton), 142–43

private sphere, transfer of clothing styles to public sphere, 16, 17–19, 123, 151

production of garments: class and art vs. trade, 59, 78–79; ethics of, 59; and new distribution methods, 108; New York City as center of, 65, 108; and paper pattern development, 168–70; piecework method, 64–65, 69; rise of ready-made fashions, 11; and shift to modern dress, 146; social fallout of mass production, 65, 69–70, 82–83; standard-ization of, 57–58; tech-nological innovations, 64–65; textile mills, 82–86; uniformity of clothing effect, 149; in Wharton's work, 5; women's role in, 51–53, 59–60, 76, 78–79. *See also* Labor in garment production

Progressivism: and self-empowerment, 90–91; Wharton's, 5–6, 79, 86, 92; Wharton's ambiva-lence, 82, 96–97; and Wharton's charity work, 92–93; and white slave narrative, 70. *See also* Production of gar-ments

Prud'hon, Pierre-Paul, *119*

psychology of shopping, 111

psychology of wedding dress, 159, 161

public sphere, women's presence in: and aes-thetic dress, 61, 136; transfer of private sphere clothing, 16, 17–19, 123, 151; Whar-ton's style as example of, 21, *22–23*

publishing process for Wharton, 171

puffed sleeve, 24, 66–68

Pulitzer Prizes, 177, 178

Pullman, George, 91

purity leagues, 70

Rachel powder, 140

railroads and garment dis-tribution, 108

reading dress, 6, 11–12

*Ready-to-Wear and Ready-to-Work* (Green), 59–60

ready-to-wear fashion: as art vs. industry, 59;

designer shift to, 11, 146; men's, 60–61; sewing patterns, 11, 123, 168–70

realism, literary: French creation of, 33; in Wharton's work, 68, 92, 179–80

reform dress. *See* Aesthetic dress

Réjane, 17, *24,* 147

Rhinelander, Lucretia Stevens (Mrs. G. F. Jones) (mother), 8, 41–42, *43,* 44, 61

Rhinelander, Mrs. (great-grandmother), *40*

Ribeiro, Aileen, 157

Robinson, Hector (charac-ter), 173

Roosevelt, Theodore, 75, 108–9

Rosenthal, Ida, 135–36

rue de la Paix couture houses: and garment production, 57–58; House of Doucet, 8, 9–11, 104; Maison Paquin, 126; mother's shopping in, 41; post-WWI shift to mod-ernism, 146, 151, *152*; rise of, 8; Virot's hats, 73–74; Wharton's shopping in, 7, 9–10. *See also* House of Worth

Sainte-Claire du Château, 154

*Sanctuary* (Wharton), 34

Sand, George, 124

sartorial codes and social status, 6–7. *See also* Fashion

satire: as common element of Wharton's style, 5; and obsession over things, 114–15; and Wharton's critique of leisure class, 93, 115–16; Wharton's use of fash-ion for, 52, 79, 88–89

*Scribner's,* 35

seamstresses, 6, 57, 59–60. *See also* Labor in gar-ment production

*The Secret World of Haute Couture* (Kinmonth), 7

*A Sense of Things* (Brown), 2

sensuality: fashion as focus for, 142; tactile rela-tionship to clothing, 141–42, 143, 164–65; in Wharton's work, 1, 3, 9, 142, 143, 144

sewing, 11, 59–60, 100. *See also* Production of gar-ments

sewing machine, 64–65

sexuality: American cul-tural ambivalence, 178–79; and beauty, 40; and class, 86, 121; clothing as enhance-ment of, 118, 122; and desire for things, 113; and dressing up in front of mirrors, 103; fashion symbol of, 164, 174; and feel of clothing, 143; marriage as outlet for women, 71; vulner-ability of women, 70, 72; in Wharton's work, 68, 155–56, 171

sexual slavery, 70

shirtwaist, 18, 25, *27*

shopping: in *The Custom of the Country,* 99–100, 103, 108, 109–16; de-partment store devel-opment, 104–8; and sewing patterns, 123, 170

shoulders, draping clothing from, 48, 79

silk dress, 69–70

simplicity, Wharton's com-mitment to, 32

Singer, Isaac Merritt, 64

slinky gown style, 150

smoking, Wharton's love of, 26, *27*

Social Darwinism, 72, 120–22

white slave narrative, 70
Wilde, Oscar, 125
will, Wharton's, 2, 180, 183n3
Wilson, Caroline Scher-
merhorn (née Astor), 52–53
Wilson, Marshall Orme, 53
Winterhalter, Franz Xavier, 8, 9
Wolff, Cynthia Griffin, 5, 164, 179
*Woman's Home Companion*, 171
women: adoption of men's clothing styles, 61, 124, 148, 149; and clothing from outside in, 142; fashion as definer of, 44, 109–10, 136; in garment production, 51–53, 59–60, 76, 78–79; liberation of modern clothing for, 79; and marriage, 71, 72, 122, 173; sexual and social vulnerability of, 70, 72; social restrictions on, 80–81; and Wharton's critique of popular taste, 31–32. *See also* Freedom for women; Public sphere, women's presence in
women's magazines and middle-class access to fashion, 169, 170
Woolf, Virginia, 144
working class, 68–70, 80–81, 96–97. *See also* Labor in garment production
World War I, 6, 36–37, 92–96
Worth, Charles Frederick: ball gown design, 54; death of, 150–51; dress creations, 10; and Empire style, 134; establishment of, 8; fashion influence of, 41–42, 187–88n12; gown of

Wharton's designed by, 24, 25; photo, 42; and treatment of labor, 57–58
Worth, Gaston-Lucien, 151
Worth, Jean-Philippe, 47–48, 54
writing: as identity for Wharton, 44–45; non-fiction, 29–31; philanthropy as distraction from, 97–98; realism in, 33, 68, 92, 179–80; Wharton on, 29, 33–34, 179–80; Wharton's early storytelling abilities, 15; Wharton's gender-based letter-writing styles, 183–84n4; Wharton's looseness with facts, 120. *See also* Ironies; Naturalism; Satire; *individual works*
*The Writing of Fiction* (Wharton), 29, 33–34, 179–80